# The Meaning of Freedom

# The Meaning of Freedom

## A Study of Secular, Muslim and Christian Views

### J. Andrew Kirk

paternoster press

First published 1998 by Paternoster Press

Paternoster Press is an imprint of Paternoster Publishing,
P.O. Box 300, Carlisle, Cumbria, CA3 0QS, U.K.
http://www.paternoster-publishing.com

04 03 02 01 00 99 98      7 6 5 4 3 2 1

**British Library Cataloguing in Publication Data**

A catalogue record for this book is available from the British Library.
ISBN 0-85364-844-1

This book is printed using Suffolk New Book paper which is 100% acid-free.

Cover design by Steve Rigley
Typeset by Design2Print, Droitwich, Worcs.
Printed in Great Britain by Clays Ltd., Bungay, Suffolk

# Contents

# Preface

The bulk of this book was written in the summer months of 1994, and later revised, during a time of sabbatical study leave from my normal responsibilities in a busy teaching department at the Selly Oak Colleges, Birmingham. This uninterrupted period of reflection and writing was made possible by others sharing out my particular work-load. I want, therefore, first and foremost to thank all the members of the department who took on, in addition to their normal duties, those I had been able to shed, and in particular Dr. George Mulrain who deputized for me in the overall running of the 'show'.

Like most authors who seek to put into writing a systematic piece of investigation, I confess that it is difficult to know where to begin in acknowledging one's indebtedness to others. Obviously all those whose books or articles I have read in preparation for writing have contributed to widening my horizons and deepening my understanding of a complex, controversial, pervasive and portentous reality. But on a subject such as freedom, whose meaning becomes clear as much in the living as in the talking, so have ordinary people who, by their transparent lifestyles made possible by the history they have inherited and the privileges they enjoy, witness to the prevailing assumptions of their culture. Not least my understanding of the meaning of freedom is clarified by those, living in hunger, insanitary conditions, illiteracy, unemployment, discriminated against, exploited and fearful of violence, whose cries against their situation of deprivation and physical and psychological coercion announce the essence of freedom by its absence. Though without recognized names and not featuring in any bibliographies, their precarious lives speak volumes.

A number of my colleagues at the Selly Oak Colleges have generously given time to read all or part of the manuscript: Dan Beeby, Martin Conway, Denys Lindsay, Philip Seddon, David Thomas. I am greatly indebted to their helpful suggestions and necessary corrections. If they read the finished text, they will find that most of their recommendations have been incorporated.

My earnest desire is that this study of diverse ways of viewing freedom may be the cause of a significant debate among those whose ideas about and practices of freedom differ at certain important points: non-religious people, Muslims and Christians. In particular I hope that people who have knowingly or tacitly imbibed a secular set of beliefs will be willing not only to recognize the strengths of their own perspective and the weaknesses of those they do not share, but also the strength of argument of those who criticize their views and the weakness of some of their own convictions. I am saddened by the apparent unwillingness of many convinced religious sceptics to understand, let alone engage with, a coherent alternative to their own position. Of course, on this subject, as on many others, there are beliefs held in common, but at the level of the world-view and system of values that sustain these beliefs there are divergent outlooks which urgently need addressing. I trust that neither a secular person, Muslim nor Christian is afraid of honest, critical debate. The subject of freedom, perhaps above most others, definitely merits it.

J. Andrew Kirk
November 1997

# Introduction

The enjoyment of an expanding range of freedoms is one of the most prized of human possessions. People all over the globe have, to coin a phrase, 'fallen in love' with freedom. Those who live under the rule of brutal and corrupt regimes wish to determine their own future. Those who live in the degrading conditions of urban or rural poverty long to be free of the cycle of deprivation in which they are trapped. Women, experiencing domestic violence, seek ways to free themselves from the inhuman treatment they are forced to suffer. Young people crave to break free from the fussy and critical attention they receive from their parents. The directors and managers of industry and businesses battle to be free from legislation that inhibits their economic freedoms. Trade unions struggle to free their members from the imposition of inhuman working practices and exploitative wages. Many see the search for the greatest possible freedom of choice in education, jobs, leisure activities, satisfying personal relationships, medical care and financial security for retirement, as a sufficient purpose in life. How often we hear the familiar cry, 'I want to keep my options open.'

Who can doubt that the permanent establishment of multiple freedoms has been an overriding consideration of modern political movements, of almost every ideological hue? Organizations that monitor basic human rights and catalogue and publicize abuses gain our admiration and, as a result, receive widespread support. Almost daily people are clamouring for additional rights to be added to the long lists that already exist in various international and regional conventions. Massive amounts of money are spent on campaigns to free whole populations from the scourges of insanitary housing, rampant diseases, illiteracy, polluted water supplies, ignorance about family planning, poor agricultural techniques and inadequate diets.

Everywhere freedom. Is it too much to postulate that for modern human life freedom constitutes, maybe even defines, the most fundamental good? For, without freedom, it is not possible to pursue other worth-while values in life. All in all, the quest for freedom figures near the top of the agenda of individuals, political parties, economic institutions, governments, nations and regional political organizations. It is a value to be highly esteemed, experienced, defended and extended.

However, in spite of its high standing, how often do we citizens of the modern world pause to ask ourselves what precisely we understand by freedom? Is its meaning entirely self-evident? Is there not more than a whiff of rhetoric in our many references to the term? On closer inspection, we find that people do not always mean the same thing: that in the realm of human rights, for example, there are unresolved clashes of interpretation. What should count as freedom? Are we content with a fairly minimalist definition that wishes to restrict its meaning to freedom from legal and constitutional limitations placed by the state on the personal liberties of its citizens? Or, should those who hold the reins of political power aspire to implement a variety of freedoms where they do not yet exist? What place, if any, does the notion of an inner freedom play, where a person may be able to conquer various controlling habits such as excessive drinking, smoking, compulsive eating, an unmanageable temper, jealousy and irrational fears? How does one link freedom to the great issues of life: personal identity, a sense of worth, the search for meaning, the inevitability of death, the nurture of children, cultural, religious and ethnic diversity, equality and inequality and so on?

There are many legitimate and significant questions to be explored. As far as I am aware, no major study of the meaning of freedom has been undertaken within the last few years. Even if one, or more, does exist, each writer will come with his or her own particular experience of life, distinctive perspective and motivation to add something fresh to the discussion. My concern is to look at freedom from a number of different angles, focusing on the origins, growth, present reality and future prospects of that ideal of human freedom which may be called typically Western. It is a notion that has come to fruition within a kind of society entirely unique in human history – one we have learnt to call 'secular' in a modern way, meaning a society in which religion 'has become marginal . . . where to be irreligious is to be normal . . . where neither status nor respectability depends upon the practice or profession of religious faith'[1].

Such a society has not emerged out of nothing. It is the result of a particular set of historical circumstances that over a number of generations have come together to form a wholly original pattern of events. A watershed between two worlds was passed with the birth in the seventeenth and eighteenth centuries in Europe and North America of what, with hindsight, we have come to call 'modernity'. This is simply a shorthand term for an assortment of new ways of looking at all aspects of human life, such as religion, knowledge, education, the family, the arts, economics, the exercise of political power, national and ethnic identity, international relations, technology and the handling of change. Modernity, even when some are proclaiming its demise (somewhat prematurely), has come to dominate the consciousness of those living in the West (geographically) or the new 'Wests' (culturally). Indeed, all who aspire to the kind of lifestyle projected by Western commercial advertising and political propaganda have thereby enlisted themselves in the project of modernity. That includes almost everyone at least in the use of machines to cut out hard and repetitive physical work.

I believe that the priority given to freedom is fundamental to the experience of life in the distinctively modern world. To such an extent is this so that the pursuit, conquest and preservation of individual freedoms in a 'free' society has become humanity's chief goal. As an all-encompassing ideal it has become an end worth following for its own sake, not merely a means to some other end.

This study begins with an impressionistic picture of how people view and live freedom today. It goes on to seek some clues as to its meaning and implications among some of the greatest thinkers who have, prior to the modern period, shaped

---

[1] A.D. Gilbert, *The Making of Post-Christian Britain: a history of the secularization of modern society*. London. Longman. 1980. p. ix.

European culture. Next it looks at the influences which in their different ways provoked the transition from a pre-modern to a modern view and experience of reality. In a subsequent chapter, the basic dimensions are exhibited of a variety of traditions which, at least within the last two hundred years and sometimes much more recently, have contributed to the debate about freedom.

After this I look at a number of the consequences for culture, society and the individual of the modern experience of freedom, noting those outcomes which provisionally might be judged as both positive and negative. Chapter Six surveys some of the present trends which have arisen as a result of what many consider is taking freedom 'a step too far'. It would be naive to think that freedom is a static reality that, once granted and assumed, remains a constant experience of human life. There are very real obstacles to freedom: they may be belief systems, intellectual processes, historical movements, cultural changes, political upheavals, institutions or enterprises. They are continually shifting, interacting among themselves and changing the shape of human communities. Some of these may, in a general way, be identified in the public mind as obstacles, whilst others may also represent real limitations, though not so readily recognized as such.

Most of this study focuses on views of freedom that have come to be believed, not necessarily apart from religion, but certainly outside a consciously accepted religious framework. In chapters Eight and Nine, I look at distinctively Muslim and Christian understandings, both of which in their own way challenge some of the secular assumptions current today. In the first case, I put forward the reasons for considering Islam an important player on the stage of the modern world, before going on to discuss its own particular world-view and, springing from this, the way it approaches the subject of freedom. I recognize that there are different Muslim attitudes and therefore seek, as far as possible and within the constraints of one who stands outside the Muslim community, to allow a variety of Muslim authors to speak for themselves. In the second case, though recognizing the severe decline in its influence in the Western world, I pick up some of the main convictions of the Christian faith which have undoubtedly contributed to and, I believe, should go on contributing to further understandings of the meaning of freedom and, where necessary, to a correction of its distortions.

The final chapter attempts a recapitulation of the main items discussed throughout the book and, in an exchange between secular, Muslim and Christian views, asks about the future of freedom and who are the genuinely free. As a final consideration, I put forward a number of choices which I believe modern societies have to make at this juncture of their history, if they want in the future to have the freedom to make choices at all.

I do not wish at any point to try to hide my own convictions. The book is not meant to be a dispassionate investigation of a set of hypotheses about which one should strive to adopt a neutral stance. How could it be? Freedom is part of life. It affects me in numerous ways beyond intellectual reflection and academic research. I happen to believe, I hope as the result of adequate study and thought, that freedom presents itself as a rather ambiguous reality, with many positive features, but also some destructive ones. I believe that the pursuit of freedom, in so far as it becomes a self-referring goal, is also intrinsically self-defeating. It can come into proper focus only when set in the context of a higher good which gives an adequate perspective for answering the question: freedom for what? I also believe that it is the Christian faith, rightly understood (and, no doubt, properly tempered by its encounter with secular thought and life), that can best answer that question.

# One

# A Modern Passion

In everyday conversation, when someone feels their liberty of choice or expression is being challenged, they often make the stock response: 'Well, this is a free country, isn't it?' The rhetorical question articulates a common assumption, deeply rooted in the collective consciousness of Western culture, that each individual has an inalienable right to certain fundamental freedoms, and that no other person or institution has the authority to restrict or take them away. Indeed, this assumption may be taken as the chief characteristic or definition of Western, or 'modern', culture;[1] although, to understand this necessarily as a virtue would be to beg a question that needs to be explored and either verified or contradicted.

I believe that the historical study of social and political movements and of scientific, religious and philosophical debate suggests that the pursuit and defence of freedom in its many forms has been the dominant global movement of human societies world-wide over the last 300 years. One of the purposes of this book is to examine this proposition; another is to look at the various understandings of, or intuitions about, freedom that pervade the expectations of people who are in any way touched by the Western way of life.

---

[1] Cf. S. Hall and B. Gieben (eds), *Formations of Modernity*. Cambridge. Polity Press. 1992, p. 277.

## Images of freedom

A good way to begin is to examine some of the most common pictures that the notion of freedom creates in ordinary human life. Take, for example, a fairly ordinary household with teenage children. Accept the probability that the family possesses several TV sets, a deep-freeze and a microwave oven. Imagine also that, for the optimum convenience of all the family, the evening meal (at least during the week) is pre-prepared from a packet. Put all this together and, although there may be some exaggeration to make the point, we have the ultimate picture of the bliss of free choice. Each member of the family, returning home at different times, takes out of the freezer the evening meal of their choice, slips it into the microwave, puts it on a tray and settles down in splendid isolation in front of their chosen TV programme. If any member of the family, even when faced at the press of a button with the various options of the normal TV channels, cable and satellite stations, does not fancy any of the programmes, the video, designed to free us from the constraint of time, is also available. In the near future, to expand choice even further and save time and effort, videos will be accessible immediately on the screen, 'down line', without the need to go round the corner to the local video shop.

When it comes to food, the modern supermarket conveys a delicious experience of freedom. It offers an immense choice of cuts of meat, cheeses, biscuits to go with them, different kinds of fresh and frozen vegetables, fruit, bread, cakes, ice-creams, alcoholic and non-alcoholic drinks, not forgetting the pre-packaged meals. The shelves are stacked high with a bewildering variety of other goods, all competing for the attention of the dedicated shopper. The only restrictions relate to one's skill at manoeuvring trollies around the aisles and to the time required to wait in the check-out queue.

Young people may experience freedom most acutely when they get the opportunity to leave home. Then comes the time when they can be at liberty to organize their own life, liberated from even the minimal requirements laid down by those who, since birth, have controlled every part of their existence. Or may come with their first taste of freedom the chance to earn money, so that they may purchase, entirely on their own initiative, their own style of clothes, music on disc and other goods and entertainments.

Though this is not confined to young people, the end of cultural constraints on the choice of sexual partners has given rise to the common pattern of serial sexual relationships. If and when two people decide to marry each other, the chances are that they will have exercised a freedom to have slept already with several different people. If, at a later stage, the marriage does not seem to work out well, current divorce laws allow them a separation relatively easy in legal terms, though often costly emotionally, and the chance to try again.

Given a favourable economic climate, many people delight in the freedom provided by a market economy to create their own business. This freedom consists in the ability to try out their entrepreneurial skills, as yet unproven. If the venture is successful, their freedom will have been enlarged by being self-employed and by being in control of the income they will feel justified in paying themselves. An additional satisfaction may be that through them other people may experience the freedom that comes through employment.

To many people with a social conscience and political concern, the destruction of the Berlin Wall may well supply the most powerful symbol of freedom in the modern age. A wall, covered with layers of barbed-wire, guarded by heavily armed soldiers, who are ordered to shoot on sight anyone trying to escape across it, and mined in depth on both sides, is the epitomy of unfreedom. Prior to the crumbling of the wall, thousands of ordinary people set out by different routes from Eastern Germany for the West in battered cars, determined to achieve liberty from a uniform and regimented existence. At the time a poignant joke was circulating through the former Communist countries: Why is the sun so happy today? Because it knows that by this evening it will be in the West!

The car is another icon of freedom. There, a few paces from the front door, stands a machine which is able to transport at least four adults in comfort and speed to places which in former times they could have reached only with difficulty and after much time. The car means I am free to choose when to leave the house and where to go. I am not dependent on the good-will, whim or timetable of others. By myself or with others, I can go shopping where I like, visit friends and relatives, go to a sporting event, eat out or escape from the city into the highways and byways of the countryside. The car has revolutionized the lives of children. They can now be taken with some ease to swimming lessons, ballet classes, football coaching, music lessons, friends' birthday parties, theme parks or to enjoy their favourite pizza. A recent plan to encourage people in Edinburgh to cut traffic congestion by giving other people a lift to work failed. Few motorists were induced to reduce their petrol costs or the general level of pollution, believing that car-sharing would deprive them of freedom and flexibility. Most people, when challenged, alleged that sharing would tie them down to specific arrangements which would prove too restrictive in practice.

To offer a final example: thinking about images of freedom also evokes the life and work of artists. No longer constrained by the notion that there is a normative aesthetic judgement before which they must bend, artists are free to explore in colour, tone, shape or sound their own individual tastes and personal preferences. They may give free expression to their own experience of the world, interpreting as they please their own inner sensations of reality. In one sense, and to be realistic, or maybe a trifle cynical, their freedom is bounded only by their ability to persuade buyers, collectors, patrons, sponsors or the disbursers of government grants to share their enthusiasms. Art has also been freed from being the domain only of the aesthetic elite or the professional connoisseur. Potentially, everyone can enjoy both classical and modern art, being free to make up their own mind whether they like it or think it worthwhile.

## The language of freedom

The way in which language influences culture and, in turn, is influenced by it makes a fascinating study. There can be little reasonable doubt that the extensive vocabulary associated with modern notions of freedom in itself helps to extend and cement that freedom. A *pluralism,* or more correctly plurality, of beliefs and *lifestyles* is something that most people have come to expect and accept. We freely acknowledge that *alternative* ways of looking at and relating to the world enriches life and our own appreciation of it.

Each person lives a *unique, autonomous* existence. They have a right to be free from the interference of others, as long as they respect other people's equal freedoms to the same extent. A free society is, almost by definition, a *permissive* one. As the saying goes, what I do in the bedroom (or kitchen, living room or garden) is my affair. If others learn about it, and do not like what they hear, they have neither right, responsibility nor duty to impose their definitions of immorality upon me. Freedom should mean a certain space, *liberated* from invasion by the community, to live out my system of *values*.

It follows from this that a free society is one in which people are consciously *open-minded* about differences and *tolerant* of other peoples' choices, always granted that they are acting within the minimum constraints of the law. And if the law in some instances seems to be burdensome or unfair (e.g., in the opinion of some, the age of consent for sexual activity), then the citizen in a *democratic* society should be able to *participate* in getting the law changed.

Although by no means universally agreed either in principle or in detail, the concept of *human rights* as guaranteeing freedoms and hindering their violation is increasingly a concern of national politics and international relations. One of the rights most often spoken about, in order to achieve an *egalitarian* social order, is that of *free access to information*. Many people consider this to be not merely a passive right, in the sense that information should be in the public domain and easily available, but an active right in which, through the educational system and government initiatives, information becomes common property. In an increasingly competitive world, where diverse types of knowledge may make the difference between success and failure, information is the gateway to intelligent *decision-making* and expanded *choice*.

In the realm of employment, *equality of opportunity* has now become widely accepted in theory, if not always in practice. *Discrimination* on the basis of a person's religion, political opinion, colour, ethnic origin, gender or disability is no longer acceptable. Indeed many institutions in their employment practice set themselves the goal of ensuring, where possible, that a short-list of candidates for a job represents a wide variety of different backgrounds. Anti-discriminatory practices also serve to promote the interests and concerns of *minority groups*. As has often been pointed out, even when a society has achieved universal voting rights, it is still in danger of exercising the tyranny of the majority. However, a society is not free, until those who do not feel that they belong to the dominant ethnic group, religion or class are heard and their genuine needs attended to.

Many social historians and analysts[2] would say that the concept which most sharply sums up the modern passion for freedom is that of *individualism* (i.e., the philosophy of life which emphasizes the priority of the individual's concerns over those of any community). *Self-determination* in the political sphere, necessary though it is, is unfinished business, unless the individual is *emancipated* from the social pressures of group loyalty, with its often subtle system of rewards and punishments, claiming *control* over his or her own choices of what religion to follow, if any, whom to vote for, whom to marry, where to live and what kind of career to pursue. To be free is to be *independent*. In the last resort, freedom means accepting restrictions only on a purely *voluntary* basis.

Alongside the language of freedom, we have to acknowledge increasingly in today's world the freedom of language. Language has become something of a battlefield between those who contend that communication is possible only in so far as a community maintains strict control over the traditional meaning of words and the rules of grammar, and those who believe that inherited patterns of signification stultify *creative* thinking, *imaginative* story-telling and *expanding* vocabularies.[3] Indeed, this latter group, no doubt, would think the title of this book entirely misconceived, for there is no one meaning of freedom; everyone is at *liberty* to make their own *options*.

---

[2] E.g. R.H. Preston, *Religion and the Persistence of Capitalism*. London. SCM Press. 1979, pp.73–74.

[3] Cf. J.J. Gumperz, *Discourse Strategies*. Cambridge. CUP. 1989, pp. 204–10; R. Carter, *Language and Literature: An Introductory Reader in Stylistics*. London. George Allen and Unwin. 1982, pp. 4–10, 13–14, 160–176; B. Carter and P. Simpson, *Language, Discourse and Literature: an Introductory Reader in Discourse Stylistics*. London. Unwin Hyman. 1989, pp. 8–17, 66–69; R. Hodge and G. Kress, *Language as Ideology*. London. Routledge and Kegan Paul. 1993, *passim*.

**Instances of freedom**

Whatever may be the power of language and the expectations that it invokes, actual practice is even more important. To what extent is freedom a reality in the daily lives of people in modern societies? Without wanting to anticipate at this point an adequate discussion of the perceptions and meaning(s) of freedom in today's world and to what extent they have a solid substance, we may note that a significant number of people living in highly 'developed' societies experience freedom in ways undreamed of by their forebears.

To begin with – though the order is unimportant – we have more years to enjoy freedom than in any previous era. Through the advent of modern medicine we are largely free from many of the former killer-diseases, such as diphtheria, meningitis, scarlet fever, poliomyelitis, smallpox and tuberculosis.[4] Although it is true that new scourges seem to have taken their place, and some people wonder whether we are, after all, a healthier race than before, there is always the expectancy that in a not too distant future gene-therapy may help to eliminate many grave and hitherto incurable disorders, particularly those that are transmitted genetically.[5]

One of the most characteristic figures of the modern age is the traveller. First the motor car and then air travel has enabled many to enjoy an enormous expansion of their horizons. The advent of the package-holiday, the lessening of visa restrictions, the lure of the exotic and an obsession with the camera and camcorder have lured people to cross frontiers, cultures and languages to experience in brief the pleasures of other parts of the globe. Airports have become symbols of a sea of humanity on the move. Every few seconds an announcement is made in several languages of the departure of a flight north, south, east and west. By this time tomorrow we can be in any part of the world.

---

[4] Tragically, incidents of tuberculosis are, for the first time in decades, again on the increase. The main sufferers seem to be those living in insanitary housing or who have no permanent housing, a group living in, or on the edge of, poverty.

[5] Cf. D. Harti, *Basic Genetics*. Boston. Jones and Bartlett. 1991, pp. 434–8.

Of course, we are only visitors. We travel because home can become stultifying and monotonous. So, we long for wings. Nevertheless, home is also a reassuring place of security and stability. To be a tourist, or engaged on business, is one thing; to emigrate is quite another. In the first case we can be geographically extravagant without disturbing our roots; but the second commits us to a replanting, which is a much more serious, unsettling and problematical choice.

The tourist industry is one aspect of the whole leisure revolution, which has grown exponentially within the last quarter of a century. Leisure has to do with freedom from what is, strictly speaking, necessary for existence. Peripheral to 'real' life, it is the sphere of relaxation, in which I can exercise a personal choice to enjoy myself in my own way.[6] Whatever may be the strains and stresses of everyday working-life, come Friday evening I am free to indulge my interests and hobbies. I am free to play, or watch others play, to entertain or be entertained, as I wish.[7] By referring to this space as 'the weekend', we demonstrate an interesting attitude to the relation between work and play: first, comes the week of five days, in which we earn 'a living', then comes the 'end of the week' when we are free to 'live' by what we have earned. There is a sense in which the freedom of Friday to Sunday is made more sweet by the knowledge that we have already paid for the rest.

Nowhere, perhaps, is the creation of freedom more apparent than in the creation of wealth. Increasingly, since the industrial revolution, the realm of necessity has been transformed into the realm of liberty. For those who possess it, wealth offers a substantial measure of financial security against the uncertainties of life. Through taxation and national insurance programmes the present is secure in the provisions of the welfare state and the future is taken care of through pension plans, insurance and annuity schemes. Wealth gives the flexibility necessary to cope with unforeseen and unwelcome

---

[6] Cf. D. Lyon, *The Steeple's Shadow: on the myths and realities of secularization*. London. SPCK. 1985, p. 61.

[7] Admittedly, this paints an ideal picture which is somewhat modified by having to fit in the necessary tasks of weekly shopping, cleaning and household repairs.

events, such as a protracted illness, the loss of employment, a divorce or a forced early retirement. The possession and enjoyment of private property also helps to expand choice and increase security.

Finally, modern societies have freed individuals from the arbitrary and oppressive obligations formerly demanded by the communities into which they were born. Freedom means liberation from the accident of birth, as a result of which people have often been bound to observe the traditions, customs and regulations of past societies. This new reality has been particularly liberating to women, traditionally confined to well-defined roles in the home on behalf of the family. The right to equal education, to the pursuit of a career, the choice of whether, whom and when to marry, access to methods of family planning, paid maternity leave and, in some countries, free or cheap nursery provision for pre-school children has revolutionized the life and expectations of women.

Though modern societies are prepared to recognize the legitimately diverse cultural norms of different ethnic groups in their midst, they are also quick to point out that there are some rights that override these: for example, a person is no longer expected of necessity to follow the religion, political beliefs, job expectations, choice of marriage partner or circle of friends of his or her parents. The acknowledgment of the right to be different not only holds between cultures, but also between generations; what is sauce for the goose is also sauce for the gander.

**Common understandings of freedom**

Apart from the images, language and instances of freedom that we have already touched upon, freedom is also taken to imply a number of other highly desirable aspects of the common life of society. In this section we shall survey a sample of some of the most significant examples that have essentially changed the way people react to their circumstances and view their place in society. I should emphasize that this whole brief, introductory survey is not intended to foreclose a proper discussion of the meaning of freedom, nor to hide the suspicion that it is not as straightforward or commonly accepted as this first glance might suggest.

Academic or intellectual freedom is highly prized. This is particularly the case in tertiary education. Freedom means that both students and staff are released from having to subscribe to either a set of religious beliefs or a particular ideology, before they can study and teach. In theory, at least, the individual is free to pursue his or her own line of investigation, even when that seems to go against currently received views in a particular discipline. By its very nature research cannot be restricted by preordained hypotheses; a hypothesis is only as strong as the evidence warrants and must therefore be corrected or abandoned if it does not match the evidence. The scholarly ideal is to begin any investigation, in so far as is possible, by suspending judgement. This should mean that, in theory at least, a person's religious, political or moral views should not be allowed to distort their research.

Gradually, over a period of some 400 years, the genuine freedom of conscience of the individual has become more respected. This respect has been built, as we shall see, on the struggle for the free exercise of religion, on giving critical human reasoning priority over inherited dogmas from the past, on the refusal to delegate moral responsibility to others (such as religious authorities) and on the legally protected rights of minorities to dissent. But freedom of conscience has not been won easily, and in not a few countries its recognition today is still problematical over a number of issues. For example, an individual refusing to be conscripted into the army of a nation he deems to be waging an unjust war has often had to pay a high price for this civil disobedience . In recent times, refusal of the draft in the USA at the time of the Vietnam war and refusal to do military service in the South African Defence Force, when engaged offensively in Namibia and Angola, have led young men to imprisonment and ostracism from their communities.

One reason for the development of the modern world has been the desacralization of structures. No longer is any institution considered completely immobile and irremovable. Permanent change is part of the present expectation of civil society. The pragmatism that springs from a technologically oriented world has also contributed to a mood which strongly affirms that institutions should be restructured, if they no longer serve a useful purpose, or cease to exist, if they no longer fulfil the objective for which they were originally created. The authority of inherited, ancient and protected institutions (even those as venerable as the monarchy) can and should be questioned.

Modern people are not prepared to offer uncritical acceptance to anybody who appears to be a self-appointed guardian of tradition, customs or values. Every institution must be potentially open to public scrutiny and public debate. Any form of secrecy or the special pleading of interest groups are especially suspect in the public's mind. Essentially, institutions are there to serve the needs of free people, and not the other way round. Freedom is ensured by making certain that this distinction is carefully maintained.

One institution clearly the object of much discussion and controversy is the welfare state. People disagree about the relation between welfare support and the freedom of the individual. To enter this debate in depth, one would need to review many of the details of state provision, such as education, health care, unemployment benefit, income support, state pensions, transport facilities and investment in industry; this will be possible only to a limited extent in the ensuing chapters. In general terms, however, experience of diverse systems in different countries over at least half a century has led to the formation of two major opinions. Some people argue that freedom ensues from welfare, because redistributing wealth to those in need puts them back on their feet and, once the crisis is past, gives them a new opportunity to take a full and responsible part in society. Others take the opposite view, namely that welfare support in many cases makes people dependent upon the state in a way that deadens their initiative and blunts their urge to take personal responsibility for their own future. Such people become trapped in a cycle of deprivation and hopelessness which is the very opposite of freedom. According to this line of reasoning, to be free is to be self-reliant through confidence-building measures which release a person from dependency on state 'hand-outs' or 'private charity'.[8]

---

[8] For a recent discussion of welfare provision, cf. J. Holmwood, 'Welfare and Citizenship' in R. Bellamy (ed.), *Theories and Concepts of Politics: an introduction.* Manchester. Manchester University Press. 1993, pp. 98–123.

Many accounts of the coming of the modern world argue that one of the principal causal factors has been the radically different place that religion occupies in society. Most religions display at least two faces: the face of orthodox belief and practice and the face of popular devotion. In both cases the typically modern process of secularization has made a vast difference to people's perception of the role of religion in life. It is generally believed, although there is much circumstantial evidence to the contrary, that a scientific view of the world has broken people's ancient, and near universal, submission to the power of fate. Belief in fate is tied into a static and deterministic attitude to human destiny, propelling people into all kinds of magical practice. Today, however, though many forms of superstition are regularly practised, people tend either to feel ashamed of what they are afraid will appear to others an irrational approach to circumstances and events, or else try to treat the matter in a somewhat frivolous and lighthearted manner.

Orthodox and popular religion have shared a similar outcome: both are largely relegated to the realm of private belief and semi-obscure practice. We talk about religion being 'privatized', meaning that it no longer has much power or persuasion in the public arena but is owned mainly by individuals who invest time and money in it, because they think it will bring them some kind of benefit or profit. It is characteristic of a free society that religion has become, in effect, another commodity, divided into different competing brands, each trying to increase its share of the market. Individuals are then considered most free when able, without prior commitment, to test the brands to discover which one might most truly enhance their experience of life, put them most in touch with their feelings and most clearly meet their needs. For authentic belief wells up spontaneously from the depths of a person's real self. If, for any reason, it seems to be inadequate, it can be changed, without any social stigma attached, for another product.

## Conclusion

In this first chapter I have tried to capture a mood which I believe is prevalent throughout the world. Though most evident in societies where there is a high standard of living and principles of liberal democracy are operating, the mood also surfaces in other societies, stimulated by the reality and message of freedom conveyed into people's homes through the penetration of Western media (particularly by the subtle persuasion of the advertising industry), even when freedom is repressed outside the home. At the same time, it is obviously important that we do not too quickly conflate cultural perceptions of freedom with real freedom.

Deliberately, this chapter has not called into question the conviction of many people (particularly those enjoying good health and a steady income) that, within certain fairly minimal constraints, they are free to do most of the things they like doing and that their quality of life would considerably diminish, if social and political life were ever to become more restricted. For the moment, I am concerned with what appears evident on the surface of life to any reasonably perceptive observer in touch with the beliefs and aspirations of his or her neighbours. Other aspects of life, which might present a rather different perspective, have not been included in this initial incursion into the subject; they will be looked at later in the study.

# Two

# Freedom before Freedom

In a deeper search for the meaning of freedom, there is some merit in beginning at the roots of Western thought and political life. Admittedly, it would be a bold person who tried to make any direct connections between the thought of the Greek philosophical schools or that of Christian theologians, following the Constantinian unification of church and state, and the kind of convictions about freedom that we summarized in the previous chapter. Nevertheless, and perhaps this is not so surprising, these immensely influential antecedents of the Western way of interpreting reality raised many issues we still struggle with today. Plato, for example (anticipating, perhaps, the banning of 'video-nasties'), believed that in certain circumstances it was quite justifiable to censor written materials the young could have access to and particular activities they could engage in.

Few, if any, of the pre-modern thinkers made freedom a direct object of their enquiry. They were concerned more immediately with other matters. As a result, their views on freedom have to be deduced from their outlook on a number of other subjects. These are not so difficult to discover, as long as one remembers that their understanding of freedom often comes as the by-product of a reflection whose centre lies elsewhere and which happened in a situation informed by interests vastly different from our own.

## The Greek schools of philosophy

As the intention of this chapter is to indicate only a few of the most important trends which precede the much more obsessive preoccupation with freedom that is one of the marks of modern societies, I will mention only a few of the major thinkers – Socrates, Plato, Aristotle, and the Epicurean and Stoic traditions. Among these we find a remarkable commonality of language and beliefs, such that it makes sense to say that one of the pillars of the Western intellectual tradition is Greek philosophy (in the singular). However there are also some significant differences both of substance and emphasis.

Among the similarities we may note the high place given to the intellect as the agent whose task it is to discern the place of human beings in the universe. The Greek philosophers also believed that there is an essential nature to all things and that there is an absolute moral order, although they disagreed about its content. For Plato, at least in the writings of his middle period, the reality of the absolute comes through a person's memory brought from another existence of ideal forms, from which every individual instance, whether abstract or concrete, derives its meaning – justice, courage, beauty, a chair, a table and so on.

These philosophers also believed that knowledge could be acquired only through a long, rigorous discipline of mental training, for which some had more of an innate ability than others. In differing degrees they held to the necessity of life, in the sense that there is a given order and purpose in the universe, in fulfilling which people are able to find their true selves.[1] They believed that the highest goal of human endeavour was to reach out for 'the good', and that in this search alone could human beings experience true happiness.

Above all they saw a direct relationship between what went on in the inner life of people – in their reason, their soul and their desires (or affections) – and what went on in the external life of the human community. It is by bringing together the inner world of personal existence and the outer world of social existence that

---

[1] Cf. Alasdair Macintyre, *After Virtue: A Study in Moral Theory*. London. Duckworth. 1985, p. 134.

we can come close to discovering what they understood real freedom to be.

### i. The freedom within

The Greeks made a number of important assumptions which guided the way they thought about human life in the universe. There is a moral order which is not ours to invent, although we may violate it.[2] Transgressing the good, however, is tragedy. Achieving the good happens when each part of the human soul is regulated in harmony with the other parts, so that they may all perform the task which is allotted to them. Such a state, which is in accord with nature, realizes true justice in the soul and brings with it the happiness for which everyone strives.

Aristotle argued that the ultimate good is that which draws every other action in its wake. Its existence is necessary, for without it desire would be constantly frustrated, given that we would always desire what we could never attain and, consequently, our purpose as humans would remain unfulfilled. The highest good is *eudaimonia*, often translated 'happiness', but perhaps more expressively, 'well-being'. This is achieved by using our reason well in order to know what are the moral virtues and to practise them.

The difficulty with this way of depicting the good life is that it tends to be circular: if 'the good life for people is a life of happiness' and 'happiness is an activity of the soul in accord with perfect virtue', then virtue is the way people ought to behave in order to achieve happiness.[3] What seems to be meant is that a person will achieve goodness, when they use their rational faculties to control their desires, so that what they actually do also fulfils what they are destined to be as human beings.

Stoicism emphasized even more the danger of the passions, which spring from external impulses (we might use the word

---

[2] Socrates, according to Plato, seemed to believe that no one would willingly turn against the good. If they acted wrongly, and therefore against their own best interests, it was due to ignorance about their own good. Cf. Dion Scott-Kakures (et. al.), *History of Philosophy*. New York. Harper Collins. 1993, p. 25.

[3] Cf. R.H. Popkin and A. Stroll, *Philosophy*. Oxford. Butterworth-Heinemann. 1993, pp. 8–10.

'temptations'). Again, according to this philosophy, it is the mind that oversees our lives, so that we know at any one time what is the right thing to do. This is happiness. Though we may be powerless to alter the external circumstances of our lives, we are able to control the correct attitude of our mind. Even Epicureanism, which has gained a reputation for consistently advocating a hedonistic lifestyle,[4] distinguished between what might appear desirable and what gives true pleasure. In some ways the philosophical advice was negative: better to avoid pain than seek out pleasures whose end product is suffering and sorrow. Individuals have the ability and duty to calculate their own best ends.

That person is free who acquires wisdom through the right use of reason. This means putting the different aspects of life into a correct relationship with each another. Freedom then is true mastery of the self (*autexousion* – power over oneself).[5] For Plato its opposite is the unruly spirit, which allows mere desire to triumph over reason. In this respect he disagreed with Socrates, believing that, even when one knew the good, one could fail to do it.

In Aristotle's thought freedom is bound up with knowing one's true end. In his theory of the four 'causes' (the material, formal, efficient and final), it is essential that each be brought into the proper relationship with the others. Human beings have an essential nature (the material and formal causes) which can only be fulfilled when it performs certain characteristic functions (the efficient cause). To achieve this is the human being's purpose, what he or she is supposed to be for (final cause). Freedom, then, is knowing the purpose for which one came into the world and achieving it.

In contrast to Plato's more idealist, theoretical or abstract notion of knowledge, Aristotle believes that one's true end is discovered through experience and is to be empirically tested. In

---

[4] 'Epicurus . . . was a secular evangelist who had to preach the secret of true happiness.' J.O. Urmson and J. Ree, *The Concise Encyclopedia of Western Philosophy and Philosophers*. London. Routledge. 1989, p. 93.

[5] Later, in different circumstances, Cicero expressed a similar belief: 'What is freedom? The power to live as you will. Who then lives as he will except one who follows the things that are right, who delights in his duty . . .' Quoted in R. McKeon, *Freedom and History and Other Essays*. Chicago. University of Chicago Press. 1990, p. 205.

other words, knowledge comes in the actual reaching out towards the goal. Though he would not have used the language, Aristotle would have concurred with the idea that freedom comes through the right combination of action and reflection. In his doctrine of 'the mean' (striking the right balance between opposing vices) he allows that the particular circumstances of a person dictate to a certain degree what it is right to do: 'Anger and pity . . . may be felt both too much and too little, and in both cases not well; but to feel them at the right *times*, with reference to the right *people*, with the right *motive*, and in the right *way*, is what is intermediate and best, and this is characteristic of virtue'.[6]

In the thinking of the Stoics freedom can be exercised only in relation to fate. The rational order of the universe is a predetermined order, such that everything that happens, given the pre-existing circumstances, could have happened only in a particular way. To be free is in part to recognize and accept the power of necessity. At the same time, one can build an inner citadel of freedom in which one is secure from the 'slings and arrows of outrageous fortune'. Some have interpreted this as a doctrine of *apatheia* or indifference to all external events. Freedom resides in the ability to decide whether, or not, one will be affected by others' power to restrict our freedoms.

In this sense the practice of non-cooperation with the evil acts of others amounts to freedom. And if outward coercion becomes irresistible, one can use the inner weapon of disdain towards others' actions, thereby maintaining the purity of one's own thoughts and motives. Marcus Aurelius distinguished between an outward liberty, which is the absence of restraining circumstances, and an inner freedom which is the rightness of choice. Liberty is the action of circumstances on humans, freedom is human action on circumstances. We are free to choose when to accept compulsion and how to turn it to our own good use.[7]

---

[6] Quoted in J.O. Urmson and J. Ree, ibid. p. 30.
[7] *Meditations*, viii.3, cited in R. McKeon, op.cit., p. 206.

### ii. Freedom in the state

In a real sense Plato's life-work in forming his 'Academy' in 385 BC was to reform the political life of the Greek city states (the *polis*). Both before, and more particularly after, the death of Socrates (condemned to death by the citizens of Athens on vague and ridiculous charges), Plato had come to realize that political life was at a low ebb and could be changed only by a drastic revolution in the way the state was governed.

He despised the exercise of democracy (rule by the general populace), likening it to the uncontrolled rule of the inner life by the appetites. Democracy, he thought, easily degenerates into anarchy, which in turn gives rise to the demagogue and the tyrannical rule of the strongest. The problem, first voiced by Socrates, is that decision by majority vote is doomed to failure, because most people do not have either the time, inclination or ability to acquire a necessary intellectual grasp of political issues. This fault is compounded by the unwillingness of most politicians to recognize their own ignorance. It follows that, if right understanding is all-important, freedom of discussion and action is largely irrelevant. The general public may debate and pass resolutions, but in effect they are merely trading ignorances.

Hence, the state should prepare with great care and precision those who do have the requisite gifts and training to rule. They are the guardians (or 'philosopher-kings'). Their function, mirroring that of reason in the soul, is to act after rational deliberation entirely for the good of the whole community. Such people are partly born and partly formed. At the age of eighteen, young people are to undergo a series of theoretical and practical, intellectual and moral tests to see whether they have an innate capacity to undertake the responsibilities of governing. At a later stage they will be given minor administrative posts, working under observation, until at the age of about fifty they will, if they come through all the tests successfully, be ready to assume the highest offices of state.

Plato made a number of assumptions about the implementation of his ideal state. He believed that the guardians would act selflessly in the interests of the common good. He also concluded that they would not be tempted by power, because their true love would always remain the pursuit of wisdom for its own sake. He presumed that the rest of the population would acquiesce in this arrangement, because their own functions as soldiers or artisans would be best facilitated and enhanced by the proper running of the city. Finally, he held that rigorous intellectual training through the study of higher mathematics and the Forms would be the best way of equipping people for political duties.

Freedom was the acceptance of one's given place and role in the state. The free state is the one where each individual fulfils the task for which he or she is fitted by nature. In this way individuals are freed from the pretence of being something other than they are and can develop a richer life, up to the maximum of their capacities. In order to perform each function successfully a corresponding training is necessary.

So far, we have been concerned with the Plato who is best known: the writer of the *Republic*. However, in what is generally termed his third period, in part due to a disastrous personal incursion into the actual political life of the kingdom of Syracuse in Sicily, Plato became considerably less idealistic about the possibilities of enlightened rule by an elite group of men and (significantly) women. His last work, the *Laws*, shows a realistic, or perhaps pessimistic, attitude to the way that people act in real life. In this work Plato advocated the supreme importance of laws, precisely so that the *polis* would not be left at the mercy of those who might be tempted to abuse their trust and power. The rule of law would give to the state the stability that it needed, freeing it from the destructive power of civil strife. As in many subsequent accounts of political idealism, law appears as the lesser of two evils; it is also clearly less than the best.

Aristotle agreed with Plato's abhorrence of democracy as it had been exercised in Athens. Nevertheless, he did allow for a modified form of it: he advocated a form of constitutional government, in which all citizens would have access to some office, so that they might have personal experience of being both the ruled and rulers. He believed that the most stable society would be one in which those in the 'middle', neither the rich nor the poor, held the balance of power (anticipating, perhaps, the role of the middle classes in modern societies). Notwithstanding the introduction of a greater flexibility into governance and a widening of its scope, Aristotle still believed in a hierarchically ordered society. Participation, in the measure in which it was allowed, was only for those granted the status of citizens; women, resident aliens, children and slaves were not counted. They were not fit for this position, only for the lower state into which they were born.

For the Greek philosophers, freedom implied a knowledge and understanding of the right order of things and the willingness to comply with it. Control over the prospect of disorder and disintegration was more important than that people should be allowed to act as they desired. This account of freedom leads inevitably to authoritarian regimes (even if 'benevolent' ones), for some people, appointing themselves unilaterally as the guardians of the rest, will have to decide unrepresentatively what is order and what threatens it.[8] It is an illiberal freedom because it assumes that some, by virtue of considering themselves more enlightened than others, have acquired the right to decide what is in the best interests of the rest.

### Freedom in the style of Hippo and Rotterdam

In the nature of the case it is impossible to determine a set date for the beginning of the modern period of Western history. This is due to the fact that many disparate elements – economic, scientific, social, political, religious and artistic – contributed to a way of being and thinking that gradually took shape, but without any of them exactly coinciding in time. For example, the Italian 'Renaissance' (from the early fourteenth century onwards), although it began to introduce a critical methodology into the study of documents and encouraged a flowering of new artistic ideas and forms, was little interested in the developing natural sciences.

In some ways the Renaissance was 'late-medieval' and in some ways 'early-modern'. It was a period of transition in which the stability of the medieval world was coming to an end 'with the growth of nationalism, the breakdown of the feudal order,

---

[8] According to J. Barnes, 'Aristotle . . . was an authoritarian. His state will determine whether and when I may play the flute.' D. Miller (et al.), *Encyclopaedia of Political Thought*. Oxford. Blackwell, p. 23.

the expansion of trade and towns, the decline in the authority of the Church and Empire, and the emergence of an educated laity'.[9]

Arbitrary though it may appear, I will take the figure of Erasmus as exemplifying the situation immediately before the birth of modern Europe. A giant of learning and culture, he was strongly opposed to the Protestant Reformation in the form it took. Thus he resisted what was undoubtedly the most cataclysmic event that happened in the intersection between two worlds; one might describe him as remaining on the threshold, but refusing to enter the new emerging reality.

Just as Greek thought has been, and remains, enormously influential in later stages of European culture, and was part of the rebirth of independent study from the time of Petrarch and Boccaccio onwards, so Augustine also towers over the whole Western tradition of personal and social development, uniting in himself (as well as neo-platonic thought) the other two major influences on Europe, the Hebrew-Christian and the Roman.

Our preview of pre-modern conceptions of freedom begins with a rapid survey of the contributions of these two formidable figures who stand, as it were, at either end of the long post-classical and medieval period of European history.

## i. Augustine

In some of his assumptions Augustine stood close to the range of thought associated with Plato's philosophy, more particularly in its neo-platonic dress. This can be seen, for example, in the way he gave the invisible and eternal world priority over the sensible and mutable. However, in many respects his thought diverges quite radically from that of the philosophical schools. If his own spiritual pilgrimage ends with the famous dictum that the heart is restless until it finds its rest in the eternal God, then God becomes central to all his convictions. Though he shares with Plato and others the belief that the goal of life is the pursuit of the good, he differs from them about both the true destination and the path to take.

---

[9] Roger Lockyer, *Hapsburg and Bourbon Europe 1470-1720*. Harlow. Longman. 1974, p. 91.

What distinguishes Augustine is his conviction that human beings are not on their own when trying to discover the reality of life; they do not have to depend either on the memory of another life or on reason to discover the form of the good. God has taken the initiative and spoken to the human race through the Hebrew prophets, through Jesus of Nazareth and through his apostles. What God speaks is true. It cannot be either discovered or verified by reason, for reason has become corrupted by sin, turned in on itself so that it becomes self-contemplating and self-absorbed. Ultimately the truth can be apprehended, or rather one is apprehended by it, only through believing.

However, reason is neither suspended nor contradicted on the way to understanding truth; yet neither is it the measure of that which has to be found. Comprehension dawns only as one actively takes the risk of believing. Hence both versions of Augustine's immortal saying are true: *Credo ut intelligam:* one believes *in order to* (*ut*) understand, and *Credo et intelligo:* one believes *and so* (*et*) understands. But the act of believing is not a leap into the unknown, but a coming to know the one who is already there, who has revealed himself: one knows, because one is already known (from conception). The final truth is not an idea, ideal or supreme moral virtue, but a personal being.

The initiative which God takes is called grace. As a result of God's grace, a human being is free to be able to choose a life of blessedness. Augustine accepted and developed the classical Christian doctrines of creation, the fall of humanity through Adam, liberation in Jesus Christ and the hope of the future kingdom of God. It is because all have inherited Adam's sin of pride and self-love that the belief of classical Greek philosophy in the capacity for rational self-control and just self-government is naive. Human nature has become corrupt, biased towards the pursuit of self-centred enjoyment. It is now innately dominated by passions which bring all kinds of confusion. Thus humans cannot make their own way back to the one true source of well-being, God. The human will is free to turn away from selfless love (God's love and love of God), but not towards it. Only grace draws back human beings to the true source of their life and the fulfilment of their being.

The world is divided into two realms or cities, one inhabited by those who have experienced the grace of God and believe that he is their ultimate vision and point of rest, and one by those who do not. Although they live in the same nation, their fundamental foci are opposed: one group seeks for the blessing of social life as God has ordained it, the other the values of corrupt earthly existence, such as honour and patriotism. Since the fall there have always been two cities, distinguished by two loyalties and two objectives:

> Two cities have been formed by two loves . . . love of self . . . (and) the love of God . . . In the one, the princes and nations it subdues are ruled by the love of ruling; in the other, the princes and the subjects serve one another in love.[10]

Augustine was writing his *City of God* approximately one century after the Roman empire adopted Christianity as the official religion of the state. Before that time, the supreme ruler was regarded as divine, or as partaking of divine functions. Christians, though they refused to worship the divine nature of the state, in their own terms remained loyal members of the civil order. Augustine reflects the separation of the two cities, each with functions particular to its own purposes. The state as an institution has been ordained by God to administer justice, but, in contrast to the eternal city, has no ultimate value.

Augustine did not make the mistake, committed by the religious thinking of a later more autocratic age, of identifying the city of God with the Church, or of suggesting that the secular city should be subordinated to the Church. Each has its own autonomy and should be free from undue interference from the other. The secular city is not totally deprived, through sin, of rational deliberation – it can, for example, discuss and implement the principles of the just war (*jus ad bellum* and *jus in bello*, the justification of the use of force and the use of force in the event of hostilities); and the city of God is itself a mixture of wheat and tares. The secular city is also blessed by the implementation of distinctively Christian principles and by the presence within it of Christians holding office in the state. The just war is itself an interesting mixture of Roman law (just cause, right authority, and proportionality) and Christian convictions (the inviolability of the innocent, and just intentions).

---

[10] *De civitate Dei*, xiv.28

The state, when left to itself, is informed only by love of this earthly existence in its diversity and duplicity. It is not founded on justice, and can realize justice only partially. It is the life of Christian faith that makes citizens just and good. The state, therefore, is dependent upon 'the citizens of the kingdom of heaven . . . (being) engaged in the affairs of Babylon'.[11] Augustine seemed to see a kind of *modus vivendi* existing between the two cities:

> The Christian empire is not a divine politeia, nor the herald of a new age of peace and security, but a pragmatic union of two entities essentially different in their ideals and destined for two quite different ends.[12]

Perhaps the most subtle, and yet deeply significant difference concerning freedom between the classical pre-Christian thinkers and Augustine does not reside in the belief that attaining order is the mark of a free society, but in the fact that for the former 'sin' is to be defined as the upsetting of order, whilst for the latter it is sin which is responsible for upsetting the divine order. The relationship between order, sin (in its different forms) and freedom will continue to be part of our study of the meaning of freedom.

## ii. Erasmus

In his own right, Erasmus has not made such a formative contribution to the underlying assumptions of Western culture as Augustine. The latter, because his views on creation, the fall and redemption in Christ and their significance for the whole life of humanity were rediscovered and promoted anew in the Reformation and later Puritan writings, has moulded central aspects of Western belief. The former has become more a symbol than an original creator of another way of looking at the world.

Nevertheless, Erasmus is important because of what he represents. He has been called 'the first conscious European . . . the ablest champion of the humanities and of a spiritual

---

[11] On *Psalm 51.6*, quoted in F. Copleston, *A History of Philosophy: Volume II*. London. Burns Oates and Washbourne. 1950, p. 88.
[12] L.G. Patterson, *God and History in Early Christian Thought*. London. Adam and Charles Black. 1967, p. 119.

ideal'.[13] He combines within himself two important elements
from his background, both of which immensely influenced his
own assumptions and stayed with him for the whole of his life:
the 'pietistic' spirituality of the Brethren of the Common Life
and the discovery of the Renaissance world of learning:

> 'There are two Erasmi: one an ardent, erudite classical scholar
> . . . the other a sincere and devoted believer in the 'philosophy of
> Christ'.[14]

He is often classified as one of the first of the early
'humanists'. This is satisfactory, so long as one understands that
he strove, according to his own lights, to combine the 'two
Erasmi', and that the word in his case does not have the modern
connotation of agnosticism or atheism. The 'humanist' tag
comes from his identification with the ideals of the Renaissance,
particularly the surge of new interest in the spirit of classical
antiquity and the many attempts made to relate the thinking of
the Greek and Latin philosophers and political theorists to
contemporary life:

> Humanism . . . stands for the rediscovery of poetry, rhetoric and
> epistolography as marks of the man of learning . . . It included as
> well a clear emphasis on ethics.[15]

Standing within this tradition, Erasmus held a number of
assumptions which are of paramount importance in
ascertaining his views on freedom. He was a firm advocate of the
power of education to strengthen and elevate the noble aspects
of human nature. He had an optimistic view of the potential of
human endeavour, 'since by the use of reason (as long as it was
accompanied with humility and devotion) man could hope to
attain knowledge and understanding of God'.[16] He believed that
the times in which he lived needed to be rescued from doctrinal

---

[13] S. Zweig, *Erasmus*. London. Souvenir Press. 1979, p. 1

[14] M. Spinka, *Advocates of Reform. from Wyclif to Erasmus*. (Library of
Christian Classics, Vol. XIV). London. SCM Press. 1953, p. 281.

[15] H.O. Oberman, *The Dawn of the Reformation: Essays in Late Medieval and
Early Reformation Thought*. Edinburgh. T and T Clark. 1992, p. 66. In his own
work Erasmus spent much time applying the critical literary methods to the
original sources of Christianity, producing the first annotated version of the
Greek New Testament.

[16] R. Lockyer, op.cit., p. 101.

dogmatism and conflict and from the intellectual obscurantism into which it had fallen. Because he set such great value on independence of mind and the rational, critical interchange of the scholarly community, he detested all forms of fanaticism, whether these flowed from the speculations ˉof the medieval schoolmen or from the new theological 'orthodoxies' of the reformers.

He was a tireless, though detached, champion of reform within the Church. He was genuinely appalled at the arbitrary authority of the Church, the manipulation of the sacraments for gain and the hypocritical life of the clergy (of which he, being the illegitimate son of a priest, was one result). The best known of his highly entertaining satirical works is his *Praise of Folly*, which 'aims at reforming the current Christian world by shaming men into a life of reason and true inward piety'.[17] In the last analysis he believed that the structures of the Church were inessential, 'that through education, attacks on religious abuses and a return to the original sources of Christianity, the church would be restored to purity'.[18]

However, though Erasmus was sympathetic to many of Martin Luther's criticisms of the Church, the two were separated by different temperaments, styles and ultimately convictions about those central elements of the faith of early Christianity which were being so devastatingly compromised by the doctrine and practice of the Church. Erasmus's main response to Luther, *De libero arbitrio* (*On Free Choice*, 1524), was not designed so much to refute the reformer's belief in the 'slavery of the will' as to warn against theological contentiousness. One of the reasons why he broke with Luther was the latter's willingness, as he saw it, to stir up theological and social unrest and, in the last resort, to separate from the Church.[19] Luther, on the other hand,

---

[17] M. Spinka, op.cit., p. 287.

[18] J.C. Keene (ed.), *The Western Heritage of Faith and Reason*. New York. Harper and Row. 1963, p. 495.

[19] Erasmus could be said to represent a kind of religious *via media*. Nothing within religion should be either accepted or rejected out of hand, although attitudes were important. Thus, in a celebrated passage at the end of the *Enchiridion* (or *Handbook of the Christian Soldier*) he says, 'Monasticism is not godliness, but a kind of life, either useful or useless to anyone depending on one's habit of body and of temperament. Certainly just as I do not urge you to it so I do not urge you against it.' (Text in M. Spinka, op. cit., p. 378)

objected to what he saw as Erasmus's humanist attitude of uncommitted scholarly enquiry.

Not only were the two motivated by different ideals, the question of the freedom, or bondage, of the will was a matter of major controversy between them. It reopened the polemic between Augustine and Pelagius which, in different forms, is still with us today. Erasmus argued that to declare the human will free, in the sense that it could accept or reject God's offer of grace to lead a morally righteous life, was necessary for a number of reasons: to emphasize human responsibility for the practice of good; to absolve God from the accusation of creating evil wills, and to prevent people falling into either despair or an undue sense of security.[20]

The two opinions represent a dichotomy in the Western view of human nature, which has 'ever oscillated between two extremes – either God is all in all, and man is nothing, or man is at the centre, and God plays a secondary role'.[21] At that time, and for at least the next 150 years, the Augustinian thesis of Luther held sway. The tradition represented by Erasmus (though not so strongly in his own writings) also lived on, developed and eventually came to the fore at another time and in another generation. To this we will also return in due course.

---

[20] Cf. M. Spinka, op.cit., p. 292.
[21] Ibid., p. 291.

# Three

# Origins of the Modern View

Endeavouring to trace the sixteenth and seventeenth century precursors of those experiences of freedom taken for granted in contemporary Western societies is a hazardous business. For every example of greater liberties and toleration won many more could be given against such a trend. By the second half of the seventeenth century, for example, 'absolutist'[1] monarchy seemed to hold sway across most of Europe. Thomas Munck has made the perceptive comment that Western society is prone to emphasising those aspects of its history that in the end become dominant or prove "correct".[2] Hence, it is tempting to rummage around in every conceivable corner of the history of the period to discover instances of a more general tendency towards freedom than the evidence unfortunately admits.

The aim of this chapter is modest and its conclusions mainly circumspect. Historical investigation cannot rely upon an abundance of easily accessible, self-explanatory facts which can be marshalled to demonstrate unequivocally certain theories about the historical development of human societies. Too many

---

[1] The word is disputed, because it has been made to refer to different kinds of regimes. Though the term itself did not appear until the very end of the eighteenth century, it is used of sovereign authority in a state largely unlimited by either representative institutions or constitutional controls. Such authority was characteristic of the period of European history between the Treaties of Westphalia (1648) and the French Revolution (1789).

[2] *Seventeenth Century Europe: State, Conflict and the Social Order in Europe 1598-1700*. Basingstoke. Macmillan. 1980, p. 298.

## Economic developments

It is clear that what we know as modern capitalism had its beginnings from the mid-eighteenth century onwards in the Industrial Revolution. Now for the first time the necessary factors of production were in place, as the rapid changes in manufacturing processes began to take hold. This new event was also accompanied by a conceptual change in outlook from the 'mercantilist' opinion[4] – that top economic priority should be given to the balance of trade, achieved through protectionist measures and the granting of monopoly rights to trading companies – to a belief in genuine free trade through open competition. The relative stability of the population, or even its decline, through war and plague, the enormous incidence of poverty across the whole continent,[5] the large agricultural sector having to be self-sufficient in terms of living needs, the difficulties of transport and the uncertainties caused by prolonged or recurring conflicts, were additional reasons why the creation of wealth, which is both a requisite for and result of capital expansion, was sluggish during this period.

Nevertheless, many of the elements of a pre-capitalist 'capitalism' had been operating since the rise of the independent economies of the Italian city states in the fifteenth century. Some trace the incipient development of capitalism as far back as the twelfth century when the drainage and utilization of wet soils increased yields and produced a surplus.[6] At a later stage, the rising 'bourgeoisie' of the urban centres (the merchants, bankers, tax-officials, owners of transport and others) began to invest surplus capital in rural development. Thanks also to a new agricultural revolution that began in the north of the Low

---

[4] Cf. D.II. Pennington, *Seventeenth Century Europe*. London. Longman. 1970, pp. 73–75.

[5] A British economist of that time, Gregory King, calculated that in 1688 more than half the population of England were 'decreasing the wealth of the kingdom' – 'a term which may denote those earning no surplus from their labour and thus living, without savings, around or below subsistence level' (T. Munck, op.cit., p.103).

[6] Cf. S. Hall and B. Gieben, op.cit., p. 101.

such theories have in the course of time bitten the dust, mercilessly shot down by counter-arguments demonstrating how some 'facts' have been selectively used and others totally ignored. Human life is complex and, particularly when not immediately available to us as personal observers, ambiguous and uncertain.

Rather, historians have been left with different forms of evidence which are random, incomplete and often coloured by the chroniclers' own views of events. The historian's task is 'to achieve the highest level of probability congruent with the state of the evidence'.[3] Bearing in mind these cautions, I will look at five main aspects of the life of the European continent during these two centuries: economic developments, political independence, religious diversification, scientific investigation and intellectual debate. Because history is continuous, though not rigidly determined, we shall discover in this period the *seeds* of those freedoms which in the next 300 years have germinated to become the freedoms we enjoy, reflect upon, take for granted or regard with confusion and fear.

Historical reconstruction is also complicated by the way in which different forces intertwine and affect each other. In the nature of the case, none of the five areas I want to explore are independent. Each has a significant bearing on the others. It would be tempting to concentrate on the intellectual debate: partly because writings give more clearly presented evidence, partly because doing so would entail less conjecture, partly because of the sheer fascination of ideas. However, adopting such a procedure would be a serious mistake, for ideas too are influenced by circumstances, and this was as true (perhaps more so) for this period as for others. For this reason I will treat it last; otherwise, the order is not intended to support any particular theory of the relative importance of these different facets of human social life.

---

[3] E. Ives, 'The Gospel and History' in H. Montefiore, *The Gospel and Contemporary Culture*. London. Mowbray. 1992, p. 20.

Countries from the late sixteenth century onwards, the land began to yield much more than a mere subsistence level of output.[7]

In spite of restrictions on trade through tolls, tariff exactions, restrictions on some trades and the encouragement of monopolies (designed to protect national commerce) and the debilitating structures of the medieval guilds, there was a substantial increase in trade during this period. Two major factors stimulated this growth. Waterways, including newly constructed canals, began to be used increasingly. This expanding form of transport was exploited by better designed barges, which raised the ratio of goods carried to the manpower needed to operate them and thus increased profitability.

The second factor in growth was overseas trade. Two potent factors in this development were the discovery of the sea route to the East via the Cape of Good Hope and the beginning of the European colonization of the continent of North America. At the beginning of the seventeenth century the Dutch had supplanted the Spanish as the main overseas trading nation. They had at that time both a superior military capability at sea and a superior design in ships. The relative flexibility of their political system in comparison with other nations also enhanced trading opportunities: for example, the Dutch East India Company (established in 1602) was not so publicly accountable as, for example, the equivalent English East India Company. They even achieved some trading concessions with Japan, taking over from the Portuguese and Spanish, who had been banned from the Imperial realms as a result of aggressive missionary work and political intrigue.

By the end of the century, however, the British had established themselves as the dominant maritime power. The Dutch did not have a population large enough to sustain either a preeminence of power at sea or a substantial permanent migration to overseas territories. In this latter case the settlements of largely British

---

[7] 'The agricultural revolution itself was achieved through a combination of livestock husbandry using special fodder crops, large-scale dairying for export, the adoption of complex crop rotations and convertible husbandry combined with heavier manuring using industrial by-products and urban night soil, and the extensive cultivation of pulses, root vegetables and various industrial crops which improved soil balance' (T. Munck, op.cit., pp. 88–9).

migrants on the Eastern sea-board of North America created a substantial market. As a result, London became the centre for re-exporting goods from across the Atlantic.[8]

Entrepreneurial activity was perhaps most closely evident in the financial sector of the economy. The relative freedom of the autonomous city states of Northern Italy (such as Venice and Genoa) from imperial dynastic controls and the growing commercial ports of Antwerp, Amsterdam and Hamburg encouraged individuals into the money-lending market. Their activities were stimulated by the desperate need of heads of state to secure funds to carry on major conflicts, such as the Thirty Years War (1618–48), or long-running internal struggles like that between the Catholic kings of France and the Protestant Huguenots. Banking became increasingly accepted as a necessary way of life as the religiously inspired ban on usury was weakened. A convenient distinction was made between usury, defined as extortionate interest, and acceptable levels of monetary gain.

War was also the occasion which industrialists like Louis de Geer used to build up a considerable financial empire. De Geer acquired control of gun-making in Sweden during the latter period of the Thirty Years' War and supplied arms to 'most European belligerents regardless of religious or political implications'.[9] On the back of this, he also diversified into other industrial enterprises in Sweden and abroad.[10] The arms industry was built on the Swedish copper and iron-ore mines. Coal-mining capacity and output in Britain and Germany also increased during this time and encouraged some technological innovations, although the scale of operations cannot be compared with what occurred some 150 years later.

Apart from mining, the other major industry of the time was the manufacture of textiles. The techniques employed were unsophisticated and labour-intensive, as they were in other industries such as glass, furniture-making and metal working. These were often carried out in home-based workshops by families, which passed on the necessary skills from one generation to another. As wealth was gradually accumulated by

[8] Cf. T. Munck, ibid., pp. 377–380.
[9] T. Munck, ibid., p. 125.
[10] Cf. Pennington, op.cit., pp. 59–60.

traders, small-scale manufacturers, wealthy farmers, bankers and others, so the demand for goods rose and the result was a diversification of output.

These professions began to represent a new social 'class', quite independent of the nobility and the land-owners. They increasingly embodied an alternative set of political interests to those of the traditional established families. Their increasing importance in the economies, particularly of Northern Europe, began to have political repercussions.[11] At the same time, poverty was endemic and, as the cities grew, an increasing problem. The vast majority of the population, even when women and children contributed to the earning power of families, was at or below the bread-line. The presence of this marginal stratum of society also had its political impact.

## Political independence

An embryonic system of capital accumulation and individual property rights encouraged a tendency towards economic diversification and independence. This period coincided with a breakdown of political centralization in some parts of Europe, the gradual recognition (though with many setbacks) of a plurality of beliefs and allegiances, new institutionalized ways of calling authority into question and an increasing demand for an account of political legitimacy. Together, given time, much suffering and conflict, these amounted to a frontal assault on the restriction of civil liberties and the concentration of political power.

The first and major cause of the broadening of power bases was the Reformation. In some ways this simply hastened factors already leading to the creation of new political entities in central Europe, as princes utilized the combination of religious fervour and nationalism engendered to make themselves independent of

[11] Not least in the political and social implications of the status of private property. Alan Ryan believes that the invention of property rights has been one of the greatest of freedom-creating acts, for it enlarges choice, allows people to plan ahead and gives them the incentive to innovate (cf. 'Liberty and Socialism' in B. Pimlott (ed.), *Fabian Essays in Socialist Thought*. London. Heinemann. 1984, p. 109).

the all-embracing Empire. At the same time, it made the birth of the modern nation-state a permanent reality. The Peace of Augsburg (1555) formulated the famous maxim, *cuius regio, eius religio*, whereby either Catholicism or Lutheranism would become coextensive with the confession of the ruler of a particular territory.

As the bitter controversies of the next 150 years demonstrated, this by no means settled the issue of religious and political plurality. The Augsburg agreement did not include Calvinists and left undecided the political status of both the independent ecclesiastical territories (such as Magdeburg), should the ruler convert, and the secularization of church property. These irritants, together with an active campaign of reconversion to Catholicism, following the Council of Trent, led to the establishment of the antagonistic Protestant Union and Catholic League of States in the first decade of the seventeenth century.

The Emperor's repression of the Protestant minority in Bohemia, despite the Letter of Majesty giving religious autonomy to the Estates there, brought on war, which lasted for thirty years and devastated much of central Europe, between two parties largely divided along confessional lines. Complete defeat of the Protestant forces was averted by the brilliant military campaigns of the Protestant king of Sweden, Gustavus Adolphus. Eventually the two sides signed the Treaties of Westphalia (Münster and Osnabrück) which established that each prince would retain power over church life in his territory, irrespective of his own religious beliefs. Certain religious freedoms were guaranteed for minorities (which meant Calvinists, but not independent religious groups), with the one major exception of the Habsburg hereditary lands. This latter settlement meant the virtual elimination of the Protestant cause in Bohemia which, fifty years earlier, had experienced a rare state of religious tolerance, and in Austria. A further by-product of the signing of the peace was Spain's final recognition of the political autonomy of the United Provinces of the Netherlands.

The end of war brought a return to a precarious *modus vivendi* between highly antagonistic religious systems. Genuine freedom of religion was still a distant prospect; however, independent political regimes were now taken for granted. No longer was there any possibility, even if there ever had been, of uniting the

Holy Roman Empire again under one confessional banner and one authority.

Another stage in the gradual limitation of absolute political power was marked by open discussion of the concept of legitimacy. Again, the Reformation played an important part in this debate. In one sense, the curtailment of power was based on the precept of the right to disobey (ecclesial) authority, when this refused to reform itself in line with God's will as revealed with clarity in the Scriptures. But in the gesture of the reformers, and their willingness to pay the ultimate price of martyrdom, is enshrined the principle of the critique of all authority. The way was open to contest and oppose belief in an immovable, divine order, hierarchically constructed, and having the right to expect unquestioning obedience. The Church could err, and did, and so could princes. Adherence to the divine Word meant inevitably a lessening of allegiance to human powers. Human authority was no longer sacrosanct. This was one of the elements in what Weber called the 'disenchantment (or de-supernaturalizing) of the world' (*Entzauberung der Welt*).

Furthermore, the reformers' emphasis on the corruptibility of human nature also had implications for political power. Their pessimistic (or realistic) view of the all-pervading extent of human self-deception led them to distrust rulers. It was the forerunner of what today we might call a doctrine of suspicion by which one assumes that those in authority tend to wield power first and foremost in their own interests. At the same time, the reformers urged the 'godly princes' to be genuine servants of the welfare of the community. The emphasis on the depravity of human nature, taken specially from the writings of the apostle Paul and Augustine, led in time to the concept of the separation of powers ('checks and balances'), whereby different branches of the executive, legislative and judiciary powers would constitutionally be held in different and counterbalancing hands.

Political authority thus came increasingly under the scrutiny of the people. On two major occasions during this period the willingness to challenge political legitimacy led to the overthrow of monarchy and the institution of a republican form of government. The population of the Netherlands in general, and particularly in the United Provinces of the North, maintained a long conflict with Spain, aimed at becoming independent of

Spanish rule. The remoteness of government, especially after Philip returned to Spain in 1559, never to leave it again, together with high taxes and religious persecution of the people, who had in large part become Calvinists, prompted a revolt against Spanish rule.

By 1609, the fighting between the two sides had temporarily blown itself out and a twelve-year truce was agreed. In effect this left the United Provinces as an independent and sovereign state (although, as we have seen, the Spanish presence continued for another forty years). Its structure was federal: through representative ambassadors the States General (i.e. the seven provinces) conferred on matters of common policy. Though the influence of the provinces was unequal (Holland being the most dominant), none could exert a centralizing tendency. From 1650 to 1672 the provinces adopted a republican government under the leadership of Johan de Witt, the Grand Pensionary. Each one gave up a certain amount of autonomy by refusing to appoint a head of state. After the end of the reign of Prince William of Orange (William III of England) in 1702, the United Provinces reverted to a republican model of government.

Britain also experimented with republican government. The eleven-year Commonwealth Protectorate under Oliver Cromwell arose out of a desire by parliament both to reform the government of the church and to limit the powers of Charles I, when the latter refused to come to a satisfactory compromise with the Commons. However, it had little chance of becoming a permanent institution: there was no genuine accord between the civilian government and the army, and in addition there was no mechanism for formalizing a proper succession when Cromwell died in 1658.

At this time, a significant movement of radical political reform, the Levellers, emerged. Influential in London and within the New Model Army, they 'represent the first substantial emergence in Britain of "the people" as a secular political force'.[12] Under the intellectual leadership of John Lilburne, Richard Overton, William Walwyn and John Wildman they put forward in a number of pamphlets a long-term programme of

---

[12] Iain Hampsher-Monk in D. Miller (et al.), *Encyclopaedia of Political Thought*. Oxford. Blackwell. 1987, p. 283.

reform that included the abolition of the monarchy and the House of Lords, an increase of the voting franchise (though not yet universal), a broadening of educational opportunities, the abolition of trading monopolies held under royal charter, a wide degree of religious toleration and a variety of legal and fiscal reforms, including a rudimentary welfare system. In an aptly named document, 'Agreements of the People', they proposed the reconstitution of political and religious authority on the basis of the voluntary consent of citizens. These ideas were clearly too early for their times. They were resisted by Cromwell and the army and the Levellers' writings censored. The Bill of Rights, which followed the revolution of 1688–9, did however enshrine in law certain guarantees of individual liberty against the encroachment of the state.

Meanwhile, on the other side of the channel the death of Louis XIII in 1643 was followed by a series of revolts against the regency of Anne of Austria and Cardinal Mazarin, known as the Frondes (1648–53), which might, if they had been successful, have curbed the growth of the monarchy's power in France. However, the revolts were not co-ordinated into a widespread resistance to the crown, were largely the work of disaffected nobility who wished to see a return of their own privileges and did not propose reforms radical enough to gain the support of the rural and urban marginalized polulations. Only in Bordeaux was there for a period of two years (1651–3), when the citizens dissolved the city parliament and ran the city by means of an elected assembly, a hint of a more democratic regime. However, factional squabbles and the reimposition of order from the centre soon brought the experiment to an end.[13]

## Religious diversification

In terms of the advancement of freedom, there are two main ways of looking at the sixteenth century Reformation: it can be seen either as the culmination of a long process leading to the eventual recognition of liberty of conscience, or as an innovative new stage in the fraught relationship between religion and

---

[13] Cf. Pennington, op.cit., pp. 274–9.

political life. Either way, it supplied a major impetus to the ultimate acceptance of a plurality of beliefs within the common life of a nation, even though at the beginning confessional fanaticism on almost every side held back hope of progress towards genuine toleration.

During that long period of European history when religious and civic belonging coalesced, religious conviction was not a matter of personal choice but of birth and soil. Religious identity was dependent on the territory into which one was born. If one belonged to a religion other than Christianity, one could not be a member of the commonwealth. By this token, Jews and Muslims were foreigners, because they were outside *Christendom*.[14] This continued to be so, after the period of the Reformation, in different regions of Europe, for two to three hundred years. However, although at the time the radical dissenters may not have grasped this, the seeds of the end of the territorial nature of Christian faith had been decisively sown. In this respect the Reformation proved to be a unique event in human history, for never before had the question of religious belief become ultimately, and in principle, divorced from that of belonging to a particular social group.

In our study of freedom, three major elements within the Reformation and the subsequent impact it made on social, political, economic and cultural life are especially significant. First, the emphasis on an unmediated relationship between individuals and God fundamentally challenged the notion that religion could be carried out 'by proxy'. Luther's celebrated 95 theses, nailed to the door of the church in Wittenburg, contained a sustained attack on religious formalism. His protest against the commercialization of indulgences signified his rejection of a practice that symbolized the belief (or hope) that the individual could enter into a tacit contract with the church by which the

---

[14] Cf. Lamin Sanneh, *Encountering the West. Christianity and the Global Cultural Process: The African Dimension.* London. Marshall Pickering. 1993, pp. 184–6.

latter would guarantee salvation if the former performed the necessary obligations with respect to its various sacraments.[15]

In terms of the common practice of religion, the Reformation constituted a frontal assault on a spiritual deceit. Henceforward the individual alone was held accountable for what he or she did with God's offer of free grace in Jesus Christ. No other person nor institution could act on their behalf. The doctrine of justification was much more than an esoteric religious belief: because it became the centre of the Reformation churches' preaching and teaching, the centre of religious gravity shifted decisively from the corporate religious body to the individual and in the process individualism was implicitly born. The church was deprived of its assumed right to judge salvation and coerce conscience. Moreover, the preaching of the Reformation presented a complete religious alternative to current Catholicism. It gained formal expression in the drawing up of confessions and catechisms which, however tragically they became polarized, represented the end of an overarching religious hegemony and opened the way to an increasing plurality of belief.

Secondly, the authority of the church was further undermined by the Reformation principle of the 'open' Bible, actualized by the new vernacular translations, the spread of the printed word and increased literacy. Inevitably, the so-called principle of 'private interpretation' led to a proliferation of different views

---

[15] In the light of much sophisticated research into the medieval background of Luther's understanding of justification by grace alone through faith alone, this account may seem crude. On the scholarly side, H.A. Oberman, op.cit. (Chapter V: 'Luther and the Scholastic Doctrines of Justification'), has argued convincingly that Luther was not contending against a 'man of straw' of his own creation; there was a fundamental point of disagreement concerning the *iustitia Dei* and the *iustitia Christi* between him and the whole medieval Catholic tradition, reaffirmed at the Council of Trent (cf. especially pp. 114–120).

One also has to remember that Luther was not chiefly concerned about the intellectual niceties of scholastic debate, but about the way salvation was proclaimed by the church to the common people and how they responded in practice. To pretend that the Reformation was somehow due to a massive theological misunderstanding is to put oneself outside real historical processes by having no adequate account of the immensely strong convictions on *both* sides.

about the central issues of Christian faith. Predictably, this was exploited for more or less political ends by those who wished to see the break-up of Christendom. However, the deeply polemical, theological question of the balance between the unity of the church and perceived issues of truth and error is irrelevant in terms of the social and cultural effects which the splits produced. The disunity of the Church and the disintegration of the Empire were steps towards the eventual acceptance of difference, a fundamental part of the modern cultural basis for freedom.

Thirdly, the Reformation doctrine of 'the priesthood of all believers' conferred equal sacredness on all vocations and affirmed the equal worth of all people. In consequence, a revolutionary attitude to both work and status was (implicitly) sown within the collective conscience of the people; no longer were the monastic or priestly vocations considered superior to all others. Although Luther himself, in his dealings with the 'Peasants' Revolt', did not accept the politically egalitarian implications of justification, others certainly did. In what has come to be called 'the Radical Reformation', minority groups (Anabaptists, Moravians and Mennonites) sought to establish new communities based on equality among their members. Tragically for them the religious and political changes were happening too rapidly and were too drastic. Society could not at that time cope with the apparent or real threat of a breakdown of order implicit in such radically alternative styles of life. As a result, the Protestant princes, the Calvinist magistrates and the Catholic monarchs (particularly after the Counter-Reformation), became in differing degrees, intolerant and brutally repressive of the minorities in their midst.[16]

The 150 years that followed the beginning of the Reformation were thus marked by considerable persecution of those groups that refused to abide by the terms of the Treaty of Augsburg.

---

[16] The northern part of the United Provinces became the major exception: 'Anabaptists consistently stood for individualism and tolerance and were able, little by little, to cause those in power to recognise their claims. In Holland, for example, where persecution had been as bitter as anywhere, toleration became so fully established by the seventeenth century that that country was the refuge for individualists as the Pilgrims and such advanced thinkers as Spinoza and Descartes' (J.C. Keene, op.cit., p. 546).

However, the different situations were never clear-cut and there were periods of toleration as well as periods of brutal suppression, as can best be illustrated by the fate of the Huguenots in France. The fluctuations in the fortunes of the Protestant Reformation in France is complex and cannot be chronicled here;[17] suffice it to say that the best that the non-Catholics achieved in terms of religious liberty were the terms of the Edict of Nantes (1598), which guaranteed a certain freedom of worship to all the subjects of Henry IV, mixed courts and the right of the Huguenots to defend themselves in about a hundred fortified places that they garrisoned at the state's expense. Less than 100 years later the Edict was revoked and replaced by the Edict of Fontainebleau (1685),[18] causing some two hundred thousand to find refuge in the United Provinces, England, Sweden, Denmark and Brandenburg.

Genuine religious toleration as a deliberate policy of the state was almost non-existent until the late seventeenth century. However, the growth of nonconformity in England, in particular the new Quaker movement under the leadership of George Fox, generated increasing pressure against the enforcement of uniformity.[19] Nevertheless, it was not for another nearly forty years after the beginning of the Commonwealth, under the terms of the Bill of Rights, which followed the 1688 Revolution, that freedom of religious conscience became respected in law.

Religious freedom became the first and most basic liberty allowed in modern Europe. The path to it was strewn with barricades often fiercely and uncompromisingly defended. The

---

[17] Cf., for example, R. Briggs, *Early Modern France 1560-1715*. Oxford. 1977; D. Parker, *The Making of French Absolutism*. London. 1983.

[18] 'Under its terms Huguenot ministers were required to accept conversion or go into exile; all remaining Huguenot schools and churches were to close; and protestant worship, both private and public, was to cease . . . After more than a century of existence there was no longer – in law at any rate – a protestant church in France. The 'Most Christian King' had shown the world how unity and orthodoxy could be restored' (R. Lockyer, op.cit., p. 487).

[19] The way in which significant communities of Jews in all parts of Europe were discriminated against, harassed and persecuted was a constant reminder of the terrible consequences of intolerance. The refusal of many of them to convert to Christian faith or otherwise to assimilate into the majority culture was also an important factor in every minority group eventually achieving properly guaranteed civil liberties.

seeds of a real plurality were undoubtedly sown in the theological emphases of the Reformation, even when the full implications of a radically changed world-view took much time to permeate the consciousness of society, tipping the balance away from the deeply ingrained idea of the sacredness of order and stability and towards the risks of freedom.[20] By the end of the seventeenth century, 'one may suggest that the first steps in the direction of freeing the state from narrow theocratic uniformity had been taken in the British Isles and parts of Protestant Europe'.[21]

---

[20] 'Whatever his [Luther's] intentions, the result of what he taught and did favoured much that has appeared in the modern outlook. The central principles of the Reformation – salvation by faith alone without priestly mediation and the authority of the Scriptures privately interpreted – are the foundation stones of religious individualism . . . These principles . . . contained the seeds of the modern assertion of the right of private judgement' (J.C. Keene, op.cit., pp. 545–6).

   Ali Mazrui (*Cultural Forces in World Politics*. London. James Currey. 1990, pp. 35–6) puts forward the interesting thesis that, as long as the Old Testament is dominant as the inspiration for political and religious authority (equally in Judaism, Christianity and Islam), theocracy is triumphant. The doctrine of God was unitary and this was reflected in a unitary heaven and earth bound together by God's law and implemented by God's direct representatives. Among other things, the Reformation rediscovered the trinitarian nature of God. Here diversity could be matched politically by a federalist concept of power. The liberationist theologian, Leonardo Boff, has also drawn anti-hierarchical and participative implications from the early elaboration of the Christian doctrine of the trinity (cf. *Trinity and Society*. Maryknoll. Orbis Books, 1987).

[21] T. Munck, op.cit., p. 370. The standard reference work on the rise of religious liberty in England is W.K. Jordan, *The Development of Religious Toleration in England*, 4 vols. Harvard University Press. 1932-1940.

## Scientific investigation

At no time during the beginning of the modern period of scientific discovery (from Copernicus (d.1543) to Newton (d.1727)) would those engaged in investigation of the material world have seen any conflict between their work and their faith. They would have reasoned that as God had put in place all that is, but was himself separate from his creation, there would be no contradiction between exploring the natural order and worshipping the one who had given it. It was Francis Bacon who inspired the concept of the dual revelations of God: in his laws revealed in Scripture and in the laws revealed in nature.[22]

Moreover, the twin commands given at the creation of human beings, according to the Genesis accounts, to 'rule over and subdue the earth' and to 'work and take care of the garden', were perceived as excellent grounds for treating the world as a place for human inquiry. The naming of the animals by Adam has been interpreted by some as the beginning of the science of taxonomy. As God, in the biblical stories of creation, did not count humanity as a rival but as a collaborator, there could be no objection to allowing natural curiosity to lead human beings into the unknown.

Or so one would have thought. The Church, however, disastrously for itself as it turned out, had other ideas. Beginning with Copernicus (d.1543), who by a process of mathematical deduction concluded that the sun, not the earth, was the centre of the solar system, scientific investigation called into question the old cosmic certainties about the relationship of the earth to the universe. Kepler (d.1630) advanced the work of Copernicus and Tycho Brahe (d.1601) by describing the motion of the planets. It was the views of Galileo (d.1642), however, as every schoolchild knows, which felt the full force of the Church's opposition.

---

[22] He set down the methods for a painstaking experimental and inductive approach to the understanding of natural phenomena. At the same time, he cautioned against the acceptance of our experience of reality either on the basis of our own inclinations, or of inherited wisdom, or the use of language, or even what appears to be common sense. In this respect he elevated prior suspicion into a methodological principle.

It is possible that the pope, Urban VIII, believed Galileo to have been more severely restricted in his scientific activities in 1616 than was in fact the case; in addition there were disagreements within the papal hierarchy; and Galileo himself had a somewhat controversial style of writing – for various reasons he was forced in 1632 to confess that he did not hold to the heliocentric (or heliostatic) view of the universe. Although at the time the astronomical theories of Galileo and others would not have been readily accepted by the entire scientific community,[23] the Church was undoubtedly wrong to take such a dogmatic stand in an area where it was potentially so vulnerable, namely that of the experimental verification in principle of the observation of material objects. Had it not felt that Galileo's findings (in the fields of astronomy and atomic particles) threatened what it considered fundamental truths of faith, including the doctrine of transubstantiation, it might have reserved judgement. Failing to do so it made a colossal mistake, which hastened the break between science and Christian faith to the intellectual impoverishment of both.

Nevertheless, the freedom from theological scrutiny which scientific investigation gradually won for itself has played a fundamental part in creating an open society (although, as we shall see, such freedom is much more problematical today). The very nature of science requires that the scientist must be allowed to pursue experimentation free from confessional considerations. If his or her conclusions are confirmed by methods of proof acceptable within the scientific community, they may not be rejected simply because an institution does not like the consequences.[24]

The effects of the scientific revolution of the seventeenth century have been incalculable in the creation of the modern world. In spite of the basic compatibility between science and

---

[23] Cf. Pennington, op.cit., p. 134.

[24] This proposition has also to work within the scientific community, in which there have been notable cases of resistance to new theories. It is said that Einstein, being convinced that the laws of physics were logically necessary, saw the notion of contingency in scientific thought as a threat to belief in the rationality of the world (cf. I.G. Barbour, *Religion in an Age of Science*. London. SCM Press. 1990, p. 141). The question of the ethical dilemmas of certain techniques in science is another matter, though undoubtedly related, which we will look at further on in the study.

faith, the latter has had to come to terms with a momentous shift of perception in the way human beings relate to their environment and interpret their whole experience of life. The natural world has been made into a separate autonomous sphere, open to investigation by principles of research universally valid and free from the constraint of beliefs that are not open to the same methods of verification.

As more and more of daily life became explicable in terms of easily understandable causes, God became less necessary as a hypothesis to fill the gaps left by events the mind could not reason out. Inevitably God became increasingly remote from the affairs of human beings. Science took over the world of divine immanence: the world of sense perception, of the data of observation and everyday experience. For most educated people God retained a role in the overall providential guiding of history and as a necessary factor in sustaining a categorical ethic, but it was only a matter of time before he would be required to give ground in these realms as well. Then that supreme characteristic of a truly modern world – the separation between the necessary truths of reason and personal beliefs concerning the meaning of existence – would become a reality.

The decisive blow in the argument about the independence of science from ecclesiastical control was given by the French philosopher, René Descartes, in developing his reasoning concerning the primacy of mathematical calculation. In his celebrated argument that began with the principle of systematic doubt and ended with the affirmation, *cogito, ergo sum* (I think, therefore [I am certain that] I exist), he was seeking to establish the validity and competence of reasoning beyond any possibility of questioning. He was attempting to establish the complete independence of reasoning by seeking an answer not only to the question, what is the world like, but how do I know what it is like?

Descartes perceived no discrepancy between his Catholic faith and his scientific work: for example, he sought a similar rigorously rational approach to the existence of God, in order to put the reality of God beyond the possibility of even suspended belief. However, it is clear that by making the autonomous reasoning self into the final judge of the validity of any proposition he cuts himself off, in principle at least, from any notion of an authority, whether the church or the word of preaching, which imposes itself on him from beyond his own self-enclosed world.[25] Nothing should be believed on the authority of another.

This claim for reason produces the ultimate intellectual freedom, but also the supreme intellectual responsibility.[26] As has been generally agreed in most areas of human inquiry three hundred years later, the powers of reason are much more fragile and precarious than this bold pioneer, and those who followed him, ever would have imagined.

## Intellectual debate

During the sixteenth and seventeenth centuries we find a number of severe contradictions in the theory and practice of political power. Not only did absolutist regimes establish themselves more firmly (such as that of Louis XIV in France), before being swept away in a tide of public revolt one hundred years later, but a number of able apologists defended them. At the beginning of our period Niccoló Machiavelli (d.1527) wrote his famous political treatise, *The Prince* (1513). As author of the most famous of all books ever written on political matters, he has given his name as an adjective describing certain political strategies (machiavellian). Some would describe his thought as realist, others as cynical. He has often been accused of arguing cogently for the view that the ends justify the means. However, it is probably truer to say that Machiavelli was simply observing that, if a political ruler is successful, those he governs are likely to excuse the means he uses. Machiavelli was a pragmatist who believed that rulers had to adapt their policies so that they bent

---

[25] 'It was his own sense of certainty alone that he was willing to make his final authority, and that for the subjective reason that it was clear and distinct to his mind' (J.C. Keene, op.cit., p. 557).

[26] 'Descartes was in fact regarded by both disciples and enemies as the principal author of the "bargain" by which the study of the material universe could continue unimpeded by faith in an immaterial one – a bargain which intelligent divines came to recognise as being to their advantage, but which the churches in general never accepted' (Pennington, op.cit., p. 136).

in the direction in which the prevailing winds of destiny were blowing:

> . . . so for Machiavelli political *virtu* has nothing to do with moral virtue or traditional prudential behaviour but consists in boldness, courage and flexibility.[27]

Students of Machiavelli's thought disagree about the extent to which he espoused a republican rather than a monarchical form of government. In practice the difference may be theoretical in the sense that, even in a strongly centralized, monarchical state, the prince never rules alone. If his model was the Roman republic, he was certainly advocating a powerfully controlled political machine. At the same time, he was not unaware of the importance of including the governed in some way in the affairs of state, even if the motive for this was to secure their cooperation with policies already decided.

Whereas Machiavelli espoused early humanist ideas, critical of the impracticality of trying to implement absolute Christian moral values in politics, Jean Bodin (d.1596) based his view of political authority on 'natural (i.e. divine)' law. The ruler of the state takes as his model the absolute sovereignty of the ruler of the universe. The general subjects of a state have no right to give or withhold their consent to be governed. Nevertheless, a wise governor will consult and listen to a group of experienced counsellors, who in their turn will listen to the people. Moreover, the ruler will follow God by practising justice, lest discontent should break the divinely ordered harmony of society, which functions only when each part is contentedly fulfilling its role within the whole. Bodin's notion of political life was essentially traditionalist in the mode of the divine or natural appointment of some to rule and others to be ruled.

The last of the great defenders of non-accountable power was Thomas Hobbes (d. 1679). Like *The Prince*, his book *Leviathan* has become one of the most notorious essays on political reality ever written. Living through the upheavals of civil war and regicide in Britain, he was concerned to establish a scientific doctrine of the state that would limit strife and the constant disputes that threatened to pull a nation in the direction of

---

[27] A. Brown in D. Miller (ed.), op.cit., p. 305.

anarchy. His main assumption about political life derives from his basic convictions about human nature – that the most powerful desire or motivation of humankind is that of self-preservation, and that this in turn springs from the overwhelming fear of ceasing to exist.

Self-preservation, however, may operate in two contradictory directions: on the one hand, it provokes a desire for those conditions of peace in which a person may continue to live without threat of harm; on the other hand, it leads to conflict and violence, because survival when resources are scarce will cause people to fight to gain an advantage for themselves. In a state of nature, human life is in effect a war of all against all; humans are like wolves who will turn and devour those weaker than themselves, or even, preemptively, those who appear to be stronger.

Here, there appears to be an irreconcilable conflict: self-preservation seems simultaneously to dictate that we make war and yet long for peace. Hobbes's solution to this conundrum is that all members of a civil community agree a contract in which they limit their natural aggression on the grounds that, as they cannot secure all that they may desire without eliminating one another, it is better to desist from violence. To be effective this common contract must be secured by a guarantor with sufficient power to make sure that it is strictly adhered to. This power has to be absolute, for balanced centres of power would generate the kind of self-preserving, antagonistic factions that the contract is designed to eliminate.[28]

Hobbes thus argues for political authority on the basis of the worst possible interpretation of what human beings may do with the fundamental freedom they have to use their own power to preserve their own nature. Once authority has been conceded to the ruler under the terms of the contract, the general populace does not seem to be much further involved in political life. However, in extreme circumstances, where the aggression of a ruler threatens self-preservation, the people have a right to defend themselves. In other words, they may act when the sovereign power betrays the one principle for which it was established in the first place.

---

[28] Cf. Pennington, op.cit., p. 184.

Although the idea of a contract would seem to provide a basis for some kind of democratic process, it appears to be more of a theoretical device to justify the use of effective power in restraining anarchy than a practical reality. There is, for example, no concept of the periodical renewal of the contract, as, for example in the case of general elections through universal suffrage. However, although Hobbes was a powerful advocate of strong government, his basis for this was universal consent, rather than a doctrine of divine right. In this sense, at least, he had crossed over one of the principal thresholds into the modern world.

Another champion of the idea of the social contract was John Locke (d.1704).[29] Locke, however, placed the social contract in a quite different framework from that of Hobbes. In general terms the concept affirms the necessity of citizens freely agreeing to government on their behalf before that government is able to claim legitimacy for itself. Contract theory can be traced back to the strong link that Augustine forged between personal will and consent. It also receives rather weak echoes in the thought of William of Ockham (d.1349) who argued against arbitrary power on the basis of the consent of the people, and in the political thought of Francisco Suarez (d.1617). It has to be said, however, that in the case of both these latter men the idea is greatly undermined by the fact that the people have no right to revoke the power they have surrendered to the rulers.

Locke, like Hobbes, begins from a particular understanding of what it means to be human in a state of nature. Although he dismissed the idea of human beings being born into the world with a set of innate ideas, he did hold to a belief in one specific factor inherent in human nature – that of the unconditional right to 'life, liberty and estate'.

Before any political organization existed, human beings recognized a moral law in which the rights of all others should

---

[29] Cf. A.J. Simmons, *The Lockean Theory of Rights*. Princeton. Princeton Univ. Press. 1992; J. Lively and A. Reeve, *Modern Political Theory from Hobbes to Marx: Key Debates*. London. Routledge. 1993, pp. 64–71, 81–102; V. Chappel (ed.), *The Cambridge Companion to Locke*. Cambridge. CUP. 1994, Chapter 9.

be respected.[30] A person has a right to property, for example, because of the labour he has expended upon some natural object. Most people will in most cases recognize the equal rights of others. Where, however, they fail to do so, there is a need for established government to make sure that those rights are properly protected. People, therefore, will be willing to come together to institute a properly appointed authority to act on their behalf. This authority will determine the laws of the society and inflict appropriate punishments for their infringement.

The most well-known of Locke's writings, *Two Treatises of Government* (1689), was written at the time of the overthrow of the Stuart monarchy and has been seen as a theoretical justification for the revolution. For Locke, unlike Hobbes, did not see political authority as being exercised solely on the basis of the status of the one invested with power. His essay also strongly disputed the idea of the divine right of the supreme governor: it is not the case that God has entrusted certain individuals with the right to rule; what God has done is to entrust each individual with natural rights, which it is the duty of the ruler to guarantee. It is the individual, not the collective body, which possesses rights and therefore the individual alone has the prerogative to keep them or give them up. These rights include the right of religious freedom. Locke was a strong proponent of religious toleration, arguing from both basic Christian principles and from the inborn nature of human liberties that religious faith could not and should not be compelled.

This emphasis both on the natural rights of the individual and also on the limitations of government, due to the function for which it is constituted, makes Locke the father of modern 'liberalism'. He was the first who seriously and systematically began to argue for limited government[31] and an open society. He was not yet, however, the father of modern democratic processes.

---

[30] Locke deduced the reciprocal obligation of people to behave in certain ways from the fact that natural law also laid upon people certain duties to be fulfilled (cf. T. Baldwin, 'Toleration and the Right to Freedom' in J. Horton and S. Mendus, *Aspects of Toleration*. London. Methuen. 1985, p.37).

[31] The French philosopher Montaigne (d.1592) advocated a more radical task for government, that of protecting people's freedom to live more or less as they pleased. This makes him a precursor of libertarianism, rather than liberalism.

The influence of Locke on the subsequent development of rights, liberties and democracy has been incalculable:

> [Locke] provided the intellectual defense of the English revolution of 1688, the theoretical foundation for a radical attack on vested interests in France, and the basis of the principles that guided American colonists.[32]

Certainly one of his most important contributions to subsequent reflection on freedom has been the connection he made between freedom, natural law, rationality and religion. Natural law is God's will and, since we are God's creatures, we have been created to fulfil this law. To be free is to act as we have been made. Consequently, the natural law does not inhibit, but actually enlarges freedom. When we know the ends for which we have come into the world and act in accordance with them, we are truly free.[33]

## Conclusion

This brief overview has touched on some of the most significant factors that have contributed to modern practices and understandings of freedom. Because of the momentous place that religion possessed in every aspect of life during the two centuries under review – all along we have noticed how it has woven in and out of most of the crucial events and debates of the time – it is not surprising that the first civil freedoms secured, in something approaching the modern sense, were freedoms to believe and practise religion according to one's own personal convictions. Whatever additional factors may in subsequent centuries have enlarged and solidified the external freedoms to which the Western world has become accustomed (and we will continue to explore these), at the root is the conscience of the religious non-conformist. In his magisterial Gifford Lectures, Owen Chadwick sums up the position:

> In western Europe the ultimate claim of the liberal was religious. Liberal faith rested in origin upon the religious dissenter. Liberalism on its more important side was a criticism of the

---

[32] J.C. Keene, op.cit., p. 567.
[33] Cf. T. Baldwin, op.cit., p. 39.

medieval world of all-embracing religious orthodoxy. Dissenters won a free right to express a religious opinion which was not the accepted or prevailing opinion . . . Freedom of religious opinion is impossible without freedom of opinion. Liberalism might or might not be religious. It must demand the right to be secular . . . If the right to be irreligious is won, then the institutions, privileges, customs, of a state and society must be dismantled, sufficiently dismantled at least, to prevent the state or society exercising pressure upon the individual to be religious if he wishes not to be religious. The liberal state, carried on logically, must be the secular state.[34]

In terms of our study so far, however, to say this is to anticipate a future still some way off.

---

[34] *The Secularization of the European Mind in the 19th Century.* Cambridge. Cambridge University Press. 1985, pp. 26–7.

# Four

# Many Perspectives

Up to this point in the book we have assumed that the meaning of freedom is, more or less, clear and unproblematical. It has been used with reference to various modern perceptions; to ideas and ideals in ancient Greece and in the thinking of Augustine and Erasmus; and also to economic, political, scientific and religious theory and practice from the beginning of the Reformation to the end of the seventeenth century. It has served as a link concept, bringing together the material collected. It is open to question, however, how far the concepts and realities involved are the same, or even similar. Certainly the word has been much more broadly used in subsequent times.

Before continuing this exploration into the meaning of freedom, I will review some of the different ways in which the term has been used in the modern period of European history. We shall see that the word has acquired a wide range of interpretations and applications in both common and more reflective language in recent times. For the idea of freedom, though usually treated with deep veneration, is much disputed.

## The negative view

Many argue passionately that the only legitimate way to understand freedom is as 'freedom from'. Isaiah Berlin has been one of the stoutest defenders of this view that the idea of freedom has to be limited to its negative application: i.e. freedom from any agent external to myself determining what is in my best interests and forcing me to comply. People are free to the extent that no individual or group interferes with their activities. To be prevented doing what one would otherwise do or to be restricted or hindered in doing it is to be unfree, coerced or enslaved:

> The only freedom which deserves the name is that of pursuing our own good in our own way.[1]

This view places the emphasis on curbing all authority external to the individual. People must be allowed their own space to think for themselves, to come to their own conclusions and decide which courses of action they are going to take. Freedom is genuine, when people's actions are truly their own, when there is no hint of their having been unduly persuaded against their wishes to believe or act in certain ways.

The model of the unfree person is the slave, unable to decide individually how to use time or gifts, or what goals to set for life. A slave is constantly under the authority and power of another, and therefore has no chance of altering his or her situation in life. It follows, conversely, that 'having some share in the government of oneself (is) constitutive of *liberty* properly speaking'.[2]

The term often used for this particular belief about freedom is self-determination. It is the self alone that decides which boundaries to set to its actions. People are free, therefore, when they are no longer under the restraints or compulsion of others' beliefs and decisions, whether these come from their immediate family, from the wider ethnic community into which they were born or the even larger community of the nation. These restraints or compulsions may be the expectations of parents or the customs of culture or the demands of the state. A person may, of course, decide to abide by some or all of these. If so, their freedom will remain intact, as long as they remain governed by their own decision taken after due deliberation and in the absence of pressure to move in any particular direction. In the last analysis, a person is free only when able to will an action without pressure or duress.

---

[1] I. Berlin, *Four Essays on Liberty*. Oxford. Oxford University Press. 1969, p. 127.
[2] Alan Ryan, 'Liberty and Socialism' in Ben Pimlott (ed.), op.cit., p. 104.

As this concept of freedom has gained popularity in modern societies, it has increasingly come to mean the absence of limits: one should be free to do what one wants, with the sole proviso that one's actions do not interfere with the freedom of others to pursue their own goals. In the process of human development from childhood to adulthood, a gradual loosening of external constraints is a continuous procedure. Erich Fromm calls it the process of 'individuation', in which people gradually emerge from primary ties to stand on their own feet and take their own decisions. They become separated from the wants of others and thus independent.[3]

In common jargon this is expressed as the right to do as I please with my life, as long as I do not harm others. This right has come to be widely associated with and even focused on sexual liberty. When two people, above the legal age of consent, freely agree to perform sexual acts with one another, it is claimed, they ought to be free from any concern about the inherited moral tradition that reserves intimate sexual acts for heterosexual relationships within marriage alone. Interestingly, although this view of freedom holds good both for casual relationships and the more permanent state of cohabitation, adultery after marriage is still widely viewed as unacceptable misconduct.

Belief in the general absence of limits has given rise to what has been called 'the permissive society'. The unrestricted pursuit of individual happiness is legitimate, provided that the equally legitimate pursuits of others are not thereby infringed. This conviction is based on two apparently self-evident truths: first, that no one else can decide for me what constitutes my happiness, and secondly that society, regarded as a collective will, has no business to be involved in the way I choose to live my private life. In other words, the state has no valid reason to arbitrate in my affairs, nor defensible mechanism by which it could do so. The state should not decide what are acceptable and unacceptable lifestyles, when these concern the mutually agreed decisions of responsible adults.[4] Therefore, the law should be silent about many aspects of an individual's choices. One might summarize this view comprehensively as follows:

---

[3] *Fear of Freedom*. London. Routledge. 1960, pp. 19–25.
[4] Cf. J.R. Lucas, *Freedom and Grace*. London. SPCK. 1976, p. 106.

> Freedom is the right to do as one pleases whether or not it is thought for any reason that one should do what one chooses to do.[5]

Three major assumptions, then, underlie the negative concept of freedom. First, there is the belief that the scope of the state's legislative power over the individual should be restricted to a minimum. Berlin warns against the danger of a super-personal entity regarding itself as more real than the individual, with a greater sense of what is morally right and wrong. When the state believes that it knows what a person needs better than that person, we are well on the way to a regime that claims rights superior to those of the individual.[6] Secondly, there is the conviction about the sovereignty of the individual conscience: that one cannot be an authentic individual unless one is at liberty to obey the dictates of one's own sense of right and wrong. Thirdly, because modern societies are, in the nature of the case, pluralistic, it follows that various options for the way one leads one's life should be equally valid as far as the state is concerned.

## The positive view

Whilst not disagreeing with the principle of negative freedom, many other people argue that freedom should mean much more than the absence of restraint. For Ben Pimlott, non-coercion is only half the story about freedom; the other half is about the expansion of choice. He argues, for example, that the invention of property rights is a freedom-creating act, not because it diminishes coercion, but because it enlarges possibilities.[7]

This way of looking at freedom is often referred to as 'freedom for'. According to this vision, freedom is really about possibilities and potency. The problem with the negative account of freedom is that it is reductionist, and therefore cannot provide any adequate statement. It is based on a dubious double negative – not being prohibited from a particular action. This means, for example, that as long as she is *not banned* by the rules or

---

[5] R. McKeon, op.cit., p. 54.
[6] Ibid., pp. 133–4.
[7] Op.cit., p. 109.

*inhibited* by prejudice, a woman is free to join an all-male club or society. However, non-prohibition is quite different from acquiring a positive opportunity (such as, in this case, the ability to pay the subscription fee). Real freedom to be a club member is clearly based on both the negative and positive freedoms.

To use a related definition, if freedom is 'the power of acting . . . according to the determinations of the will',[8] then creating conditions for making a choice real is part of actual freedom. This is known as 'effective' freedom:[9] if I need certain resources, powers or abilities in order to achieve self-realization, then having these resources constitutes part of freedom itself.[10] On this view, the welfare state becomes a necessary instrument in making people free, since the resources that it commands (in education, in supplying certain services, in health care) expand choice.

Freedom, then, entails more than the liberty to act without sanctions being applied. It also requires the acquisition of goods and abilities that make certain actions possible that otherwise would have been impossible. If I am free to follow a particular profession, this is because I have achieved the necessary qualifications, not because in principle there are no restrictions on who may enter. Speaking generally, I can be free to act as I want only if I have a proper chance to develop my capacities. Otherwise, freedom becomes a frustrating fiction, as I am left contemplating what might have been.

There are certain freedoms 'from' which do not exist without the positive action of others. The most obvious, perhaps, is freedom from sickness.[11] In this case, unless other people, organizations or institutions take positive action to deal with my health problem, then my freedom is certainly limited, for I know that I am not able to treat myself. The decisions that governments take, or fail to take, on our behalf can also enlarge or restrict our freedoms. I cannot be relatively free from the danger of inhaling dangerous exhaust fumes, unless the

---

[8] *International Encyclopedia of the Social Sciences*, Vol.5. Macmillan. 1972.
[9] J. Gray, *Liberalism*. Milton Keynes. Open University Press. 1986, p. 32.
[10] Ibid., p. 58.
[11] Others would be debt, destitution, disabilities, mental traumas. Cf. N. Anderson, *Freedom under Law: the role of law in man's quest for freedom.* Eastbourne. Kingsway. 1988, p. 7.

Department of Transport decides to build a bypass round the town where I live. I cannot, as a young person, be free from the dangers caused by inadequate exercise, unless the education authority provides adequate sports facilities and the time in the school curriculum to use them.

These arguments for an extension to our understanding of freedom are controversial, because logically they may require the curbing of some people's freedoms in the interests of a greater distribution of freedom for all. Thus land reform in poor countries, enabling more people to gain a living from agriculture; or the prohibition of smoking in confined areas; or (to give the most significant example) levying a tax on income, all entail curtailing negative freedoms in order to increase positive freedoms. Freedom is related to the relative power one has in a society to effect certain ends. This means that we can increase freedoms only by redistributing the means of power: wealth, status, privilege, patronage, knowledge and decision-making mechanisms. Redistribution is always coercive and restrictive of individual freedoms. One of the main reasons why many have argued cogently against the notion of positive freedoms[12] is because of the inherent tendency of central authorities to take more authority for themselves and to deprive individuals of the power to make decisions.

The advocates of positive freedoms counter this argument by pointing out that to limit freedom to the negative idea is to be naive about the place occupied by unequal power in determining choice. Most people judge instinctively that the non-restriction of freedoms (the negative view) can be achieved ultimately only by the extending of freedoms to as many as possible (the positive view). Otherwise, the meaning of freedom is ideologically determined by those seeking to defend their powers. Historically these two versions of freedom have been elaborated and defended in the liberal and socialist (or social democratic) traditions respectively.

---

[12] In recent years, the case has been put most forcefully by Robert Nozick in *Anarchy, State and Utopia*. Oxford. Blackwell. 1974.

## The liberal tradition

According to David Edgar, the original liberal ideal affirmed that it is possible for the individual, either alone or in voluntary association with others, to cope with the eternal dilemmas of the human condition.[13] Historically, liberalism is bound up with a strenuous protection of the rights of the individual against more powerful collective forces:

> The most conspicuous attribute of liberalism that distinguishes it as much from conservatism as from socialism is the view that moral beliefs concerning matters of conduct which do not directly interfere with the protected sphere of other persons do not justify coercion.[14]

The tradition, therefore, is characterized primarily by its interest in the individual liberties of the person. Ronald Preston spells out the main assumptions as follows: the capacity to be human is determined by a person's freedom from dependence on the will of others; freedom from dependence means freedom from any relations with others except those entered into voluntarily with a view to fulfilling one's own personal interests; the individual is the proprietor of his or her own person and capacities without prior obligations to society; an individual's freedom can rightly be limited only by such obligations and rules as are necessary to secure the same freedom for others; political society is a human contrivance designed to protect the individual's life and property and to maintain orderly relations of exchange between people.[15]

In more general terms, liberalism asserts the rightness of parliamentary government on the basis of universal suffrage against any concentration of either inherited or acquired power by any person or group within society. It believes in the rule of law, particularly in the protection of freedom of association and private property rights. Civil society is a society of free men and women, equal under the law, bound together by no common

---

[13] 'The Free or the Good' in R. Levitas (ed.), *The Ideology of the New Right*. Cambridge. Polity Press. 1986, p. 66.
[14] Hayek, *The Constitution of Liberty*. London. Routledge. 1976, p. 402.
[15] *Religion and the Persistence of Capitalism*, London, SCM Press, 1979, pp. 73–4.

purpose beyond that of sharing a common respect for each other's rights.[16]

Emphasis on the rights of the individual has now become an established part of political moral debate. Given that, in terms of humanity's long history, this is a new conviction,[17] always under threat from the centralizing tendencies of power, liberals are keen to maintain it always high on the political agenda.

Organizations campaigning for an increase in civil liberties argue that where rights are in question, the presumption must be in favour of individuals, because the state should never arrogate to itself powers beyond those that individuals, following their own self-interests, would allow it if they were the legislators. The individual is a concrete reality, whilst society is an abstraction. Individuals are born into the world as ends for themselves and, therefore, should be free to pursue their own ends, rather than those of some other entity:

> Every plea for civil liberties and individual rights, every protest against exploitation and humiliation, against the encroachment of public authority or the mass hypnosis of custom or organised propaganda, springs from an individualistic conception of human beings.[18]

The assumptions of individualism affirm the moral primacy of the individual, against the claims of any collective organisation; an equal moral status for every person, regardless of the differences which are accidents of their birth; and the moral unity of the human race; whatever may be the distinct histories and cultures that people spring from. Liberals also believe in the possibility and necessity of improving social institutions and political arrangements, so that they reflect ever more clearly in practice these general ideals.[19]

---

[16] Cf. J. Gray, op.cit., p. 12.

[17] The notion of rights for individuals is a phenomenon arising in the seventeenth century. The gradual breaking free from social and religious conventions began to happen at least two centuries earlier: 'The achievements of the Renaissance . . . were the products of unfettered individuality seeking to taste and express fully what it means to be human.' J.C. Keene, *The Western Heritage of Faith and Reason*. New York. Harper and Row. 1963, p. 496.

[18] I. Berlin, op.cit., p. 128.

[19] Cf. J. Gray, op.cit., p. 3.

Individualism is a deep and pervasive modern, spiritual force.[20] From whence, then, has it come? It is generally conceded that one of the writers most influential in giving it a sound intellectual foundation was the German philosopher Immanuel Kant (d.1804). He wrestled (not the first or last to do so) with the apparent contradiction within human nature and society between causation and necessity in the physical world and the freedom required for human beings to act morally. The world of external phenomena gives no guidance about moral behaviour, and yet human life would be inconceivable without a respect for the 'good will'. Kant, therefore, accepts that, if morality is to make sense to reason, human beings have to be free in their 'spirit' (within what he described as the noumenal world) from compulsion in their material existence.

Kant also argued that individuals can expect their freedom to be respected by other individuals only if they concede to each one an equal freedom to their own. In other words, my own freedom is compromised and in jeopardy, unless I am willing to grant it in the same measure to all others. If I believe it right to restrict the freedom of others, I have no reasonable defence against their decision to limit mine. From this, Kant's 'critical reason' deduces the 'categorical imperative' that I must act in a way that I would be prepared to see universalized. Thus, for example, if I were to argue that I am free to take articles from a shop without paying, I must allow others an equal freedom to take what belongs to me without my permission. The imperative is based on the logic of consistency of action: because I expect to be treated as an end and not as a means to someone else's end, I have an obligation to treat others in exactly the same way.

It is important to realize that Kant was not arguing from the merely pragmatic basis that it is in the interests of the individual to treat others well. If this were so, human actions would not be moral, for they would be based on the calculation of what was in one's own best interests or what happened to be convenient at a particular time and place, and such calculation and convenience could equally well give rise to immoral acts. An act is moral when performed because it is the right thing to do, regardless of a person's inclinations at the time. It follows that the free

---

[20] Cf. A. Storkey, *A Christian Social Perspective*. Leicester. IVP. 1979, p. 152.

individual is the one who chooses to do good, for no other reason than that it is good. In other words, everyone lies under the obligation to choose the right action and the truly free person is the one who decides to fulfil this responsibility. On the other hand, a person who merely follows his or her desires is not free, because then they are not acting out of the realm of the 'spirit' but are bound by the determining forces of the natural world.

Individualism has also been an important consideration in the ethical stance of another philosophical system, utilitarianism. For utilitarianism, good is brought about by maximizing the amount of happiness within society. It assumes that everyone desires happiness as their chief end. It also assumes that, when the greatest degree of happiness is being achieved for everyone, the individual's own happiness will also be increased. If it is objected that people do, in fact, desire other ends rather than immediate happiness, such as the opportunity to alleviate suffering, even when they put their life at risk as a result, the utilitarian would answer that even in such a case the deepest motivation is still the achievement of pleasure. The argument is, of course, circular for once the thesis is granted that everyone always acts to maximize their own happiness, any action must of necessity be interpreted as contributing to this end; there is nothing that could disprove what is, in effect, a tautology.

The general principle of the greatest happiness of the greatest number has also been criticized on the grounds that it might well conflict with individual rights. To this the utilitarian responds that there can be no happiness without a sense of individual security, and no security without individual rights. It would, therefore, be a contradiction in terms to suggest that the repression of rights could ever be in the interests of maximizing happiness.

The weaknesses in the classical account of utilitarianism (as put forward by Jeremy Bentham and J.S. Mill) were so pronounced that the theory has been considerably modified subsequently, to give a more sophisticated basis for judging the overall utility to society and to individuals of particular actions. Some kind of notion of an intrinsic good has to replace that of happiness, because of the latter's vagueness and ambiguity. Also, in terms of people's perceived needs, reducing the greatest amount of overall misery (as in the alleviation of hunger and homelessness) is considered to be an important ingredient in calculating utility.

Notwithstanding these significant developments in the theory, all versions of morality based solely on the criteria of the consequences produced from particular actions are flawed: first, because consequences can never be predicted with any degree of accuracy, and secondly because notions of good and bad still have to be smuggled into the argument, for clearly these latter cannot be determined on the basis of the kind of consequences produced without arguing in a circle.

In spite of the obvious inadequacies of the theory, it enjoys enormous popularity in a culture which reinforces both individualism and hedonism. Thus, for example, arguments justifying experimentation on human embryos, or the creation of female human embryos for the sole purpose of using the eggs for subsequent fertilization, are settled for many on the consequentialist, utilitarian basis that the probable outcome will be to give a great deal of happiness to infertile couples, without causing any corresponding harm to anyone else. A consequentialist ethic has difficulty in assessing the worth of the moral outrage that this kind of experimentation causes to those who believe that the intrinsic dignity of human life is being violated. Such people might argue that their human sensibilities are indeed being harmed. The consequentialist might then respond that, because they have no personal stake in the treatment process for infertility, they should not feel involved. It is not their affair. They are not directly parties to the action. Therefore, they should not become part of the ethical equation.

Such an argument, increasingly common in the secular West, highlights the dilemma of extreme individualism. It assumes that ethical concern is the prerogative only of those whose personal interests are at stake. It takes no account of the sense of belonging to a common humanity, so that the violation of the dignity of one affects the dignity of all. Individualism may also be one of the main reasons why people who are 'pro-choice' in the abortion debate signally fail to understand the depth of moral disgust caused by abortion to those who are 'pro-life' or the terrible inconsistency between performing abortions one day and fighting to save the life of a threatened foetus the next. Thus, individualism and utilitarianism mutually reinforce one another.

The ethics of intrinsic, or absolute, right and wrong are regarded by the liberal spirit as generally tending to infringe individual liberties.

Another fundamental aspect of liberal thinking surrounds the crucial notion of economic freedoms. Freedom in the market place embodies a number of interlocking liberties: the individual ownership of property and the right to dispose of it according to individual desires, the possibility of unfettered bargaining between employer and employee concerning the price value of labour (a minimum wage would hinder freedom), the ability to transfer capital assets across national boundaries, the maximizing of net income across the population in order to stimulate economic growth through consumer choice (taxes should be kept to a minimum), the desirability of the market's determining which research projects will be undertaken.

The desire for a free market is based on a number of assumptions. First, that the market is a spontaneous, natural process which, if allowed to work according to its own laws, will produce the greatest benefit to all in terms of economic prosperity. Second, that the market is the mechanism which most effectively distributes the knowledge needed for economic transactions to take place in a way which maximizes efficiency and therefore wealth creation. Third, that the individual political freedoms that are contained in the various ideals surrounding human rights can be safeguarded only in the context of corresponding economic freedoms. Once the state begins to interfere in the free exchange of goods and services, limiting people's power to act in their own interests, then, it is argued, government will want to regulate other areas of people's lives. A recent example of this, according to some people, is the legislation passed in Britain, and several other nations, obliging divorced fathers to pay maintenance to their ex-wives for the children of the marriage. Not infrequently, freely negotiated settlements between husband and wife, prior to divorce, are not taken into account. The state simply overrides the individual participants' agreed contract.

The liberal tradition strongly advocates the minimal state, an open society and the priority of the individual. The twentieth century has seen such a degree of terror against and control over the population of whole nations in the name of various high-sounding ideals, that it would be irresponsible not to be suspicious of all ideologies, and especially those advocated in the name of mass movements:

> Never before in history had any form of tyranny managed to combine all the characteristics that bear the signs of physical and spiritual death – the official ideology, the single party, the secret political police, the breakdown of society, the submission in childhood, the militarisation of knowledge and the stranglehold on opinion. Everywhere, when men tortured and people admired the torturers, when words lost their meaning, the mark of totalitarianism has weighed heavily on this century.[21]

Given the tendency towards autocratic government, in which small groups of people assume the right, on the basis of a superior vantage-point, to govern in the best interests of all, it is better to err on the side of the protection of the individual, even if some social injustices are consequently not rectified. The maintenance and extension of liberty in society demand an eternal vigilance, in which the implementation of democratic ideals is carefully and constantly monitored.

Effective democracy requires a press free of political pressure from government, such as the threat of censorship through the law. It requires a government by consent, where consent does not mean simply a general election every four to six years, but a constant listening to the wishes of the whole population on delicate issues and the promotion of open debates on controversial moral and legal concerns. It requires a judicial system, wholly independent of political interference, where legal processes are seen to be swift and fair, where every member, and not only the rich, has recourse to the courts for the redress of civil wrongs and where it is generally agreed that punishment should be commensurate with the crime committed. There is an increasing recognition that every nation needs to have a readily enforceable Bill of Rights, enshrining the legal protection of free speech, free assembly, mobility, citizenship, the presumption of innocence when accused of a crime, legal representation in

---

[21] J-P. Rioux, 'The Tragic Century: Suffering and Upheaval' in Leonardo: *The Age of Discoveries*. Supplement to *The Independent, El Pais, La Repubblica, Le Monde*, April 1992, p. 48. (Henceforth, this will be referred to as *The Independent.*)

court and access to all information, save that which, if in the public domain, might threaten the livelihood, lives or freedoms of others.

A democratic society which is functioning well is also one where people not only recognize quickly when legitimate rights and freedoms are being curtailed, but are able swiftly to put the matter right. Such a society will have in place mechanisms of official opposition, scrutiny, information, participation and processes of law with the ability to deter unscrupulous people in their determination to impose their will on others.

If minimal government is an ideal of the liberal tradition, it follows that in some sense those who govern have a responsibility both to promote a general tolerance in society and themselves to maintain an indifference to many things that happen. Tolerance is a society's capacity to sustain dissent without tearing itself apart. It should not necessarily be confused with an amoral pragmatism, for it can express a profound moral choice to treat other people as serious moral agents, whose opinions and way of life should be respected, even when not shared. Intolerance, on the other hand, can easily be a cover for deep, unacknowledged prejudices, a desire to impose opinions through the use of superior power and unwillingness to risk exposing one's beliefs to the challenge of being found inadequate.[22]

Indifference may seem to be the epitomy of moral apathy. However, in terms of the liberal tradition, it is intended to signal a genuine refusal to judge too swiftly and too categorically. The aim of a liberal society is to give people the benefit of the doubt in matters of behaviour that do not impinge on the need for a common consensus. Purposeful indifference stems from a conviction that the state should be extremely careful before intervening to curtail people's pursuit of enjoyment or seeking to meddle in the goals they set themselves. It is not the government's duty to generate a system of moral demands for society. Wherever this has happened in history, whether for religious or ideological reasons, it has resulted in an uncontrollable fanaticism. Then the value of real people has

---

[22] Cf. P. Nicholson, 'Toleration as a moral ideal' in Horton and Mendus, op.cit., pp. 158–167.

been sacrificed, supposedly for the sake of an unassailably sublime good, but in reality on the altar of expediency.

Today we call this 'fundamentalism', a fervent devotion to an extreme political radicalism combined with an unquestioning commitment to religious or ideological slogans.[23] Fanaticism of all colours cheerfully subordinates means to ends; it treats accusations as proven guilt; it rewards the betrayal of friends and relatives in the interests of the cause; its end product is the inquisition and summary execution. It is a return to the kind of barbaric society from which the historical processes of the last 300 years have delivered us, often at great cost.

## The socialist tradition

It needs to be said at the outset that in many aspects socialism is not opposed to the liberal rights and freedoms that we have been considering. There is no historical, logical or semantic reason for identifying the socialist tradition with, say, Stalin's Gulag, the massacre of student protesters in Tiananmen Square, the 'Shining Path' guerillas of Peru or the 'killing fields' of Cambodia. Socialism has an honourable and serious record, and possesses intellectual and political credibility.

What distinguishes the socialist view of how to run society is its belief that liberalism has gone too far in protecting the rights of the individual, is too narrow in its definition of rights and is too naive in its assessment of the use of power in society. Socialism builds on the positive view of freedom as requiring some government intervention, albeit well-defined and properly regulated, in the righting of inequities caused by an unequal distribution of power among individuals and groups in society.

---

[23] Cf. e.g. C.B. Strozier, *Apocalypse: On the Psychology of Fundamentalism in America*. Boston. Beacon Press. 1994; M. Marty and R. Appleby, (The Fundamentalism Project): *Fundamentalisms Observed* (Vol.I), 1991; *Fundamentalisms and Society: Reclaiming the Sciences, the Family and Education* (Vol.2), 1993; *Fundamentalisms and the State: Remaking Politics, Economics and Militance* (Vol.3), 1993. Chicago. University of Chicago Press; M. Marty and R. Appleby, *Accounting for Fundamentalisms: The Dynamic Character of Movements*. Chicago. University of Chicago Press, 1994.

While valuing individual freedoms, in the last analysis this tradition believes that justice is a higher, or at least an equal, good.[24] Indeed, it asserts that social justice is needed in order to preserve the kind of harmonious social order in which alone freedom may flourish. Great inequality is likely to produce social unrest amongst the disadvantaged, who will end up having their civil freedoms repressed, unless the situation is righted by, at least, a minimal redistribution of wealth. Such unrest, however, will also cause the privileged to lose some of their freedoms, since they will have to take measures to protect themselves and their possessions from violence, theft and damage. Social disharmony is also economically harmful; as maintaining a strong police presence, imprisoning dissenters and protecting lives and property will become prohibitively costly. Indeed, a socialist might well argue, with a wry smile, that economic liberalism is possible only on the basis of a measure of distributive justice.

More importantly, the socialist tradition invites the liberal to consider a deeper meaning to freedom and rights. J.R. Lucas claims that

> . . . we have been pursuing the wrong political goals – productivity, efficiency, equality – and have neglected the cardinal political virtue of justice, which together with liberty is the condition under which I and every man can identify with society . . . and accept its rulings as my own.[25]

Justice, Morris Ginsberg argues, is an innate sense that we owe something to others, which is theirs by right because they are supremely worthy of respect.[26] In Rawls's well-known theory,[27] justice is based on the concept of fairness. In order to avoid equating justice with my own self-interest, or that of my group, I and all people have to imagine that we are governed by an imaginary social contract to which we have all put our name. It would be based on a series of principles or values that we would all choose for our own lives, *prior* to knowing whether or

---

[24] Cf. J. Milbank, *Theology and Social Theory: Beyond Secular Reason*. Oxford. Blackwell. 1990, p. 201.
[25] *On Justice*. Oxford. Clarendon Press. 1980, p. 1.
[26] *On Justice in Society*. Harmondsworth. Penguin Books. 1965, p. 80.
[27] *On Justice*. Oxford. Clarendon Press. 1971.

not we were going to gain from them. Assuming that we might receive the worst possible outcome, and in order to safeguard our own interests, we would think it only fair that opportunities and resources should be distributed equitably. That, in a nutshell, is the programme of the socialist option.

However, the socialist tradition is also based on the justified criticism of liberalism, where this latter seeks to avoid the accusation that the market is unjust in its dealings. The Austrian economist and philosopher, F.A. Hayek, argues strenuously that, because a true market economy is spontaneous (i.e. unfettered by arbitrary political intervention), it cannot be coercive. Thus, according to his line of reasoning, to be disadvantaged in a market society is not a limit on freedom.[28] On this basis, economic liberals have argued that, because free exchange is a natural human process, the workings of the market have nothing to do with morality and justice:

> Most differences of status or position or wealth can be regarded as a product of chance at a far enough remove.[29]

The argument hinges on a particular interpretation of intention: because the system as such clearly does not intend there to be any limitations on freedom, due to an unequal distribution of economic power, there cannot be any question of holding people or institutions to account; such a procedure would make sense only when the human will makes deliberate decisions.

Socialists dispute this defence against the accusation that an unfettered market works unjustly. First, they argue that lack of direct intention is not a sufficient justification, since knowledge of the probable effects of a system also amounts to culpability. If it is known, for example, that the dumping of toxic waste in the sea is going to decimate the stock of fish, it is no defence to argue that there was no intention to kill fish. Secondly, they point out that the legitimation of inviolable property rights is usually

---

[28] Cf. *Law, Legislation and Liberty*, Vol. II, pp. 31–2.

[29] M. Friedman, *Capitalism and Freedom*. Chicago. University of Chicago Press. 1962, pp. 165–6. Some people, generally identified politically as 'New Right', hold that substantial inequalities of income are not merely an inevitable outworking of unfettered market forces, but are desirable in order to attract the best qualified people for the most important jobs.

based on a presumption that the correct procedures have been followed for acquiring and transferring assets: i.e. that no due legal processes have been violated. However, the laws which define and defend the absolute right to private property are created by humans in particular circumstances, according to certain beliefs and may thus be vulnerable to criticism.[30] Unless the economic liberal can give an adequate justification, showing why the law should be what it is, not merely an historical description of what it happens to be, then the position is open to being challenged on moral grounds.[31] The third socialist argument is that the primitive accumulation of capital is inevitably the result of a process in which the fruit of some people's human labour is expropriated by others. Thus, a person becomes rich, not necessarily at the total expense of others (for the creation of wealth delivers communities from an economic zero sum game), but at least through failing to reward others' efforts equitably.

It is thus part of the socialist case that the relative redistribution of wealth should be interpreted not as robbing Peter of what is legitimately his, in order to pay Paul, but as returning to Paul what has been taken from him by an unfair and violent process. In other words, workers have a right to the freedom involved in receiving a just reward for their part in the process of creating wealth. The tacit agreement of the worker to sell his or her labour by acceding to the terms of a job is not a fair procedure, in case where there is an inequality of power on either side of the bargain. The worker has just as much right to be protected from the coercive power of the market, as the property-owner has to be protected from the coercive power of the state.[32]

Socialism is based in part on the labour theory of value, which Marx took over from the British economist, Ricardo, and elaborated further. However, it does not necessarily adopt either the Marxist deterministic reading of history or its 'quasi-messianic' beliefs. Refusing to give credence to ahistorical

---

[30] Cf. G. Ponton and P. Gill, *Introduction to Politics*. Oxford. Blackwell. 1982, pp. 196–7.
[31] Cf., Samuel Brittan, *A Restatement of Economic Liberalism*. Atlantic Highlands. Humanities Press International. 1988, p. 220.
[32] Cf. J. Milbank, op.cit., p. 193.

theories of the way societies must develop, socialism limits itself to redressing the disadvantages which certain sectors of society suffer by virtue of the unequal balance of power in an unregulated market. It claims to be concerned about making freedoms more available by being more equivalent across the whole of society.

## The perspective of 'Existentialism'

Modern notions of freedom are associated, not only with political and economic ideas and movements, but with philosophical thought and artistic endeavour. These latter have been, and continue to be, influential in shaping general cultural perceptions. Thus one of the most potent twentieth-century expressions of human defiance against the creeping loss of freedom through intellectual conventions and bureaucratic controls has been existentialism. It has emerged as a serious statement about the reality of human life in a universe that appears to be absurd. Extentialism is linked with the names of philosophers like Heidegger, Jaspers, Sartre and Marcel; writers like Camus and Osborne; theologians like Bultmann and Tillich; film directors like Buñuel, Godard, Fellini and Bergman. It is also the framework for the 'Theatre of the Absurd' and for artistic movements like Abstract Expressionism and Tachisme.[33]

Over and above these explicit manifestations, extentialism, as a prevalent approach to life, is spread quite widely throughout the general populace. Resembling in some respects the romantic movement of the early nineteenth century, it has been influenced by the religious thought of Kierkegaard, the philosophy of Nietzsche and the insights of Dostoievsky and Tolstoy and has much in common with 'post-modern' thought. It is difficult to categorize all these different elements under one single rubric. Nevertheless, existentialism, which has made a particular view of freedom into one of its distinctive features, captures and

---

[33] Cf. H. Osborne, *Abstraction and Artifice in Twentieth-Century Art*. Oxford. OUP. 1979, pp. 111–124; R. Hughes, *The Shock of the New: Art and the Century of Change*. London. Thames and Hudson. 1991, pp. 310ff.

promotes a distinct mood in the modern world.

Like most movements within a culture, it is a reaction (or perhaps a revolt) against several tendencies which have become powerful influences since the eighteenth century. One is *empiricism*, which suggests that only what is observable, measurable and verifiable, according to universally binding criteria, is real. Another is *rationalism*, which holds that the human mind, unaided by beliefs based on revelation, is able in principle to comprehend the unity and meaning of everything that exists. We should also mention *materialism* with its strong emphasis on understanding existence by looking for human origins exclusively in nature with its rigid sequence of cause and effect.

Each of these tendencies has, in its own way, built an impenetrable wall between fact and meaning, between 'being-in-itself' and 'being-for-itself'.[34] The modern person experiences life as a series of unrelated encounters with the material world, unified neither by an integrated inner person nor by an unchanging transcendent reality. In Heidegger's famous phrase, humans are 'thrown into being', as if by chance. For Sartre, 'existence precedes essence'. By this he means that there is no specific, given human nature which precedes the actual, concrete action of human beings in the world.

Without an external reference point or even a stable, continuing internal reference point, life is a ceaseless flux in which, potentially, meaning, purpose, moral values and human relations may change arbitrarily from day to day. This would seem to spell a complete loss of freedom, for freedom is related to what is *worth* choosing, but without an overall, given purpose we cannot know what is worth while. It appears that every choice and every action is equally meaningful and equally absurd. However, the message of existentialism is that precisely in this condition the human being is radically free:

> If indeed existence precedes essence, one will never be able to explain one's action by reference to a given and specific human nature; in other words, there is no determinism – man is free,

---

34 Jean-Paul Sartre developed this terminology to refer to things that are conscious of existing and those that are not: cf. A. Castell (et al.), *An Introduction to Modern Philosophy: Examining the Human Condition.* New York. Macmillan College. 1994, p. 105.

man *is* freedom. Nor, on the other hand, if God does not exist, are we provided with any values or commands that could legitimize our behaviour. Thus we have neither behind us, nor before us in a luminous realm of values, any means of justification or excuse. We are left alone . . . That is what I mean when I say that man is condemned to be free.[35]

Freedom, then, is the decision to shoulder the full responsibility, despite the 'anguish', 'abandonment' and 'despair' implied in the human condition, of creating one's own meaning, values and being, by a voluntary act of the will. The individual is alone and cannot blame anyone or anything else for what he or she is. Sartre is categoric:

> Man is nothing else but what he purposes, he exists only in so far as he realizes himself, he is therefore nothing else but the sum of his actions, nothing else but what his life is.[36]

All who do not shoulder this responsibility Sartre accuses of 'bad faith': they are those who shelter behind the particular hand that fate has dealt them in life, fearful of accepting the challenge of being absolutely free to make something genuinely their own out of their lives, or who hypocritically submit to the imposed meanings and values of a culture captured and controlled by the media. The lives they pursue are essentially inauthentic.

## 'Spiritual' freedom

Another way of coping with a world that seems to be unduly controlled by the rational management of time, talents and resources, that does not seem to offer any alternative to ever-expanding economic growth and consumerism as the object of economic life, that appears to be endemically brutal and incapable of resolving its mounting environmental crisis and that has given up on the search for a coherent and satisfying purpose for existence, is to retreat inwards. As was taught by the Stoics, there is an inner citadel, where one can be free from the pressures and seeming irrationalities of the most rational of predetermined existences.

---

[35] J-P. Sartre, *Existentialism is a Humanism*, quoted in A. Castell, ibid., p. 107.
[36] Ibid., p. 108.

This kind of freedom, says Berlin, is either a way of life we decree for ourselves, or one that is prescribed by a group to which we willingly submit. However circumscribed our life may be by the outward circumstances in which we live, and over which we have little control, within this inner sphere we can dedicate ourselves to our own emancipation. It is, he says, the kind of self-transformation promised by ascetics and religions like Buddhism. Through meditation, right thinking, healthy eating, care for the environment and the building of small intential communities, individuals can transcend the limitations of a culture which has no values beyond those of material progress. They can, as it were, move outside[37] 'the circle of idolatry'. They are free, in so far as they have consciously chosen to reject a life dedicated to self-gratification. Now, they have control over their desires and affections.

In this view, freedom is not a commodity that someone else can give or withhold, it is something I lay hold of within myself. In some ways, this perspective is the opposite of existentialism in that it appears to be based on a belief that there is a given selfhood which exists prior to social influences; this self is able to accept, reject or mould external forces. Closely related to this view is the freedom some people experience, even when they are outwardly constrained. Thus, when unjustly confined as a prisoner of conscience or when living under a dictatorial regime, it is possible to be free both from acquiescence in the political status quo and from the hatred and bitterness that engenders a destructive passion for revenge.

Some people define 'spiritual' freedom in terms of the interaction between a supposed higher and lower nature. People cannot experience genuine freedom until they have come to terms with themselves. If they are not at ease with themselves, are unable to forgive themselves their failures, despise their inability to make genuine friendships, are frustrated by the weakness of their will, their irrational fantasies and inhibitions and are fearful of breaking free from conventional norms, they

---

[37] A clear example of disengagement from the normal routine of 'civilized' social life is given by the 'Travellers', associated in recent years with a spirituality provocatively called 'New Age'. Both the spiritual underpinning and the lifestyle itself are consciously chosen as alternatives to mainstream assumptions about what is important in life.

are not in control of themselves. The truly free person is the one who is confident about their goals in life and is able to fulfil them. Such a person would be in control of his or her own intellectual processes of reflection, memory of the past and imagination of the future.[38] In this view of the two natures at conflict with one another, derived from Greek philosophy (as already mentioned), the 'thinking' person is more truly free than the 'feeling' person. Deliberate reflection is placed above emotions and instincts. A person cannot claim to be free unless they can reflect on their lower impulses, criticize them rationally and do something about transforming them. Freedom is experienced in the act of knowing and coming to terms with oneself, and then changing oneself to the person one really wants to be.

**Aesthetic freedom**

Another way of looking inward is by exploring the entire range of one's emotional life, not in order to bring it under the control of a supposedly higher rational self, but in order to allow it free expression. All forms of art, therefore, if they are to be authentic must originate in the spontaneous, imaginative side of our nature. Artists are at liberty to use any style which suits their mood. Images may flow freely, producing in principle an infinite variety of different collages. It is, of course, acceptable to impose a form on the artistic medium being used, not because of some external compulsion to do so, but as an expression of individual choice. In the last resort, the artist is accountable to himself or herself alone. What another person does with the result of the creative processes is the other side of aesthetic freedom. They may see the art-object in another light. This freedom is equally permissible. Nevertheless, some artists, engaged in much more than an intellectual struggle to understand themselves, are disappointed, or even hurt, when the viewer or listener appears to show little awareness of their processes of self-exploration or harshly judges their work as immature, crude, imitative, confused or stylistically contrived.

---

[38] Cf. E. Barker, *The Making of a Moonie: Choice or Brainwashing*. Oxford. Blackwell. 1984, p. 137.

Modern aesthetics is, in many ways, a child of the romantic movement, which was itself a rebellion against the rationalist notion of an objective, minutely ordered, intellectually accessible universe.[39] Like the scientist, the artist may engage in constant experiment; unlike the work of the scientist, however, there are no accepted criteria for validating the results. There is thus a sense in which judgement, particularly moral judgement, is out of place, apart from an expression of personal preference. Art flows essentially out of a subjective experience,[40] and therefore the only possible form of 'bad' art is that which is insincere, which copies past styles and expresses other people's views. Art is corrupted, when it is forced (as in Stalin's Russia) to express a particular ideology:

> The artist . . . far from accepting a brief to defend the virtues of the present or the past claims freedom, and uses it to indict the present by proclaiming the future . . . The work of art is itself authentic by reason of an entire self-definition: it is understood to exist wholly by the laws of its own being. The artist sets the highest value on intensity of feeling and finds that, in his search for ever greater intensity, more ordinary experiences disappoint him.[41]

The prevalent contemporary emphasis on the priority of personal experience as the starting place for making sense of reality, and the invitation to be in touch with one's feelings and impressions, are part of the heritage derived from romanticism. It fits well a culture convinced of the equal validity of all choices, all ways of expressing oneself, all patterns of believing and all ways of living that is the hallmark of what is called 'postmodernity'. After looking at some of the major consequences which spring from the views of freedom we have been outlining in this chapter, we will devote a further chapter to considering freedom after the modern world.

---

[39] Cf. J. Marquet, *The Aesthetic Experience: An Anthropologist looks at the Visual Arts.* New Haven. Yale University Press. 1986, pp. 172ff.

[40] 'Schlegel wishes to see the creative potential beyond every particular sensuous object, *which leads to an endless proliferation*' (my emphasis), A. Bowie, *Aesthetics and Subjectivity: from Kant to Nietzsche.* Manchester. Manchester University Press. 1990, p. 54.

[41] B. Mitchell, *Morality: Religious and Secular.* Oxford. Clarendon Press. 1980, pp. 38, 40.

# Five

# A Variety of Consequences

The modern world has been characterized by accelerating change. We have noted the emergence of various economic, political, technological and intellectual forces during the sixteenth and seventeenth centuries. During the intervening years they have imposed a radically different kind of society. In terms of the long sweep of human history a quarter of a millenium is an insignificant period of time. Nevertheless, human life and the environment have been transformed to a degree barely imaginable.

The years between 1700 and 1950 have seen industrialization, urbanization, colonialism, the intellectual revolution of the Enlightenment, the triumph of the natural sciences and the rise of the social sciences, the end of absolute monarchy and the consolidation of parliamentary democracy, universal suffrage, the emergence of a post-colonial world in the 'South', unprecedented migration, education for all and the immunization of whole populations. As if all this were not enough, the last half century has seen even more incredible changes. For those living in the Western world the result has been, on balance, an increase in formal freedoms. For those living in other parts of the world freedom may still be an ideal, a dream (or for some, a nightmare), whose time has not yet come, because economic, social and cultural circumstances do not yet permit it.

The coming of freedom in the modern sense to many societies

has brought with it a number of consequences – some enormously beneficial to those who experience them, some ambiguous and some distinctly problematical. Life in modern societies might be described as the daily struggle to understand, come to terms with and implement the implications of freedom. We continue our exploration by discussing some of the main consequences of the changes that have affected the way Western people live and think.

## The individual alone

Young people, having just crossed the threshold into adult life, are aware of the new opportunities opening up to make their life what they want it to be. They live at a time when the conventions which may have been part of their upbringing are strongly contested. As they look to the future, they concentrate on the present and the variety of experiences which are within their reach. Their thoughts are unlikely to be much on the past, nor are they generally guided by wisdom from another generation. If they are concerned about social, political and environmental issues, they are likely to propose new ideas and solutions involving a substantial break with the past. They are more likely to be idealists than realists or pragmatists. In their vocabulary continuity, customs, venerable structures, rituals, etiquettes and inherited duties are certainly not sacred words. Their first thought will not be about preserving the past, but about liberating themselves (and maybe others, including their parents) from ideas and practices they feel are outmoded.

There are many reasons why young people perceive life in this way. They have just emerged from ties that have bound them to figures of authority and to routines of life which have been set for them. Now is the time for them to experiment and take risks for themselves. They have been given, or have taken, freedom to discover who they are in relation to a world still largely unexplored. They are now on their own. Economic independence (if they are able to secure regular employment) enables them to be mobile and to live away from home. They will now establish relations with their family on their own terms. If they wish they can remain relatively anonymous.

The educational system has encouraged them to think for themselves and to make their own decisions about what they believe and what lifestyle is suitable for them. They have been taught to base their opinions on real facts and tested evidence, not on mere traditions, superstitions, hearsay or idle chatter. They will know, particularly if they have attended mixed-ethnic schools, that there are many beliefs and opinions abroad in the world. They will have been urged to respect and tolerate the convictions of others and to explore worlds with which they are not familiar:

> More people are being called on to assert a new power – the power not to believe or accept dogma – and being given the opportunity to discover a new pleasure – of feeling inside how contradictory ideas, if we are capable of assimilating them, can create an enormous mental richness. Autonomous man – *homo individualis* – is being born, and like all births, the process is painful.[1]

They live in a climate which expects them to take responsibility for their own decisions. They are unique individuals, who demonstrate a proper maturity when they are the real originators of their own actions and the proper subjects of their own moral evaluations. If they attend university, they will probably have learnt that the first priority of proper academic study is the suspension of judgement in the interests of honing a critical response to the learning process. They will learn to be suspicious of the motives of others and ever alert to the subtle ways in which their minds may be subverted and dominated by others' views. They may even drink in the idea that there are no right conclusions at which they should arrive, unless they have to do with areas where a specific body of data is open in principle to repeated testing and verification.

In applying for a job, they will expect that any religious or political views they may hold or any particular lifestyle they may follow in their private lives will not be considered relevant to their application and their chance of being selected. As long as they are professionally well-qualified, able to work with others and willing to fulfil the demands of the employer, they will be

---

[1] E.H. Teclglen, 'The Anguish of Abundance' in *The Independent*, op.cit., p. 159.

entirely suitable for the work, and other factors will, therefore, not be pertinent.

However, neither younger nor older people are prepared consistently to take full responsibility for their actions. Some accounts of freedom give the impression that liberty of choice and action also entails freedom from having to experience and face up to the consequences that may flow from them. Devices abound which enable us to deny the connections, excuse our follies and find external causes to blame. It is a matter of controversy, for example, to what extent people should be held accountable for the consequences of a permissive sexual lifestyle, such as unwanted pregnancies, suicides following the trauma of broken relations, AIDS or other sexually transmitted diseases, the break-up of marriages, or the effects of over-eating, lack of exercise, smoking and excessive drinking. How far should over-stretched medical resources be available for those who deliberately choose a way of life which is known to have a high risk of causing illness? To give an example of a different kind: personal and legal redress for the victims of corruption and violence has not advanced far in modern societies. It is amazing that dishonest business people, having acquired people's savings by fraud and deception, spent them on an extravagant lifestyle and then gone bankrupt, can find ways to trade, the following day, under a new name, as if nothing untoward had taken place. Responsibility inevitably has to become an integral part of the debate about freedom, for if it is a truism that a person cannot be held responsible for an action, unless it was freely chosen, surely it is equally true that a person cannot be free, unless they take full responsibility for what they have done.

## Democracy and the dispersion of power

Freedom from all kinds of arbitrary rule has entailed a new political consciousness and new legal processes and forms of government. Emphasis on the dignity and inviolability of the individual has brought a much changed climate with respect to collective organization. We have noticed that in modern political thinking the main purpose of government is to protect the rights and freedoms of all members of a society, creating the conditions in which they may carry on their personal and economic lives with a minimum of regulation. Governments are required to protect the equal freedoms of all against the inclination of some to gain additional freedoms for themselves at the expense of others.

The dispute between liberal and social democratic political ideals has to do with the desirability, the nature and amount of state interference needed to equalize power among all sections of the population. There is certainly ideological disagreement about how far a government should go in legislating to overcome natural inequalities, but no one doubts that some collective action is needed, in order that all may be protected against excessive power.

By the same token democracy entails the implicit participation of all and the explicit participation of a cross-section of some of the population in order to ensure that the proper limits of government are observed. The worth of the individual must not be treated as an abstract ideal, but is to be allowed public, as well as private, expression. The significance of individuality is acknowledged only in those democratic systems which genuinely allow all to participate in government, whatever their status and background. Democratic freedom is severely curtailed when election to government is dependent on personal financial resources or on political patronage, or when the actual or potential economic rewards are excessive. Regular and fair elections are not, in themselves, sufficient ways of ensuring genuine democratic participation. The voting population has a responsibility to remind government in the intervening years that a majority in parliament is not an unrestricted mandate to carry through any kind of legislation; not even that legislation which was explicitly included in the winning party's political manifesto at the election; a vote indicates a general approbation, not an endorsement of every detail of a policy statement.

Government implies a certain loss of freedom. Few believe that the freedom of all is best extended and guaranteed, where there is no government. Although anarchical ideas were particularly popular at the end of the nineteenth century,[2] during

---

[2] Cf. A. Carter, *The Political Theory of Anarchism*. London. Routledge and Kegan Paul. 1971 (especially pp. 60ff.); G. Woodcock, *The Anarchist Reader*. Glasgow. Fontana/Collins. 1977.

a period of intense idealism in which a belief in the spontaneous co-operative spirit of humankind came to the fore, few people today, at the end of the most violent and repressive century in human history, would realistically advocate abolishing all forms of coercive power.[3] In addition, if government and the purpose for which it is established, namely the equalization of power and opportunity[4] (implying a welfare state of some kind), is legitimate, then it has to be paid for. Taxation is undoubtedly a limit on freedom as everyone can see from their weekly or monthly statement of pay: on one side of the sheet is the gross pay; on the other, standard deductions; at the bottom comes the net pay, which in my case amounts to 76 per cent of my salary (nearly one quarter goes to central government). Local taxes, inheritance taxes, capital gains taxes, sales taxes and other forms of raising revenue take away further slices. We may grumble about budget proposals, but we know that taxation is as certain as death and that it is indispensible for the proper functioning of a free society. Naturally, taxation also has the effect of making governments more accountable; it would be strange if people did not care what happened to the money that is deducted from their hard-won earnings.

Democracy is not without its dangers. Since the birth of the welfare state, government has tended to be seen as the provider of universal benefit. This is probably most keenly felt in the area of health care, which consistently ranks first in surveys designed to discover the population's highest priority for well-being. As a result, it is extremely tempting in times of mass democracy, when engaged in the struggle for votes, for governments and opposition parties to promise to meet people's expectations, however unrealistic these may be. There is, therefore, likely to be a certain amount of duplicity in the relationship between the public and political parties, particularly at the time of an

---

[3] C. Ward (*Anarchy in Action*. London. 1973) seems to think that anarchy in the form of limited libertarian gains is probably the most that can be realistically achieved. He points to various 'liberation' movements in the West as examples of some progress in the implementation of anarchist ideals (cf. pp. 136–7).

[4] The added responsibility to defend the realm against actual or potential aggressors may be becoming redundant, due to the growing popularity of treaties based on the notion of 'common security'. Protection against internal violence (crime) remains.

election. Subsequently this may lead to political cynicism and even apathy, as a government is seen to go back on its word. The other major danger of democracy, particularly in the absence of proportional representation, is the tyranny of the majority.[5] Nothing is more threatening to democratic rule than the feeling of a substantial minority that they are effectively disenfranchised, whatever the formal situation may be.

## Loss of community

The example given earlier of family life with each member sitting in splendid isolation in front of their own TV may seem far-fetched – although it is a fact that some 70 per cent of all teenagers in Britain do have their own set. However, the reality of the family as a close-knit organism, sharing in meals and common interests and tasks is largely a thing of the past. Of course it would be absurd to generalize across different strata and geographical areas of the same country; there will always be variations in the rate that changes take place. Nevertheless, the comparative ease with which a father and mother may separate, the abundance of choice as to leisure activities, the irregular patterns of work all conspire to create a fragmented family existence. Moreover, increased concern about child abuse and an enlargement of the concept of democracy have led to the suggestion that children should have rights, established in law, against their parents, guardians and other members of their family. Whereas the idea has much to commend it, in order that the overt and covert violation of vulnerable people may be properly monitored and its incidence reduced, it also tends to breed distrust and further alienate the members of a family from one another. Of course, the implementation of rights within the most intensive and potentially explosive community of all – the family – is fraught with difficulties. The issue needs to be addressed circumspectly. For example, what are the rights and limits of the parental discipline of children? Do children have a right to a secure home with two parents living together?

---

[5] Where there are more than two major political parties competing for power (as in Britain), this can become the tyranny of the minority.

Many young people do not experience their family as a community that shares, cares and protects. Rather, they find it an arena where a conflict of interests is played out and where the power, and often brutality, of the strongest gains the upper hand. Many women also find the family oppressive and suffocating; within it they are expected to fulfil roles which conflict with their own sense of identity as a person, independent of being a wife and mother.

Social and economic freedoms have contributed to the dissolution of personal bonds between people. The pace of life lessens possibilities for making and developing genuine friendships, which can prosper only when time is spent on cultivating them. Modern society tends to make do with acquaintances and colleagues rather than friends. Hospitality and entertaining is more likely to take place, if at all, as an extension of one's employment, for here it may be justified as a necessity; in one's genuinely private life, it can be felt as a burden added to the already exhausting business of gaining a living.

So we should not assume that community is generally perceived as an ideal which has sadly disappeared into an irrecoverable, though still longed-for, past. Whether consisting of family, neighbourhood, voluntary association or religious or ethnic groups, communities are seen as entitities which demand mental and emotional energy, which many people feel they do not possess. There are probably few people who feel that one needs to be an active part of a community in order to live a full and satisfying life. We do not feel that we inherit a community to which we have a long-lasting commitment. Rather, we belong to groups, societies or associations for limited times and for specific purposes: geographically based communities (like villages) can be experienced by relatively few people, and even then the kind of people who make them up may be so diverse that a sense of common belonging becomes almost impossible. Nevertheless, there are new types of communities (if that is not stretching the meaning of the word too far) which engender passion and commitment. An obvious example would be a football supporters' club, which generates at least a kind of sense of belonging, providing perhaps a marginal sense of identity, to some entity with a vision and purpose beyond oneself.

Communities are now voluntary collectivities, created to meet the needs of individuals. We will abide by their rules only if we have joined them on our own initiative. It may be that our view of community is shaped by our daily experience that human relations are generally speaking built on calculated, economic transactions. Only rarely do we experience community as something wholly gratuitous, in which we are free to give and receive for no other reason than that such a way of relating enriches human life.

This means, as has often been pointed out, that modern society exists as a collectivity of 'strangers'. We pursue our personal interests ignorant of and unconcerned about those of others. We may know little or nothing about even our most immediate neighbours, let alone people who live further down the street or on another level in the block of flats. Indeed it is generally considered prudent not to become too closely involved in the lives of others. Individuality spells freedom from our having to divulge our feelings, beliefs, experiences, interests and occupations to others. So, conversely, we may resent others enquiring too persistently about our affairs. Not surprisingly, this lifestyle may result in intense loneliness, as witnessed by the 'lonely hearts' columns.

The celebration of diversity and plurality, already mentioned, may also detract from the celebration of community. On the one hand, people do not so readily hold to the same common opinions, values and interests as they may have done in a former age. On the other hand, diversity of views engenders competing pressure groups often actively working against one another in the public forum. It would appear also that the media in general is subversive of a community of ideas, since it is profitable to encourage the expression of antagonistic viewpoints (ostensibly in the interests of balancing opinions). It also gives the impression that controverted beliefs, although they may be held with sincerity and conviction, can never be reconciled.

## The loss of a centre

Strongly related to the loss of a community with which individuals identify, giving them roots and a sense of belonging, comes the loss of a fundamental set of convictions which sustains them through changing times. What Peter Berger calls 'the sacred canopy' has gone and, to continue the metaphor, all that has replaced it are a series of individually designed umbrellas.

Since about 1680, the Christian world-view has gradually ceased to be the normative way of interpreting life in Western culture. This does not necessarily mean, as in some theories of secularization, that religious belief has been altogether lost. It may have been relocated into very private inner experiences of the divine or the sacred. Freedom of religious belief and the spirit of the entrepreneur have combined to produce a bewildering variety of religious and semi-religious beliefs. Exposure to other cultures and immigration from different parts of the world have made it possible for the West to learn from other religious traditions. The result has been a remarkable florescence of colourful cults, combining elements from different backgrounds.

Symbols and rituals which, in former times, would have bound societies together have disappeared. Only a small minority now observes the rhythm of the Christian year, though associated festivals (or festivities) like Shrove Tuesday, Mothers' Day (not Mothering Sunday) and Hallowe'en are popular with many sectors of society. Holidays do not coincide any more with 'holy' days, so they no longer celebrate the sacred reality of the story of the saviour of the whole world, but the secular reality of rest and relaxation; no longer the healing of the spirit, but the recuperation of the body and the mind:

> a thoroughly secular culture would be one in which norms, values and modes of interpreting reality . . . have been emancipated entirely from assumptions of human dependence on supernatural agencies or influences'.[6]

Part of the explanation of this loss is that people's everyday life centres on the mundane, the empirical and the functional. By and large they distrust grandiose, universal, metaphysical claims as the solution to practical problems. No longer are they concerned about an objective condition of sin against an ever-present God whose righteous anger at injustice and corruption

---

[6] A.D. Gilbert, op.cit., p. 9.

needs to be atoned for. Suffering and misfortune as well as happiness and well-being seem to come to people irrespective of the kind of life they live. People may still have feelings of guilt, but they do not suffer from a bad conscience in the same way as in former times. Impersonal chance, rather than a compassionate providence, is what most people see as ruling their destinies. In the modern age people are looking for ways of alleviating a general sense of dis-ease, which religious people would interpret as a spiritual emptiness, but is in general experienced as a lack of significance, self-confidence and self-worth.

At times of crisis, like natural or human-created disasters (floods, earthquakes, serious road accidents, brutal killings) many, though far distant from any formal religious conviction, would feel it appropriate to use religious language to express their sentiments, even when bemused by the official content implied by it. Prayers and memorial services still figure as a major part of coming to terms with grief.

Yet modern people are not totally apathetic. Recent years have seen an upsurge of commitment to a wide variety of moral causes (from prisoners of conscience to animal rights). People are deeply moral and demonstrate it by their willingness to be activists on behalf of many issues. But often the sense of outrage and indignation fills a gap left by the erosion of solidly constructed moral principles. Since the late 1960s protest has become almost a way of life. Because life tends to be experienced as a set of discordant variations, protest supplies the missing theme.

In a world bustling with disparate information, ideas and advice, assured knowledge is distrusted. People are torn in two: they want stable values and commitments, but are afraid of ending up with illusions. In place of a creator's design for living, they grasp at the latest passing fashion. The heated debates about 'political correctness' and 'back to basics' evoke the image of a broken wheel, with a bent rim, crooked spokes and no hub.

**Progress in place of purpose**

The Puritan divines who gathered at Westminster in 1643 confidently affirmed that the chief end of humankind was 'to glorify God and enjoy him for ever'. Most people in the West are far from believing such a statement today. Modern people are doubtful whether there is a 'chief end' at all, in the sense of one over-arching purpose for living which defines the meaning of being human. Any such claim would be seen as an unwarranted interference with the individual's right to decide what goals to choose, and therefore what kind of human person to be.

For the modern world, the question of whether human beings, as such, are born to fulfil a particular destiny in life has to remain unknowable. According to modern ways of thinking, we cannot know what we are for. Our place in the world is a matter of speculation. Although it has been addressed down the ages by philosophers and theologians of different religious persuasions, in the nature of the case the debate has proved quite inconclusive. The only thing we may know with certainty is how we function physically, for that is a matter of observation and experiment. We are relatively confident that human beings can be described according to their beginnings, but not according to their ends:

> There seems little room for ideas of final causes or natural ends in a modern scientific worldview which has expelled teleology from itself, where it has not given the evidences of purpose in nature a mechanistic explanation.[7]

A naturalistic approach to human life inevitably leaves a great question mark over the question of destiny. There is nothing within the world which I observe external to myself that can guide me as to what I should do or be; even the scientific enterprise itself is founded on a set of beliefs which transcend its own method of working. A naturalistic philosophy grants that we have the ability to observe, catalogue and discuss different cultural approaches to the question of our 'chief end' and tells us to make up our own mind, according to whatever criteria makes sense to us, about what we hope to achieve with our lives. What

---

[7] J. Gray, op.cit., p. 46.

is absent is any rational basis, supported by a coherent world-view, for preferring one option to another.

Nevertheless, though the inadequacy of unaided reason to understand the experience of being human seems to be the logical outcome of a view of the world which has driven a wedge between mechanical explanation and meaning, the modern world is also marked by a tacit, yet powerful, belief in development and progress. The rise in material prosperity, staggering technological innovation and the spread of democracy lead to the conviction that the world is becoming a better place. If one were to ask what is meant by better, the response would probably be that individual freedoms have expanded. The extent of progress is measured by the amount of freedom people enjoy to choose for themselves how they will interpret the meaning of their own lives and how, therefore, they will actually live. Progress is defined by the increasing variety of dishes on the menu, not by our having at last discovered that there is more nourishment or goodness in choosing one rather than another.

Paradoxically, belief in the reality of progress, through a continual control of the natural world, presupposes that something is actually more important than freedom. If modern medicine can prolong the average life of human beings by, say, ten years over the period of half a century, one is curious to know to what end. In the overall cycle of birth, growth, decline and death, what benefit is it to live another ten years? What is worthwhile doing during those extra years, and why? If modern computer technology can devise machines able to carry out functions with ever greater speed, to store ever greater amounts of data, to recognize a person's handwriting and voice, to enable ever more sophisticated ways of communicating, why should these particular achievements be considered important? Is life in some way further enriched by these spectacular performances? To give an answer demands some idea of what enrichment would mean and this, in turn, points to questions about the purpose of existence.

'Freedom' has produced the solitary being, alone in an impersonal universe, seeking to make sense of the great questions of life, but with nothing to go on apart from the necessity, in order to live at all, of deciding something. This is not a happy position, for reason alone can neither discern an essential nature in human beings, which would help to define purpose, nor refute a complete scepticism.[8] Of what comfort is it to know that 'I am', if I only know partially *what* I am and do not know at all *why* I am?


## The split person

The absence of any substantial and coherent basis for understanding the purpose of existence is due largely to the apparently unbridgeable breach in the modern consciousness between what counts as fact and what as mere belief. This dichotomy is one of many which, perhaps more than anything else, characterize modern culture. As has been repeated numerous times by commentators on modern culture, the world of science does not provide a foundation for any particular values.[9] Although some attempts have been made to bridge the chasm between what is the case (from a phenomenological point of view) and what ought to follow (from a moral point of view), there are no conceivable logical steps that could adequately span the gap; *is* and *ought* belong to two separate kinds of discourse. The obvious conclusion has to be that moral judgements are simply linguistic survivals from the practices of classical theism, now without a context. Divorced from foundational moral claims 'ought' sentences become nothing more than forms of expression for an emotivist self alone.[10] Emancipation from the former way of interpreting human life in the universe leaves a paltry residue: the individual ego expressing desires and wishes.

The consequence has been a long slide into the realm of inner experience, conjecture and the creation of quite arbitrary values. There is no ladder leading from the pit of subjectivism to the firm ground of true right and wrong. The only recourse, one feels, is

---

[8] Cf. A. Macintyre, *After Virtue: A Study in Moral Theory*. London. Duckworth. 1985, p. 55.

[9] Cf., amongst others, M. Midgley, *Evolution as Religion: Strange Hopes and Strange Fears*. London. Methuen. 1985, pp.17–19, 81–88; R.C. Lewartin, *Biology as Ideology: The Doctrine of DNA*. Concord. Anansi. 1991, pp. 3–16; G. Grant, *Technology and Justice*. Concord. Anansi. 1986, pp. 35–44.

[10] A. MacIntyre, op.cit., p. 60.

to wave bravely to all the others struggling in their own pits and bid them 'have a good day'. Subjectivism, as we shall continue to investigate in following chapters, is a dangerous region to end up in as it gives no criteria for resisting real evil. Solid, intelligent and well-founded criticism of the beliefs of another can be only made on the basis of more substantial beliefs, not, as is often the case, as a result of emotive inclinations and illogical prejudices. On the other hand, scepticism about absolute values is simply self-refuting.

## The privatization of morality

> Freedom implies *freedom not* to accept any obligation or particular responsibility . . . The only obligations acceptable to the free man are those which he chooses to place on himself.[11]

The reasoning behind this affirmation is sound: a moral action is one which a person carries out according to the dictates of his or her own conscience, and then bears the consequences of the deed. If we are obliged to behave in a particular way, through fear of sanction or punishment, the action is not truly our own. We could be held morally responsible for not resisting the coercion, only if it were reasonable to expect that we were strong enough to resist the force.[12]

Of course, moral action undertaken after responsible and sincere deliberation and in the absence of external pressure is not necessarily right action. People, tragically, use the murder of totally innocent people as a means of furthering ends which they have consciously chosen for themselves, whether their purpose is to defeat some political power or to redress discrimination against a minority. Even when murder is committed for the dark motive of 'ethnic cleansing' or in fulfilment of sexual fantasies, the people who perpetrate such grim crimes, are still held fully

---

[11] J.C. Merrill, *The Imperative of Freedom: A Philosophy of Journalistic Autonomy*. New York. Freedom House. 1990, p. 75.

[12] There are obvious border-line cases, like torture or the threat of death to oneself or one's family, which can be considered such excessive pressure that not to defy it is hardly to be considered a moral lapse.

accountable for their actions, even though these may be unimaginable to the vast majority of people.

These examples show that there is a very real tension between private and public morality. The fact that there are sophisticated and clear-headed reasons for acting in a particular way do not give the individual the right to act thus. One of the problems of individual freedom is to give any account of public morality. If the object of morality, in consonance with modern consciousness, is to create respect for the autonomy of the individual,[13] it is difficult to give an account of a morality which, in the interests of maintaining a society free of anarchy, has to restrain that moral autonomy. Is it not true that morality is the possession of the individual? How, then, can a collective entity be moral? And yet, if it is going to enforce laws against individual citizens, it has to act morally and not just legally. If human communities cannot function on the basis of individuals choosing entirely their own morality, there has to be a commonly accepted morality which enables each person to live at peace with all others. Individual desire logically cannot be the source for such a morality.

Another area of tension between the private and the public is that of education. How can an education authority, board of governors, parents or teachers ever come to agree a moral education syllabus? As we have seen, in the absence of a foundation for an ethic of intrinsic right and wrong, actions tend to be judged on the sole criterion of their consequences. Recent debate about sex education has shown that this is an inadequate procedure.[14] Limiting the topic to describing how to prevent the unwanted consequences of sexual unions and assuming that there is a such a thing as 'safe sex' is futile. This focuses attention on the purely physical side of an intimate union between two

---

[13] Cf. S. Hauerwas, *After Christendom?* Nashville. Abingdon Press. 1991, p. 29.
[14] Educationalists from a number of religious traditions in an agreed statement drew a clear and significant distinction between stable relationships (not casual and promiscuous) and relationships of publicly recognized and permanent commitment. Cf. *Sex Education in the School Curriculum: The Religious Perspective*. Cambridge. The Islamic Academy. 1991. For the wider debate, cf. M.F. Hoffmann, 'Assumptions in Sex Education Books', *Educational Review*, 27,3, June 1975, pp. 211–20; P. White (ed.), *Personal and Social Education: Philosophical Perspectives*. London. Kegan Page. 1989, Chapter 5.

people; it does not come to terms with the many deep emotions aroused by this kind of act and their consequences, such as the sense of self-worth or self-disgust which is engendered.[15]

To speak of stable relations as the proper context in which people may experience sex together is hardly any better. How stable is stable? A friendship which has lasted three, six or nine months? What happens to the significance of the sex act within a stable relationship, when that relationship breaks apart? The tacit agreement between two consenting adults to be together for the moment is surely a wholly insufficient basis for something so fundamental to human existence as the sexual union of a man and a woman. The growth of genuine care for one another, followed in due course by procreation and child-rearing, requires nothing less than a life-time commitment within an established relationship, supported by both families and friends. To settle for anything less is to submit to the deceit of a momentary gratification, a passing fancy or, at best, a prolonged experimentation in human intimacy. The tragic, destructive remorse caused by the way in which relationships, without binding commitments, so easily fall apart is all too common. 'Falling in love' has become a catch-all phrase which seems often to have no more content than that of an individual's present feeling for another person.

In today's moral climate, how is it possible to build into a moral syllabus the notion that something is right or wrong, irrespective of our inclinations and beliefs? We are accustomed to respond to the notion of absolute values by asserting that this does not allow for difference. Respect for another's freedom, it is argued, should mean we are prepared to be open to the possibility that their view is as valid as mine, however bizarre it may appear to me. There is a new emphasis on the diversity of cultures as a reason for toleration. It is argued that values may be no more than a reflection of the particular way that a culture has evolved historically; that they represent no more than social constraints which have been introduced in the course of time to help societies function better. Interestingly enough this kind of

---

[15] Making casual sexual relations less dangerous or problematical can hardly be equated with fulfilling one's moral duty: cf. A. Bloom, *The Closing of the American Mind*. Harmondsworth. Penguin. 1987, p. 236.

reasoning is a typically Western response to moral confusion. People of other cultures often have a more definite idea of truth, as we shall see later in the case of Islam.

The privatization of morality cannot avoid serious and debilitating contradictions. For example, a hedonistic lifestyle in the private sphere, based on immediate consumption, does not easily fit the need for a rigorous work-ethic in the public life of business. Indeed, if competition rules public life, driving the commercial world to cut costs in order to be able to bring down prices, then the levels of both productivity and the work-force become the most serious consideration for survival. Efficiency demands that an increasingly slimmed-down work-force does increasingly more work. One is not one's own, one belongs to the company. But where, then, is the time and energy to live as one spends?

Freedom, seen as independence from the past, has led to a good deal of superficial thinking about morality. It can easily be a form of arrogance, which refuses to acknowledge that other people in other times may have come closer to the truth than us. Whereas it is true that people must make moral judgements their own, for them to be moral, it does not follow that a refusal to accept some moral reasoning on trust is any more moral or wiser than trying to begin a moral life as if it were a blank sheet of paper. Hauerwas likens much modern understanding of morality to functional glass buildings: cheap, easily built and efficient. But, he says, experience shows us that to be properly moral requires both initiation into a moral code and rigorous training.[16]

## Imperialism

Freedom as both the dominant value and definition of the modern world has been a significant factor in the removal of all constraints on the sheer will to dominate. It has been suggested that modern consciousness is founded not so much on the assertion of the individual reasoning subject as on the individual

---

[16] Op.cit., pp. 102–3

willing subject; not *cogito*, but *vinco* 'I conquer' *ergo sum*.[17] The whole history of the West, since the middle of the fifteenth century, can be written as episodes in the conquest of the world. In sequence, there have been the conquest of the sea, of other lands and peoples, of nature, of subsistence living, of economic markets and of space (even, it might be argued, the conquest of God[18]). The West has stamped on all other races its belief in its uninhibited right of discovery, experimentation, exploitation and the imposition of its own way of life.

However, in many ways the almost unbelievable presumptuousness of *homo occidentalis*, in taking to himself the right to extend his unlimited sovereignty over other human beings and over nature, has come back to haunt him. The West has created the notion of the sovereign state: as Ali Mazrui has put it, 'the pull of the Westphalian system continues to be for the time being irresistible'.[19] When Churchill and Roosevelt signed the Atlantic Charter in 1941, they saw the right of self-determination as applying only to those European peoples who were dominated by Nazi Germany. But this right had to be extended to those, in other parts of the world, dominated by all the European powers, however beneficial and magnanimous they might have thought their rule was. Hence, decolonization. Hence, the birth of the United Nations, though the implicitly democratic notion of 'one nation, one vote' has been circumvented by the presence of permanent members on the Security Council. Hence, the demand for non-interference in the internal affairs of a sovereign state.

It is in the realm of the world economic order that former colonized peoples most keenly feel the invincible might of the West:

> Attempts to bring development to these cultures have created a poverty never previously known. Their economies have moved from a position of austere sufficiency to a position of life-

---

[17] Cf. E. Dussel, *A History of the Church in Latin America: Colonialism to Liberation*. Grand Rapids. Eerdmans. 1981, pp. 5, 11–13.

[18] Is it easier to put God in chains, kill him off or simply banish him from the universe? In human history the latter, metaphorically speaking, has been the most successful.

[19] Op.cit., p. 239.

threatening deprivation. They experience a 'scarcity [which is] the self-fulfilling assumption of modern economic culture'.[20]

As a result of the control of the world markets in commodities, high tariff barriers to trade in the past, mono-producing economies, unskilled labour-forces, high returns to the exterior from investments, poor balance of trade, massive debt repayment burdens, many nations of the South have been net exporters of wealth. Not being able to retain sufficient of the wealth created nor to have a proper internal control over reinvestment has meant an increase in the level of poverty for the majority in many nations, even whilst some modernization has taken place and the rich élite have prospered even more.


**The question of justice**

Ever since the beginning of the modern period, freedom to possess, trade with and dispose of property privately has become one of the most jealously guarded of liberties. Apologists for a libertarian interpretation of economic policies argue that political freedoms of all kinds can be guaranteed only in a state committed to a minimum interference in the market. This argument is based not so much on any proven correlation between a free-market economy and a minimal government, but more on the combination of a centralized economy and a totalitarian state in the former Communist nations. That is, undoubtedly, one side of the story. The other side, however, suggests that commitment to the kind of negative freedom embodied in the free market actually requires strong government to enforce it. Against the powerful pull towards equalization policies that 'natural justice' demands in an open, democratic society, a strong state is necessary to ensure that the market is kept free.[21] This is also a matter of historical observation, from the time that the post-war consensus about

---

[20] J. Collier, 'Contemporary Culture and the Role of Economics' in H. Montefiore (ed.), *The Gospel and Contemporary Culture*. London. Mowbray. 1992, p. 124. (The words quoted are from A.L. de Romana, 'The autonomous society', *Interculture* 22.3 and 4 (Fall 1989).)

[21] Cf. A. Gamble, 'The Political Economy of Freedom' in R. Levitas (ed.), *The Ideology of the New Right*. Cambridge. Polity Press. 1986, pp. 27–51.

welfare-economics was broken and the economics of 'the new right' began to dominate Western nations from the late 1970s onwards.

It is often argued that capitalism can survive only if inequalities of wealth and power are sustained and the losers coerced or seduced into acquiescence.[22] It is admitted, by even the most ardent exponents of the free-market, that capitalism works on the basis of 'the survival of the fittest', a kind of economic equivalent to the comparative advantage which is the outcome of natural selection.[23] However, the inequalities that inevitably arise when freedom is given only a negative interpretation cannot be allowed to go beyond a certain point. Extremes of wealth and poverty are an affront to the conscience of any society, even those which are convinced that the creation of wealth necessitates relative inequality. Thus, even a strong proponent of a liberal economic system argues that economic freedom presupposes a just distribution of capital and that a moral defence of liberty requires that past injustices, caused by a departure from equal liberties, are rectified.[24] Unchecked inequalities of wealth are a major problem for modern accounts of freedom.

Capitalism, as a means of distributing resources, does not require as a result of its own mechanisms even the most minimum redistribution of those resources, when the powerful and the fortunate acquire for themselves a large share of the profits of wealth creation. Only the most radical on the right of the political spectrum continue to argue, in face of the evidence, that there is no injustice within the system. The call for individual compassion and generosity,[25] though it must always be part of a community's response to poverty, is never enough. It could even be argued that capitalism, within its own terms, will flourish better as a greater number of people are able to participate actively within the market as consumers. Those

[22] Cf. J. Milbank, op.cit., p. 193.

[23] Cf. B. Griffiths, *The Creation of Wealth*. London. Hodder and Stoughton. 1984, p. 105.

[24] Cf. J. Gray, op.cit., p. 89.

[25] Cf. E.R. Dykema, 'Wealth and Well-Being' in C.R. Strain (ed.), *Prophetic Visions and Economic Realities: Protestants, Jews and Catholics confront the Bishops' Letter on the Economy*. Grand Rapids. Eerdmans. 1989, p. 55.

whose buying power is almost non-existent are effectively outside the market, and therefore are non-contributors to the system. Here we find one of the many contradictions of capitalism: it is both dependent on the 'reserve army' of the unemployed, who in times of expansion can be brought in to provide cheap labour, and also on the masses having at all times disposable income, beyond what is required for sheer physical survival, sufficient to keep the economy buoyant.

Modern capitalist economics is committed to the premise that 'more is better', that human happiness is best served by economic growth. The corollary is that economic growth is dependent upon persuading people to consume. But these consumers need the income in order to 'consume'. In a situation of high unemployment or low wages (or both), the economics of spending one's way out of recession seems particularly cruel (and ineffective). Manipulating desire through advertising then becomes the equivalent of the mirage in the desert; the thirst is there, but the means to quench it is an illusion.

In one way, all modern political life can be seen as a struggle to limit the freedom of those who control large amounts of capital to act always in their own interests, rather than in the interests of the majority. In areas like health and safety, the use and abuse of the environment, compensation for redundancy, a minimum wage, the exploitation of indigenous, ancestral lands and control of the money markets and foreign exchange, the interests of the corporations, banks and finance houses are often in conflict with the interests of ordinary citizens. On the whole, though the ordinary person may wish to believe that the power of government is greater than the power of business, the reality is often otherwise.[26]


## Science, freedom and determinism

Modern societies are uncertain about and ambivalent towards the achievements and potential of science. On the one hand, there is a justified recognition of the new freedoms which

---

[26] Cf. L. Rasmussen, 'The Morality of Power and the Power of Morality' in C.R. Strain, op.cit., p. 140.

scientific method and 'discoveries' have produced. The modern tradition of science has been built on the premise that the exploration of the natural world could lead to a true understanding of the way things are, only if it were allowed to happen without either coercive pressure from non-scientific beliefs or fear of the possible consequences. The technological products of scientific experimentation in such areas as medicine, the gathering and dissemination of information, travel and industrial production have been so staggeringly effective as to leave the human race gasping for breath. Writing about European colonization, Lamin Sanneh puts the matter ironically:

> There was no better harbinger of the new creation than silent plumbing, no brighter hope than electricity and no higher symbol of a redeemed humanity than the modern bio-medical system.[27]

On the other hand, the twentieth century has also given so much evidence of both the negative side-effects of the application of science (in drug therapy, for example) and of the wrong uses to which science has been put (in the creation of nerve gases, for example) that today people have a more sober assessment of the place of science within human life. In the field of human biology, the Genome Project is raising deep-seated anxieties that we may not know how or for what purpose we should use the knowledge we will have of the entire genetic make-up of the human person. The ambivalences of present research are well illustrated by Tom Wilkie. On the one hand, he writes expansively and euphorically about the information that will be at our disposal; on the other, he urges much caution:

> Five centuries after Columbus set sail, the human race has begun its ultimate voyage of exploration. Around the globe, the search is already under way for the innermost essence of humanity . . . Teams of scientists are attempting nothing less than to unravel the secret of human inheritance itself . . . The Human Genome Project holds the promise that ultimately we may be able to rewrite this inheritance if we choose, and free ourselves of the scourge of diseases as diverse as cystic fibrosis or cancer. But if the new knowledge is not used wisely, it holds also the threat of creating new forms of discrimination and new methods of oppression.

---

[27] Op.cit., p. 22.

He quotes the words of James Watson, who with Francis Crick discovered the DNA molecule: 'As more and more things are revealed to have genetic components, we may see a feeling of losing control over our own destiny.'[28]

Information technology has revolutionized the study of both the cosmos and the microcosm and immensely facilitated communication through visual, spoken and written media. The 'birth' of new 'generations' of computers gives the promise of ever-greater 'advances' in the gathering and processing of information. At the same time, 'there are fears . . . that the privacy of the individual will be invaded and that new types of crime involving software . . . will arise'.[29]

Three major considerations are giving to scientific experimentation a more sombre face. First, there is the apprehension that advances in technological manipulation are outstripping considerations of ethical validity (as, for example, the possible use of aborted human foetuses either for experimentation or for the gathering of organs for transplantation into other humans). Secondly, and intimately connected with the ethical question, is a concern about the ends of the whole scientific enterprise: given the appalling history of the use of science for inhuman activities, sometimes with the connivance of the scientists themselves, and given the modern cultural climate of extreme uncertainty about what it means to be human, how may we know that the ends are genuinely worthy? There are two additional fears here: first, the danger that technology will be used increasingly as a force for discrimination, always giving those who possess it an advantage in the distribution of resources (for example, in the field of medical care); secondly, the tendency of technology to build up its own, ultimately uncontrollable momentum, in the sense that what can be achieved must be achieved. Technology would thus become a power to which we surrender in the long run, always being able to find ways of rationalizing our submission to *Techne*.[30]

---

[28] *The Independent*, op.cit., pp. 78–80.

[29] Cf. T. Ishii, 'Living with the Smart Machine' in *The Independent*, ibid., pp. 91–3.

[30] One of the most austere critics of the independence of 'technique' from the proper supervision of human society has been Jacques Ellul: for example, *The Technological Society* (1964) and *The Political Illusion* (1967). Others, however, have found his writings unduly alarmist.

The third consideration has to do with the suspicion that science, through its immense understanding of the workings of the human body, mind and psyche, has shown that real freedom of action is an illusion. There is the understandable fear that if events, including those within the human mind, can be understood in terms of mechanical cause and effect processes, human beings are ultimately predetermined to think and act in particular ways. Genuine choice and responsibility then become a mere fiction. Francis Crick, for example, has embarked on the study of human consciousness, asserting that everything that goes on in our consciousness can be explained by the behaviour of billions of nerve cells:

> You, your joys and sorrows, your memories and ambitions, your sense of personal identity and free will are, in fact, no more than the behaviour of a vast assembly of nerve cells.[31]

In one sense, the position he takes in the debate about the relation of the mind and the brain is not new; it is merely a reductionist view of human life. Its significance lies partly in the scientific aura which surrounds the name of the author of the thesis, partly in the assurance that human self-consciousness can be reduced to *nothing but* biological functions, however complex these may be. If everything is indeed reduceable to machine-like functions, then ethical behaviour is nothing more than a series of mental states, without any 'spiritual' value, and freedom becomes a matter of feelings, but not reality. This would be, perhaps, the last stage of the attempt to explain the whole of human life in terms of our genetic make-up and biological

---

[31] Quoted from Crick's book, *The Astonishing Hypothesis* (Simon and Schuster, 1994) by Nigel Hawkes in 'A Mind's Eye View', *The Times Magazine*, April 30, 1994, p. 21.

function.[32] Human significance would then be reduced purely to mechanical complexity. Most people, surely, would see this as a grave threat to human freedom and dignity. They would hardly be mollified by the advice that the consciousness of freedom (as long as we believe we are free) is more important than its reality.

In the light of these fears, many people do not relish the outlook for scientific work in the next century:

> Few doubt that the coming century will be the century of research into bio-ethics, the possible manipulation of genes, artificial intelligence, the prolongation of life, unknown factors in nuclear power, the creation of new lethal chemical substances or new drugs, the manipulation of the planet's resources and the conquest of space.[33]

Increasing technological sophistication seems to be in danger of putting far too much power into the hands of technicians and managers anxious to harness the findings of science for commercial profit. They will forge ahead in the vacuum formed by the lack of any consensus over the basis for ethical decision-making. If it is only by the methods of scientific investigation that we can know anything with certainty then science becomes the revelation of the only truth we can know. To what avail, then religious, ideological and moral pluralism, except as a further reason for loosening ethical controls over permissible scientific experimentation?

---

[32]  Cf. R. Dawkins, *The Selfish Gene*. Oxford. OUP. 1989. According to Dawkins, the only aspect of our lives, apparently, which saves us from 'the worst selfish excesses of the blind replicators' is foresight and, possibly, disinterested altruism (p. 200). He stretches one's imagination beyond credulity by the idea that by 'devious routes' evolution can save us from the apparent savagery of evolution. The choice to 'rebel against the tyranny of the selfish replicators' has no adequate cause in Dawkins's account of human origins. In the endnote on pp. 331–2, he confuses the description of a reality with an adequate explanation of why it has come about. By a sleight of reasoning the first is substituted for the second. Evolution as a theory of biological adaptation and development is incapable of carrying the weight of existential meaning or moral significance that the human species needs. Any ontological reductionist (such as Dawkins) ought to be consistent to his own premises, which can lead only to complete bewilderment in the contemplation of the manifold variety and complexity of the universe. For further critical analysis of Dawkin's theories, cf. J. Bowker, *Is God a Virus? Genes, Culture and Religion*. London: SPCK, 1995.

[33]  J. Arias, 'Seeking a Religious Dialogue in a World that lacks values' in *The Independent*, op.cit., p. 164.

# Six

# Freedom after Modernity

Having outlined a variety of ways of looking at the meaning of freedom and indicated some of the major consequences which follow from contemporary experiences of freedom, the next step is to take stock of where this leaves the reality of freedom in societies which are fully modern in their political and economic structures, laws, technological development and attitudes to individuals and their rights. We have noted that the human community has made solid gains in the area of real, concrete freedoms. At the same time, we have recognized that the practice of freedom, as it is understood in a secular culture, brings its own peculiar problems in a number of areas. The purpose of this chapter is to set the discussion within a wider context by attempting to take the temperature of the present moment of history, which has been categorized, not without reason, as 'post-modern'.

## The significance of modernity

A modern society is one in which technical and instrumental reason has come to define the boundaries of public life. The rational capacity of human beings has been oriented towards the domination of the natural world in order to bring to the human community prosperity, the conquest of disease, ignorance and superstition and the methodical overcoming of obstacles that stand in the way of an expanding quality of life. A modern society is also characterized by a multi-layered social stratification, social mobility, expanding opportunities for leisure activities, an increasing reliance on sophisticated means of information gathering and communication and a growing percentage of people with advanced educational qualifications.[1]

## The completion of modernity

There is a sense in which the modernizing programme, which has augmented and cemented the freedoms we have described, has now come to its denouement. All its most well-known characteristics have been in place for some time past. There is no going back to the kind of society that existed prior to industrialization, urbanization, the establishment of representative democracy, the birth of the autonomous individual and the abandonment of the public significance of a supernatural world, unless of course there were to be a major world-wide catastrophe of the order of a 'nuclear winter'.

More significantly, perhaps, the expectations of ever fresh territories to conquer, opened up by the confidence in reason, the prospects of the scientific endeavour, increased self-understanding, a more humane attitude to punishment, greater toleration of difference and the extension of equal opportunities to every member of society, have diminished. Such dreamers and visionaries as remain are treated as unrealistic idealists who have little notion of the hard realities of life. In short, modern people at the end of the second millennium no longer gaze with eager anticipation into the remote horizons of the future but keep their eyes down, fixed squarely on the unimaginative but necessary aspects of living in the present:

---

[1] Cf. L. Kolakowski, *Modernity on Endless Trial*. Chicago. University of Chicago Press. 1990; M. Waters, *Modern Sociological Theory*. London. Sage Publications. 1994, pp. 301–9; P. Sampson, V. Samuel and C. Sugden (eds), *Faith and Modernity*. Oxford. Lynx/Regnum. 1994; J. Habermas, 'Modernity – an incomplete project' in H. Foster, *The Anti-Aesthetic: Essays in Postmodern Culture*. Port Townsend. Bay Press. 1983.

the celebration of the half-millennium (1492–1992) . . . seems to coincide with the closure of a cycle. There is now no exploration, no new territory to be discovered, no frontier to cross, no new land, Utopia or idea to mobilise people . . . Prometheus has been routed. We know that man is not capable of organising his own salvation and is compelled to seek a more modest and land-based Utopia . . . There are no paradises other than the paradises lost . . . So, between pain and hope, without Prometheus but with the temptation of Faust, humanity continues its difficult path.[2]

## The birth of the 'post-modern'[3]

This sense of *déjá vu* is one of the possible ways of understanding 'after modernity'. The other refers to the cluster of ideas, beliefs and commitments that, since the middle of the 1970s, has come to be called 'post-modernity'. This represents altogether a different mood. Whereas in the first case there is a wistful recognition that the claims and expectations of modernity have to be modified in the light of experience, that reason has not triumphed as completely as once might have been hoped and that with the gains in freedom has also come the use of freedom for sinister ends, 'post-modernity' implies a conscious, positive celebration of the rout of modernity as a cultural end in itself.

Post-modernism is based on a number of assumptions about the historical development of modernity, the way to interpret the present and the way the future has to be envisioned. It promotes, for example, a scepticism towards any attempt to discover an all-embracing explanation of the world through a critical interaction with all conceivable data accessible to human reason through experimental methods. The search for certainty about

[2] Luis Bassets, 'Five Centuries of Discovery' in *The Independent*, op.cit., p. 24.
[3] For a comprehensive general description and analysis of 'post-modernity' cf. D. Harvey, *The Condition of Postmodernity: An Enquiry into the Origins of Cultural Change*. Oxford. Blackwell. 1990. A more philosophical approach is C. Norris, *The Truth about Postmodernism*. Oxford. Blackwell. 1993. Cf. also H. Bertens, *The Idea of the Postmodern: A History*. London. Routledge. 1995; P. Sampson, 'The Rise of Postmodernity' in Sampson, Samuel and Sugden, op.cit.

the reality of human life in the cosmos is not only doomed to disappoint, but is itself an intrinsically unworthy objective. The search for explanations in the age of reason have invariably been accompanied by the desire to control by acquiring and defending power over institutions, the environment and human beings. Modernity has been characterized by a recurring abuse of power in the name of an irresistible progress and an indisputable reality. As Leopold Senghor once said, 'the maker of myth is the manipulator of power'.

In place of the search for a final explanation of the universe and our place in it, we must rest content with a potentially infinite number of incomplete interpretations. The most obvious change that has taken place in the period following the emancipation in 1945 of the territories occupied by Germany and Japan is the consciousness of living in a plural world. The arrogant dominance (no longer directly military but economic and cultural) of the powerful nations of the world (those that have experienced modernization) over the rest should cease once for all, so that the diversity of world-views, value-systems and ways of living may no longer be suppressed but be heard and allowed to flourish and contribute their insights to the global intersection of cultures.

Post-modernity encourages a celebration of difference, a delight in heterogeneity, a solemnization of dissonance, a repudiation of coherence. It claims to be the end not only of the attempt of some to subject others to their definition of truth, but of the very idea that there is any truth to which people ought to be subjected. In this sense it also professes the end of ideology and indoctrination.

What is required is a multiplication of ethical stances and personal lifestyles. Freedom is not so much the formal space which is accorded by law to citizens and within which they may choose their own goals and pursue them without interference from those who 'know' those goals are wrong as the awareness that all goals honestly pursued are right. The end that is worth choosing is the one I choose, whether or not I am able to convince others of its value:

> Mourning for the eclipse of values should be replaced by a joyful and positive fooling, liberating and constructive . . . [now is the time when] new values can be born, neither dogmatic, nor

totalitarian, but delicate and relative, carved from the soul of a society freed for ever from the protective cover of metaphysics and religion.[4]

## From Romanticism to Post-modernism

Modernity is founded on a commitment to a rationalism that is universal, objective, perspicuous and orderly. Its project is to search out and harness for human use the realities of the external world as an entity entirely accessible to the human mind:

> Men had supreme confidence in the power of the human mind, unaided by revelation, to think out the truths of nature, to trace out the meaning of nature's laws, and then to employ the knowledge of these laws to human advantage.[5]

However, since the beginning of the Romantic Movement, around the turn of the eighteenth and nineteenth centuries, there have been a number of attempts to suggest other ways of interpreting and experiencing the world.[6] What they have in common is an emphasis on the integrity of inner feeling and creative spontaneity. The real world cannot be comprehended primarily as an external set of statistical data, but as something which manifests itself in a vast variety of sense perceptions which are received according to the subjective individuality of the person concerned. How objects appear to individuals is more important in the human encounter with the world of nature than the way they may be formally described, classified and catalogued.

The rationalism which characterized the Enlightenment could only grasp the world in a fragmentary way. The search for indisputable facts finished up with a series of particular instances of the world that did not begin to explain the complex experience of being human. For this reason,

---

[4] P. Frandstraller, quoted by J. Arias in *The Independent*, op.cit., p. 165.
[5] J.C. Keene, *The Western Heritage of Faith and Reason*, op.cit. p. 581.
[6] Cf. M. Cranston, *The Romantic Movement*. Oxford. Blackwell. 1994.

. . . romantic thinkers dismissed the achievements of modern physics . . . because the search for general laws, premissed upon the quantifiability and calculability of all subject matter, rendered only an impoverished, abstract notion of human persons and could give no account of the intimate and emotive quality of the relationships that bound them to nature and to each other.[7]

Poets like Schiller, Shelley and Coleridge stressed the intercommunion between human beings and nature and the need to grasp the meaning of life through intuition and empathy.

The integrity of a person's inner feelings and duty to express these with sincerity and commitment has become the hallmark of a mood which objects to a mechanistic and deterministic account of the human being. It is the cry of people appalled to think that human beings are no more than the sum of their parts, or that they can be adequately accounted for by reference to their evolutionary origins and development in the natural selection of the fittest for survival.

The Romantic instinctively reacts against the loss of freedom implied in a reductionist account of human nature. If rationalism provoked the end of a universally accepted belief in a personal creation as the act of a personal transcendent divine being, Romanticism substituted its own immanent creation, often in art-forms, in the hope of generating its own answers to the many enigmas of human experience.

Though arising in vastly different circumstances, not least those of the appalling, mindless and barbaric destruction of two major European wars and the attempted genocide of the Jews and other minority groups, Existentialism carries over some of the main characteristics of Romanticism. In particular it is an attempt to come to terms with a world that, on the assumption that human life is totally bounded by the visible universe, has no inherent meaning. Thus, for Camus,

Nothing, nothing has the least importance . . . From the dark horizon of my future, a sort of slow persistent breeze had been blowing towards me . . . and on its way, that breeze had levelled out all the ideas people had tried to foist on me in the equally unreal years I was then living through . . . all alike would be condemned to die one day.[8]

---

[7] *Encyclopaedia of Political Thought*, op.cit. p. 453.
[8] Quoted in *Living Philosophy*, op.cit., p. 170.

Unlike animals, human beings are conscious of the final reality of death. With no knowledge of any existence beyond the grave, we live our concrete finiteness with no comprehension of any meaning and with the anxiety produced by the ever-pending loss of being. The human condition is bleak: the world is intrinsically unintelligible and yet we are condemned to make some sense of it (even if only to ourselves). Here we are confronted, as we have already seen, with our 'dreadful freedom': on the one hand, we *have* to choose how we are going to live, on the other hand we can find no certain guides to shoulder our burden of absurdity:

> There is no light at the end of the road, no omniscient Being who will eventually explain all the mysteries of life. All is not to be revealed . . . Rejecting all concepts of 'ultimate reality', the task of every person thrown willy-nilly into the world is to make what he can of the freedom he possesses and create his own nature according to his own perception of values, of right and wrong conduct, and of the priorities required in human relationships.[9]

In *Irrational Man*, William Barrett sums up the modern predicament with extreme poignancy:

> Suppose . . . that there were a road and we were told we ought to walk it . . . [because] there is a priceless treasure at the end of the road, then the imperative to walk would carry overwhelming weight with us. It is this treasure at the end of the road that has disappeared from the modern horizon, *for the simple reason that the end of the road has itself disappeared.*[10]

Existentialism paints an exceptionally sombre picture of the human plight. Its mood is anxious, troubled and apprehensive, as befits a movement that reflected a world dominated by the grim reality of rampant fascism in Germany, Spain and Italy, an ideology which was, in its own terms, self-consciously rational and idealistic.

Post-modernism, on the other hand, appears to advocate a more cheerful acceptance of the impossibility of making any sense of history, or for that matter of thought itself. It is an outrageous and gleeful intellectual anarchy which claims to

---

[9] Ibid., p. 168.
[10] p. 80 ( my emphasis).

liberate Western thinking from the absurdity of imagining that there is any necessary connection between an objective world, open to philosophical contemplation, and the processes of the human mind which seek a substantial and non-contradictory interpretation of that world. It is iconoclastic in the sense of razing to the ground any and every sand-castle built to halt the incoming tidal waves of extreme scepticism;

> The position adopted by Post-Modernism is far more radical and controversial in the sense that it rejects completely the attempt of mainstream Western intellectual tradition to overcome complete subjectivity and relativity and all that that would logically entail. If a theory cannot be normatively judged by its faithful correspondence to reality, then no statement can be any more true or false than any other, and therefore no one can be any more correct or incorrect in their descriptions than anyone else – everyone's opinion is as good as anyone else's.[11]

Post-modernism puts itself forward as a radical liberation from all forms of objectivism, particularly that found in trying to give univocal meaning to linguistic symbols. Language is freed from the intention of its user, from context and from etymology. Readers of a text, for example, may create any meaning out of it that happens to make sense to them – the more, quite literally, the merrier! Derrida speaks of 'playing' with the text. It is up to us to create the coda at the end of the movement of a concerto, not this time as a set of variations on the theme of the composer's music but rather as a string of notes that, though inspired in some way by the music, may bear no clear relation to what has gone before. Moreover it is the coda, rather than the concerto, that becomes the most important aspect of the listening process.

It follows, as night follows day, that the result of the post-modern enterprise is total subjectivism:

> We are free to go with what seems at the moment compelling to us and we are guided in our articulations only by the desire to persuade, to gain a receptive following.[12]

Post-modernism and Existentialism are close bed-fellows, though this has not always been recognized. What distinguishes

---

[11] H.G. Blocker, 'The Challenge of Postmodernism' in *An Introduction to Modern Philosophy*, op.cit. p. 677.
[12] Ibid., p. 681.

them is their mood. For the former there is no more reason to be pessimistic or gloomy about existence than there is to be optimistic and sanguine. Existentialism, perhaps, is still a philosophical exercise in the Western tradition, taking the courage to stake out a meaning for life, in spite of the evident lack of anything that gives it a tangible sense. Post-modernism, on the other hand, if true to itself, is an anti-philosophy in the sense that it does not much matter whether we create or find meaning or not. The important thing is to enjoy the frolic of life, twisting and turning like a porpoise at play, savouring the sheer exhilaration of being in the water.[13] There is not a long step from this way of looking at things to the concept of nothingness – anything might be or equally it might not be. Such a conclusion is not surprising, if one starts with the presuppositions of a rationalist view of the world.

## From scepticism to nihilism

In the modern world intellectual thought typically begins from a position of doubt. Over against the great ages of faith, nothing any longer is to be taken on trust. Traditions of all kinds inherited from the past must be called into question, until and unless they can be substantiated by criteria of verification that are freed from the belief systems of former times.

This formal refusal to accept any beliefs or knowledge without questioning has given rise to the critical method of investigation, which has now become the generally accepted and required standard for anyone doing research in any subject. Particularly in the realm of ideas, the evaluation of a system of thought or values should begin by trying to penetrate the weak points of an argument, those which appear to be incoherent, inconsistent within their own terms or incompatible with observed facts. The critical method assumes deficiencies and flaws, so that the argument or opinion concerned has first to clear itself of presumed guilt, rather than being able to assume a prior innocence.

---

[13] Cf. R. Bhaskar's discussion of the recent philosophical writings of Richard Rorty, *Philosophy and the Idea of Freedom*. Oxford. Blackwell. 1991, pp. 99–105.

Though originally established as a science of ideas, the study of ideology has become a particular instance of this method of suspicion. An ideology (even when intended in a positive sense) may be defined as a systematic attempt to justify or rationalize a way of conducting human affairs that establishes some people in a position of privilege or power over others.[14] Thus, for example, every argument used to justify women taking a subordinate position in society to that of men, whether through sex-stereotyping, through fears about family breakdown or through appeal to the notion of the weaker sex, is automatically ideological. Gender discrimination simply supports the dominant patriarchy which, since the dawn of time, has assumed that women's function is to enable the freedom of men. It is particularly unacceptable when men blame women for their own misdeeds, as for example in cases of rape, where the man will quite probably claim he was seduced. In contrast to this, the movement of recent decades known as Feminism plays a cathartically critical role in exposing as invalid all assumptions, attitudes and structures which place men in positions of power over women.

The critical method is a necessary part of human knowing, by which we sort out the probable from the fantastical and learn to live on the basis of what most people judge to be reasonable assumptions about the way reality presents itself to us. Life would simply be impossible if there were no ways of distinguishing between illusions (created images that bear no relationship to normal waking experience) and actuality. However, a systematic and unrelenting commitment to doubt is also unsustainable in practice. Doubt can endure only on the basis of a claim to reasonableness superior to that implied in the object doubted. But that reasonableness itself has to be supported by a better argument which will itself be dependent on and sustained by a contrary belief. Methodical doubt ends up by eating its own tail. It has nowhere to stop in its infinite

---

[14] Cf. R. Eatwell and A. Wrig, *Contemporary Political Ideologies*. London. Pinter Publishers. 1993; M. Waters, op.cit., pp. 171–195; D. McLellan, *Ideology*. Milton Keynes. Open Univ. Press. 1995; P. Bocock and K. Thompson, *Religion and Ideology*. Manchester. Manchester Univ. Press. 1987; T. Eagleton, *Ideology*. Harlow. Longman Group. 1994; A. Heywood, *Political Ideologies: An Introduction*. Basingstoke. Macmillan Press. 1992.

regress, and therefore ceases to have any basis for doubt in the first place.

In its understandable reaction against all kinds of superstition and manipulation of power and in its determination never to lapse into credulity the modern world has tended to erect scepticism itself into a fundamental creed. This principle leads straight into nihilism, which is a view of life that holds that nothing is worthy of being believed. Objection and protest become a way of life, an end in themselves. Every opinion is reduced to mere speculation, without a foundation substantial enough to bear the weight of decision-making. Life is conducted in the spaces between an endless progression of suspended beliefs.

Nihilism represents a refusal to accept any answer to the enigmas of life. It is the *via negativa* taken to its absolute conclusion. It refuses to be comforted by any kind of superficial optimism:

> The spirit of irony is today woven into the fabric of the tragic vision. Refusing to be deluded by romantic utopianism, the cult of progress, the dream of perfectibility, the tragic vision responds to Nietzsche's call for laughter.[15]

But if we are to be consistent, not even this smile on the face of the Cheshire cat is visible![16]

## From wisdom to information

Among the chief characteristics of a world after modernity is the inflationary acceleration of fragmentary information and the relative ease with which it is attainable. Increasingly sophisticated computer technology enables anyone at the flick of a switch, the touch of a few letters on a keyboard and, where necessary, the key to certain codes to have access to a dizzying kaleidoscope of data, details, material and news. The sheer abundance of data which may flit across our VDUs has even generated a new indisposition of our age, 'information anxiety' or 'information fatigue'.

---

[15] Glicksberg, *Tragic Vision of the Twentieth Century*. Carbondale. 1963, p. 7.
[16] Cf. L. Carroll, *Alice in Wonderland*.

Information may be on a grand scale, that is it may have to do with serious issues in human social and political life, or it may be utterly trivial. It gives the appearance of being neutral – simply facts – but actually comes in the form of encoded messages, which individuals must make sense of for themselves or their businesses or political parties. Often the information appears to be contradictory, maybe because it has already passed through the sieve of someone's ideology.

Information is absolutely necessary as a prerequisite for making intelligent decisions, but gathering it is not a straightforward exercise. One needs to have a trained capacity, rather like that which historians develop in their investigation of the past, to discern which pieces are relevant to the decisions which have to be made. This is where *knowledge*, which comes as the result of painstaking analysis and shrewd integration, becomes necessary. *Information* is scattered, like a pile of papers on a windy day; *knowledge*, by contrast, is accumulated from experience, awareness and learning; it represents the process of gathering together the papers and assembling them in the right page sequence. It entails the ability to judge, to categorize and comprehend how different parts fit into patterns.

Increasing information, such as our world deems important to transmit into every conceivable corner, does not necessarily mean more knowledge. Indeed it has been said that 'the more the information the less the knowledge' (though to maintain the converse might be a trifle cynical). Moreover, knowledge itself is of dubious value if it lacks that further dimension which has traditionally been called *wisdom*.

Wisdom is a difficult concept to understand adequately, not least because it has been downgraded by a culture which has exalted functional or pragmatic knowledge to a position of preeminence. Wisdom is a matter of perspective, of fathoming out what to do with knowledge and why. Like knowledge, it is built up over a period of years, perhaps a life-time. That is why wisdom is associated with mature years and why, probably, it is not given much credence in an age which demands instant answers, craves fast solutions and believes senility sets in after the age of 40.

Wisdom is built on long experience of observing both the joys and follies of human existence. It is often captured in maxims and proverbs, such as those contained in the Hebrew scriptures: 'a gentle answer turns away wrath, but a harsh word stirs up anger'; 'he who spares the rod hates his son, but he who loves him is careful to discipline him'; 'dishonest money dwindles away, but he who gathers money little by little makes it grow'.[17] However, it is largely out of harmony with the spirit of the age, which values scientifically tested verities and accords the observations of the older ('yesterday's') generation no more status than that of merely one more subjective opinion. It is of the essence of a world 'after modernity' that information is the residue which remains after knowledge has become problematical and wisdom archaic.

## The ambiguity of science

In an age of intense uncertainty, of shifting sands and unpredictable currents, we still look to science to provide some stability and assurance of continuity. It may seem bizarre to mention it, but it is curiously comforting in a world of rapid change to know that my body will continue to function today and tomorrow, as it did yesterday. If my doctor prescribes a course of treatment on Wednesday, it will not have become redundant on Thursday, owing to a sudden and unexpected transformation of my internal workings. It is reassuring to realise that the bridge I cross every day on my way to work will not collapse tomorrow, just because the laws of mechanical engineering have altered overnight. A scientific explanation of the natural order gives some sense of security. There are, after all, some constants that we can all hold on to.

As we have already mentioned, experimental sciences have in many ways enriched the quality of life. It is intrinsically right that medical science should continue to harness all its efforts to discovering permanent cures or means for preventing killer diseases, meanwhile treating as best it may the symptoms, where there is not, as yet, any long-term cure. The attempts to utilize science in modifying or eliminating environment-threatening practices is also highly commendable. In both cases the notion of an enhanced or debased quality of life does make sense.

---

17 Proverbs 15.1; 13.24; 13.11

And yet, there is a nagging feeling that science, or rather the way that it is often used in practice or as a way of interpreting life, lessens the possibility of a widening experience of life. The problem is the incipient, creeping reductionism which seems almost inseparable from science. Let us take two areas where this has and continues to be a reality: the theory of evolution applied to human beings and certain attitudes in modern medicine.

It is an accepted dogma of the scientific establishment that human beings have evolved in an unbroken line, through proto-human forms, from the most intelligent species of animal life to *homo sapiens*. On the basis of what is taken as an established fact (though it is certainly no more than an unsubstantiated hypothesis), it is assumed that human beings are in essence no more than animals, though possessing considerably more complex brains. They belong to the same class as all other mammals, though it is admitted that, because of what the brain is able to perform, the human being stands at an apex of achievement.

It is difficult to understand this fascination with the idea of evolution, particularly in the light of the absence of the kind of concrete evidence essential if the thesis is to be verified, unless it has to do with an obstinate reluctance to give up a mechanistic explanation of cause and effect, which hitherto has ruled out any other account of human origins than that of gradual evolution. There are other difficulties with the theory: as Michael Polanyi has forcibly pointed out,[18] the advent of human beings on earth as the highest form of life by the process of evolution is the theory's most intractable, inexplicable problem. The most fundamental question, which science does not (cannot?) answer, is: how did any single individual of an immensely intricate higher form ever come into existence by chance from undifferentiated cell constructs ? The theory does not sufficiently distinguish between accidental mutations, which have enabled

---

[18] *The Tacit Dimension*. London. Routledge and Kegan Paul. 1967, pp. 47–52.

species to adapt and survive, and changes of type that achieve new levels of existence.[19]

At the highest level of personhood we encounter the moral sense of humankind which has been characterized in all cultures by a sense of duty and responsibility in defiance of self-preservation. How can evolutionary theory make sense of this apparent after-thought to 500 million years of pure self-seeking? It might appear to an outside observer that the more likely reason for continuing to sustain the theory is that there is too much *philosophically* involved in the theory of evolution for its adherents to give it up.[20]

In the realm of health care, a concentration on the mechanical mechanisms of the human body and long-running and deep divisions of thought over the nature of the human psyche has led

---

[19] 'There is nothing in neo-Darwinism which enables us to predict a long-term increase in complexity.' (J. Maynard Smith, *On Evolution.* Edinburgh. University Press. 1972, p. 89.) 'Natural selection is a theory of *local* adaptation to changing environments. It proposes no perfecting principles, no guarantee of general improvement . . . no reason for . . . favouring innate progress in nature.' (S. Gould, *Ever Since Darwin.* New York. W.W. Norton. 1977, p. 45.)

[20] This suspicion was interestingly borne out by a long correspondence in the *Listener* magazine in the early 1970s over the implications of work on taxonomy being done at that time in the Victoria and Albert Museum, London. Those who argued vehemently against the findings (which included evidence that countered the theory of evolution) did so not purely on the basis of the evidence, but on the realization that if the origin of human beings from much less complex forms of life through an evolutionary process was suspect and problematical the way could be open to a belief in special creation. In other words, the argument proceeded from an initial metaphysical base, rather than from a specifically scientific one.

Honesty and clarity would be served, if it could be admitted that the question of the descent (or ascent?) of species was of a different order from that of adaptation through natural selection. It is simply a matter of whether it is possible in principle to have the kind of access to data which could solve the conundrums of origins. Though it may be a bitter pill to have to swallow, the answer surely has to be negative·

'There is nothing one can say about an ancestor that will relate it to its descendents – the concept of ancestry is not accessible by the tools we have. . . . No one has ever produced a new species by means of natural selection . . .' That is a very profound attack on neo-Darwinism (Dr. C. Patterson, quoted by B. Leith, 'Are the Reports of Darwin's Death exaggerated?' *The Listener,* vol. 106, no. 2730, October 8, 1981, p. 391).

Obviously there is much more at stake here than scientific reputations, however important.

modern medicine to emphasize cure at the expense of healing. Cure is the restoration of parts of the body to their normal functioning. It is the elimination of pathological symptoms by means of restoring the integrity of tissue whose continuity has been interrupted by disease or injury. Healing, on the other hand, is the restoration of the whole human being to the purpose for which it exists.

The problem for modern medicine is that it has no criteria within its own professional bounds for knowing what is 'a whole human being' nor for discerning 'the purpose for which the human being exists'. It is true that medicine has in recent years given much greater attention to the social context in which certain physical or psychological abnormalities take place;[21] also, for a long time it has recognized the existence of psychosomatic illnesses. However, as soon as one supposes that illnesses may be due to, or may be aggravated by, extra-physical factors like broken relations, physical, verbal or sexual abuse, a lack of self-worth, a sense of guilt and failure, remorse, a revengeful spirit or a general 'spiritual' malaise, modern medicine does not have the specific tools to deal with the underlying problem. Maybe that is the principal reason why mainstream medicine tends to be suspicious of the proliferation of counselling services, which precisely attempt to explore an integrated account of human existence. It is true that some of them are based on fanciful beliefs and theories. Nevertheless they, along with all schools of psychiatry, work necessarily from anthropological presuppositions which defy explanation within a reductionist account of the human.

## The straitjacket of the free market

According to classical Marxism economic structures act as an infrastructure upon which the rest of the institutions of society are founded. Subsequent analysis and debate has shown that to

---

[21] Cf. M. Morgan, M. Calman and N. Manning, *Sociological Approaches to Health and Medicine*. London. Routledge. 1985, pp. 45–75; D. Locke, 'Social causes of Disease' in G. Scrambler (ed.), *Sociology as Applied to Medicine*. London. Tindall. 1991, pp. 18–30; A. Kleinman, *Patients and Healers in the Context of Culture*. Berkeley. Univ. of California Press. 1980, pp. 179–202.

imagine that the influence runs in one direction only is an exaggeration. The historical materialist reading of history is too one-sided to explain how all the phenomena of complex industrialized societies function.

Nevertheless, it would be a grave mistake to underestimate the enormous power of the economic machine as it increasingly gathers to itself the productive capacities of all nations and expands markets to every corner of the globe. Much more than in Marx's day, the world economic order today is practically indivisible. There is no nation or group of people who can play outside its rules. Even the most isolated (Cuba, North Korea?) are dependent on acquiring foreign currency (US dollars and Japanese yen). To be outside the system is to live outside all contact with modern human life.

So Jane Collier is right when she says that the discipline of economics provides the most dominant of cultural paradigms or intellectual frameworks for our age:

> If cultures are ways of living articulated in language, rituals and institutions, then our modern culture is 'economic' culture. The language of economics is the language through which the world is understood, the language by which human and social problems are defined and by which solutions to these problems are expressed. Our lives are dominated by the rituals of 'getting and spending'. Political options translate into economic decisions; political decisions are implemented by economic institutions.[22]

The belief that the ideals of a capitalist free-market system constitute the best of all possible worlds (though not necessarily the best of all imaginable worlds) is superficially attractive. In terms of actualizing it in practice the argument has been massively won. This fact remains an enigma in some ways, given the rather feeble theoretical basis of the thesis and its even more slender moral defence. The belief is professed and sustained by selecting evidence which favours the thesis, marginalizing evidence that does not, and ignoring or explaining away the adverse consequences.

The ideal of economic freedom enshrined in the texts of the 'high-priests' of the free-market (people like Hayek, Friedman

---

[22] 'Contemporary culture and the role of economics' in H. Montefiore, op.cit., p. 103.

and Nozak[23]) simply jettisons unpalatable realities. We will mention three of these. First, the distribution of resources is not largely due to the mechanisms of an impersonal set of laws, under which all may be equally involved. Despite the rhetoric that a true market economy is spontaneous (i.e. unfettered by arbitrary social intervention) and therefore cannot be coercive of freedom, distribution happens by a process of violence.

Historically speaking (and defenders of the capitalist system are not usually conscientious historians), the primitive accumulation of wealth has been achieved by those who held political power, through the exploitation of people's misfortunes, the restriction of their economic freedoms and the exploitation of tax systems by which money was raised for war and building projects. Above all, it has happened through a rigorous and unforgiving system of loans and debt repayments, under which the economically vulnerable, in order to survive physically, became dependent on those who already possessed wealth. Markets are not free-flowing vehicles of exchange in which all may participate on equal terms. They are systematically and rationally exploited by those who have secured for themselves an advantage within the system.

Secondly, capital and labour are not equivalent factors of production. Capitalism as an economic way of life presupposes that both capital and labour demand a price in the market (dividends and wages), as if they were totally separate and equal entities that somehow come together (guided by an 'invisible hand') to increase wealth for the benefit of all. Capital, however, is another name for surplus value, which is produced in a manufacturing process by labour (i.e. by human power and abilities – from management downwards or from the shop-floor worker upwards). One is the product of the other. However, under present economic arrangements the former controls the latter; what is created (surplus value) controls those who create it. The outcome is that the freedom to share in the fruits of one's labour has largely been exchanged (the exceptions would be those industries and businesses jointly owned by the workforce) for the freedom to sell one's labour for whatever price capital ultimately allows the market to offer.

---

[23] Cf. G. Hayek, *Law, Legislation and Liberty;* M. Friedman, *Capitalism and Freedom;* R. Nozack, *Anarchy, State and Utopia.*

Thirdly, the market does not work through a system in which power conflicts temporarily with power and then is resolved. The freedom of the market is not so much a self-regulating harmonious system in which all who play by the rules are ultimately advantaged, but suspended warfare. It is disingenuous of economic libertarians to pretend that firms and corporations are part of a neutral, spontaneous order which upholds basic freedoms and rights. To survive they have to push expediency to the limits tolerated by the countervailing force of popular morality, as for example in respect of the degradation of the environment, workers' contracts, ethical investment, the infringement of copyright, stock-market speculation ('insider dealing') and other dubious practices. It is a fact that business people with high moral integrity live on a knife edge of tension between the values they would like to see implemented and the pressures which the system exerts to take ethical short-cuts.

The notion that the global market is based on free access, invariably rewards imaginative enterprise, and is fair to all participants is equivalent to envisioning a game in which all are forced to compete, whether they choose to or not, whose rules they are powerless to change and where unequal abilities are rewarded by the winners taking (nearly) all. Apparently, there is no way of pretending that the economic order can basically be any way other than it is (the criticisms of the radical left are brushed off like irritating but ultimately harmless flies). All that appears to be 'left' (and this may not be insignificant) is the possibility of bringing changes into current practices which tip the balance away from the powerful towards those disadvantaged by the workings of the market.[24] Otherwise we are, rhetoric to the contrary, locked into a way of conducting economic life in which freedom of movement is severely curtailed.

It is quite possible, of course, that the majority of people (whether in or out of employment) would endorse, or at least acquiesce in, the present arrangements on the basis of the old adage of 'better the devil you know . . . '. People who advocate

---

[24] Cf. the twelve-step programme for economic recovery advocated by the Dutch economists B. Goudzwaard and H. de Lange, *Beyond Poverty and Affluence: Toward an Economy of Care*. Geneva. WCC Publications. 1995, pp. 134–161.

radical change often profoundly misunderstand the basic human yearning for security and stability, which is deemed to be seriously threatened by any kind of massive upheaval. As David Lyon says, 'The tolerance-level for uncertainty among the large majority in any society is probably fairly low.'[25]

## The ambiguity of liberal democracy

Since the early 1980s, though still fragile because of brittle economies, popularly elected, multi-party democratic regimes have returned to many countries formerly dominated by harsh military regimes. In the Western Hemisphere, for example, though sometimes only in a formal sense, only Cuba stands outside this reality.[26] Nevertheless, democracies, even in those countries where they have been in place for many years and where they appear to be firmly entrenched, are vulnerable to long-term trends and have not succeeded in overcoming potentially disturbing tensions. In the first category, I would place the rising tide of violence and the lack of any solid, agreed foundation for treating people with dignity. In the second category I would put the tensions and ambivalences surrounding the current notion of toleration.

---

[25] D. Lyon, op.cit. p. 146. Another reason for resisting substantial change is the eternal hope that 'my lucky number may come up', i.e. that the system may one day smile on me, as it has on countless others. The gambling instinct remains a powerful factor in determining social consciousness. On the other hand, it is abundantly evident over the last 30 years, since W.W. Rostow's book, *The Stages of Development*, was published – showing that the key to development is the creation of wealth through sustained economic growth based on an unfettered market – that both long-term unemployment and endemic poverty have steadily risen within developed and underdeveloped nations alike and that the wealth gap between North and South has dramatically increased. In other words, the present world economic order is 'both in theory and practice, incapable of resolving the major economic dilemmas of our time – poverty, environmental degeneration, and unemployment' (Goudzwaard and De Lange, op.cit., p. 1). In other words, as in all gambling, if the present system continues substantially unchanged, the vast majority will be the losers.

[26] Because political situations can change rapidly, I need to state that this remark is written as of September 1997.

## i. The rise of violence

Jean-Pierre Rioux, writing on the legacy of violence which the present generation has inherited from the past, says:

> The twentieth century has been violent, punctuated by great slaughter, full of dreams which became nightmares, and its gift to humankind will be a strong stench of death. The world's failure to atone for such great suffering, the revolutions which never brought justice, the inability to control developments and manage the unfolding dramas have given the century a unique and tragic dimension . . . If the horrors of war provided the thread for the tapestry of the tragic century, then it is unfulfilled hopes and revanchist temptations which formed the rough backcloth.[27]

The end of the 'tragic century' does not look promising. It is being assumed that economic and political co-operation in Europe makes major military conflict unthinkable. It may well be that the stakes of modern war are too high. And yet, whilst brutal struggles for land and power are waged on the edge of the 'common European home' in former Yugoslavia and the former Soviet Republic, and whilst the temperature of nationalism rises throughout Europe, there is no room for complacency.

Violence is by no means confined to what some people dismissively call the 'periphery' of the world order (Myanmar, Cambodia, Rwanda, Angola, Colombia, Afghanistan, Kashmir, East Timor). Systematic torture appears to be a calculated means of political control, according to recent revelations, in a sophisticated, modern democracy like Israel. In the past this has been the case also in South Africa, Chile, Argentina, South Korea and other ('developed') countries beside.

Much closer to the home of modern democracy, violence has been on a massively upward curve in the USA, Britain and many continental European countries during the 1980s and 1990s. Much of this is crime-related to drug addiction, which now feeds the second largest 'industry' in the world. Some social analysts try to comfort themselves and society by suggesting that the rise of violent crime is largely the product of a rise in unemployment. Such a relationship is notoriously hard to demonstrate and in

---

[27] 'The Tragic Century: Suffering and Upheaval' in *The Independent*, op.cit., pp. 46–7.

any case, if assumed to be a sufficient explanation, would be open to a charge of reductionism, in that the causes of violence (not only in deprived urban centres) are multiple and have much to do with rootlessness and the break-up of stable, supportive networks in which young people may be both affirmed and disciplined. Even if the economic arguments were largely true – that people resort to theft (if necessary by causing physical damage to life and property) because they are not able to buy into the good life through the legitimate means of regular work – this only takes the argument one stage further back to the cultural images of the good life and the notion of the individual's right to enjoy it.

The economic argument hardly does justice to the whole phenomenon of drug-abuse (or the more hidden violence which is the outcome of excessive alcoholic consumption). The drug culture is not confined to marginalized groups, but is prevalent also among people who have grown up in privileged surroundings. Drugs are taken for a variety of reasons, one of them being to seek experiences which might fill the sense of emptiness that a one-dimensional materialist culture inevitably produces. The expectation of self-fulfilment through choice, possessions, the taking of drugs, and even through violence, form an unstable cocktail found in advanced, modern societies.

Another arena where violence is also on the increase and which brings back horrifying memories from the past is racism, which motivates many attacks. Again, the economic realities of unemployment and the perceived flooding of the labour market by 'guest workers' from overseas may be part of the cause for this rising phenomenon. However, it would be simplistic in the extreme to imagine that this is the whole story. Irrational prejudice, deep anger and hatred and deliberate provocation arise primarily from inner impulses, not from external forces. The latter may afford an opportunity and a certain justification but they are not the deep-lying motivation. That has to be sought in the dark recesses of perverted minds and corrupted spirits – a reality we will address in the next chapter.

Racial violence is not only a matter of physical abuse – the massive physical assault on youngsters from a South Asian background or the burning down of migrant workers' hostels – it is also inherent in the racial discrimination of unequal job opportunities, immigration practices and the bias of the law. Of course much can and is being done to reverse the trends, to create the conditions for an inclusive, multi-ethnic democracy. But education and moral exhortation are insufficient, particularly when the frustration of ethnic minorities spills over into retaliatory violence, for part of the culture of racialist terrorism and ethnic discrimination is the notion that the minority communities should not react but accept their lot passively.

### ii. Why human dignity?

One of the major claims of modernity has been the notion that human communities can divest themselves of any significant belief in a transcendent God as the final ground of a moral order and yet maintain a consistent pattern of morality. Appeal has been made instead to the givenness of human nature which, because it is essentially rational, has to be respected by other rational beings. In any case, it is argued, the commandments of God would not be sufficient by themselves to establish a moral order, because there would be no additional external criteria for distinguishing between capricious and just commands. That criteria, it is argued, can be found in an essential human essence that either corresponds to or repudiates the particular demands made upon it by a divine being.

These claims are partly valid. However, the difficulty for modern thought is to conjure up out of the stuff of nature a plausible account of the reality of being human. For example, it is difficult to sustain a credible theory of natural rights, using the concept of natural law, within a framework of ideas that specifically excludes all reference to the purpose of being. But in a modern scientific world-view there is no room for a belief in natural ends, since evidences of purpose are always given a mechanistic explanation. 'The conception of natural law needed to support a theory of natural rights is incompatible with modern empiricism.'[28]

Natural rights have been based on the assumption that they embody the conditions necessary for the flourishing of human beings as distinctive creatures. Thus, we should be able to

---

[28] J. Gray, op.cit. p. 46.

discern rights by considering the distinguishing marks of the human species and the circumstances in which these are best realized. But how do we discern the distinctive traits and the order of importance in which they should be assembled? The fact that the various components of human flourishing, as we perceive them, may often conflict intractably with each other is a decisive argument against using a natural law ethic on its own as a basis for human rights.[29]

There is the added difficulty that 'as a matter of logic, no imperative conclusion can be drawn from premises which do not contain at least one imperative'.[30] In other words, the mere description of a reality, however universally agreed it may be, does not give a sufficient reason for the duty to act in one way rather than another. Respect for human dignity can come only from a recognition of the intrinsic, infinite worth of the individual. But how can this rabbit be conjured out of the hat of a world that is said to have arrived by mere chance and to be ruled by necessity? A thoroughly modern world-view is at a loss for an answer. If, as truly scientific people, we cannot admit the reality of any dimension beyond the natural, we have no adequate basis for an ultimate and invariable respect for the equal dignity of all.

Evolution (even if it were true) cannot supply it, for some people may well argue that they are more highly evolved (developed) than others and therefore have a right to a discriminatory dignity; others may argue that natural selection favours the strong and discriminates against the weak. Who could deny them? Because an adequate account of human rights is a massive theoretical problem for contemporary ideas of freedom, modern societies hover uncertainly around either a notion of contractual justice or the wistful desire that 'god' could somehow be brought back into the equation as a trusted hypothesis, but without becoming God again.

### ii. The limits of toleration

There is perhaps no greater virtue inculcated by liberal education than that of openness to different ways of being

---

[29]  Ibid., pp. 48–9; also R. Bellamy, 'Citizenship and Rights' in R. Bellamy (ed.), op.cit., pp. 47–8.
[30]  B. Mitchell, op.cit., p. 113.

human. In many circumstances, the toleration of beliefs and lifestyles with which some people may not sympathize is a necessary part of a society that is not going to tear itself apart by angry factionalism. There is a sense in which no one has been given the right to police other people's consciences. Freedom is predicated on an elasticity in understanding, forbearing and the patient acknowledgment of differences of all kinds.

Nevertheless, in practice no one allows the elastic to stretch indefinitely. There are beliefs and practices which societies do not tolerate. Perhaps the most obvious is the one mentioned above, namely racial discrimination and harassment. This is true not only for racially motivated physical intimidation but also for incitement to racist attitudes and racist discrimination in job selection procedures. There are other areas, too, where toleration is not readily admitted: certain types of pornography, the showing of gratuitous violence on TV and video and the use of sexist language are examples.

Distinguishing between what may or may not be tolerated is a matter of very fine discretion, because, whether for good or bad reasons, the consensus of societies tend to change. One troublesome feature of the debate about toleration is the attitude to be adopted towards those whose convictions do not allow them to be tolerant in certain circumstances. Some recent cases would be the burning of Salman Rushdie's novel, *The Satanic Verses*, protests against multi-faith worship in Westminister Abbey, the obstruction of the working practice of abortion clinics, the blockade of lorries carrying young calves and instances of militant industrial action against the closure of companies or the unfair dismissal of employees.

In these examples, one form of intolerance seems to be matched by another, demonstrating just how wafer-thin so called openness to the views of others really is. If it is accepted that it is wrong in certain circumstances to be tolerant of manifest evil, who is to decide where the evil lies or when it has become a cancer in the body politic? Does it have to be the majority who manage to get the law on their side? Or should a government take action, even when the majority of the population apparently remains indifferent? Certainly a culture which prides itself on the relativity of moral values will find it very difficult to distinguish serious matters of conscience from trivial fancies.

Current preoccupation with toleration as an ideal does not necessarily enhance the quality of moral debate in society; it is often the result of moral superficiality and confusion.

## The contradictions of being free

It has been pointed out that one of the consequences of modern views of freedom is a sense of individual isolation and loneliness. Being accountable to oneself alone brings with it a certain anonymity. The stress on rights without an equal emphasis on mutual responsibilities turns each of us into a stranger to the other. Individualism has led to a culture of non-interference, under the stern warning to mind only our own business and not get caught up in the affairs of others. Sharing concerns and decision-making is often portrayed as a weakness, a hindrance to developing the rugged self-confidence, self-sufficiency and self-assertion admired by modern culture. The danger of self-sufficiency, however, is that we become wrapped up in our own small world, unable or unwilling to make the time and develop the empathy necessary to listen properly to the heartbeat of the other. What we do hear is related to our own perception of our own best interests, and we filter out what we do not wish to hear. Colin Gunton expresses the peril we may put ourselves in:

> . . . taken to its logical extreme, it means that finally we are all enclosed in a kind of self-centred isolation, a form of autistic solipsism, in which there can be no real communication between people and their world, because each individual is finally unrelated to anything else.[31]

According to contemporary self-understanding, we are not born into an already established community, whose boundaries

---

[31] 'Knowledge and culture: towards an epistemology of the concrete' in H. Montefiore, op.cit., p. 97.

are determined by eternal realities.[32] That would be too restrictive of freedom. Rather we have to create communities with others on the basis of mutual self-interest. The dominant social relationship then is built upon maximizing the benefit that all will receive in the arrangement. What results is not a community in the traditional sense at all, because we become a member far more for what we may gain than for what we may contribute. 'There's nothing in it for me' is a sufficiently understood reason for a person not to join, or to withdraw. Temporary associations of this kind are not communities but contractual societies.[33]

The isolated pursuit of self-interest, in which the free flow of pleasure is maximized and pain minimized, can itself become a bearer of distress. Suppose that there were after all negative consequences to be reaped from the commitment to indulging one's every whim. Suppose that real character is formed by self-denial and by sacrifice for the sake of others, as ancient philosophies and religions have consistently taught. Then the pursuit of pleasure and the avoidance of pain leads not to the affirmation of life but to the ebbing away of life, like water gradually draining into the endless deserts of oblivion.

Most people want to leave a mark on their environment. They may be prevented from doing so either by circumstances beyond their control or because they have no means of knowing what kind of mark would be significant for future generations. Isolation, loneliness, separation, the stranger syndrome, the lack

---

[32] The Western view that family life is contingent, and fundamentally accidental, makes it almost impossible for a Western(ized) person to understand the family patterns of other cultures, which are based on the well-defined obligations of all members to the others, necessary to maintain the cohesion of the family unit. Western culture has largely accepted the reality that family life is atomistic and fragmentary, each member using the family for the pursuit of their own self-interests. This rather stark view has to be modified in the case of those (overwhelmingly women) who take some responsibility for the care of disabled, chronically sick or elderly relatives. Their self-sacrifice often knows few bounds; their dedication is a virtue to be emulated. Nevertheless, I wonder if it is entirely unfair to suggest that most people believe that it would be better if social and medical services were able to take on entirely this work, thus releasing the 'carers' to continue their respective careers.

[33] So Carver Yu, op.cit., p. 141.

of any sustaining community and the fear of obscurity then lead many either to accept the need for expert advice about achieving self-fulfilment or to give up the struggle and submit, consciously or unconsciously, to the authority of others. Then other agencies, such as professional organizations, the advertising industry, religious groups or the media are allowed by default to define what our needs are that demand satisfying.

Tony Walter demonstrates how the mechanism of submission to authority in the interests of satisfying needs operates in the case of parenting.[34] Child-rearing, he says, used to be seen as a process of educating children for life by imparting the moral standards required for them to serve and be considerate to others. Today, however, it is viewed much more as an attempt to meet the multifarious needs of the child, so that it can attain to its own potential. The parents, wishing to convince themselves that they are caring for their offspring (and thus also fulfilling their own psychological need to be considered competent parents), become dependent on the expertise of others to inform them what those needs are.

Walter further argues that the tacit acceptance of the 'need-syndrome' offers many advantages over furthering mere self-interest. It appears to be scientifically demonstrable, referring objectively to the child's psychology. It is, therefore, the way things are naturally. If the needs are self-evidently right, according to the latest and best opinion, then there is no need to worry about disputed values. If something is genuinely needed then seeking it cannot be conceived of as greed (mere desire). Choices are made for us, thus easing the pain caused by the bewilderment of so many options. The need-syndrome is tailor-made for late capitalism which thrives on consumer spending. It neatly avoids the impossible questions of meaning and purpose.

If Walter's analysis is right, then he has pinpointed many of the most enduring characteristics of late modernity, demonstrating how a preoccupation with freedom can lead unwittingly to a spirit of conformity. We do not so much map out the journey for ourselves as wait for a passing band-wagon, jump on board and see whether it might lead somewhere interesting or useful, or we follow the 'role model' currently being promoted

---

[34] *All You Love is Need.* London. SPCK. 1984.

by the opinion-formers, until such time as they are displaced and a new specification is on offer:

> Most people are very largely the creatures of their age and social environment, and only occasionally make autonomous choices uninfluenced by the heteronomy of the done thing.[35]

> Modern man is in a position where much of what 'he' thinks and says are the things that everyone else thinks and says; . . . he has not acquired the ability to think originally – that is, for himself – which alone gives meaning to his claim that nobody can interfere with the expression of his thoughts.[36]

> If I am nothing but what I believe I am supposed to be – who am 'I'? . . . I am 'as you desire me'.[37]

The confusion about worthwhile goals and the anxiety that one may allow unrepeatable opportunities to slip away amply demonstrate the paradox of freedom: unless I am certain of who I am, have deliberated long and hard about what I believe are goals worth achieving in life, I am vulnerable to the forces of suggestion which, although they leave me with formal choices, manipulate me to adopt those which others think adequate for me:

> For example, it might be said that if a woman were truly free and self-determining she would not choose to marry and keep house for a man. If she does this willingly she is suffering from false consciousness. To make her free we may have, in the first instance, to deny her certain options, or even to 're-educate' her so that she recognises that her preference for the domestic role is *not her own* but arose because of the process of socialisation to which she was subject. She must, that is, *be forced to be free*.[38]

The purpose of this chapter has been, by setting the discussion of the meaning of freedom within the wider context of the intellectual, social and economic traits of late modernity, to demonstrate something of its complexity and uncertainty. In the next chapter we will explore some of the more obstinate internal and external forces that hinder human freedom.

---

[35] J.R. Lucas, *Responsibility*. Oxford. Clarendon Press. 1993, p. 175.
[36] E. Fromm, op.cit., p. 91.
[37] Ibid., p. 219.
[38] A. Jefferies, 'Freedom' in R. Bellamy, op.cit., pp. 18–19 (my emphasis).

# Seven

# Obstacles to Freedom

## The refusal of authority

In spite of all the constraints of a largely impersonal economic system, tendencies towards limiting civil liberties and recent attempts to demonstrate that human decisions are merely the result of complex biological programming freedom for the human being is a reality. Nevertheless, freedom is not a commodity that is available without limitation: there are many actual and potential restrictions on our doing always what at any given moment we would choose to do. It is sometimes said that the real freedom is to understand and accept the proper limits to freedom.

Freedom in the modern sense has come about largely as a result of the rejection of externally imposed authority. In the sixteenth century the *magisterium* of the undivided church of the West was first questioned and then repudiated in favour of the individual's conscience in submission to the Bible. Then the teaching authority of the Bible was itself questioned by people doubtful of its veracity, credibility and relevance.

As religious belief gradually became a private matter, a wedge was driven between Christianity and the culture of the West. It became perfectly possible to be a citizen of Europe while holding no distinctively religious beliefs at all. As modern science gradually explained more and more of the cosmos, God was pushed to the margins of life. The result was both the decline of the 'public, transcendent God', who was in and over all things, and the rise of numerous 'private, immanent gods', fashioned according to the perceived needs of a new understanding of the world. The boundary between the sacred and the secular became more clearly defined, in that the state no longer imposed religious tests; it also became more fluid, in that civil religion changed in nature, rather than disappeared, and the intervention of faith convictions into ethical debates did not entirely cease.

The idea of the good gradually became disconnected from the hypothesis of a personal God and was seen as resting on a foundation either of natural rights or utility. Evil, on the other hand, was dug up from the deep recesses of the human spirit and relocated in processes that were observable and verifiable, identified with imperfections in human development, related usually to institutions that inhibited self-determination and considered amenable to processes of social elimination.

At a later stage, the birth of modern anthropological studies gave rise to attempts to explain religion as a product of human evolution, belonging to the primitive or infantile stage of human development. Religion had arisen as an understandable reaction to a world that seemed threatening and inexplicable. But once men and women began to understand truly how the natural world functioned, belief in the power of another world to influence the fortunes of people in this world could be dismissed as the superstition and magic that it undoubtedly was. For some religion remained a harmless relic from the past which was unobjectionable if it was strictly confined to a person's own internal life; for others it was nothing but an irrational, neurotic response to feelings of insecurity and unworthiness.

Under the pressure of the modern scientific world view, theism became deism; under the pressure of an enclosed rationalism, deism became agnosticism or atheism. With a sense of relief and optimism, the philosophers of the Enlightenment anaesthetized God and, to their own satisfaction, rendered him innocuous. 'But, like Macbeth, the men of the Enlightenment did not know that the cosmos would rebel at the deed.'[1] It was Nietzsche, some one hundred years later, who dealt the death-blow to God. However, 'Nietzsche replaces easygoing or self-satisfied atheism with agonised atheism, suffering its human consequences'.[2] Before Nietzsche, progressive thinkers accelerated the 'decline of God'; after Nietzsche, sensitive thinkers heralded the gradual 'decline of the West'.

It was not long before sections of the community desired to be free, not only from God, but also from innate human nature. A natural, inborn, structurally given human essence, though necessary to make sense of and guarantee implicit human rights, was felt to be too restrictive of the free flow of the human spirit: creativity, spontaneity and authenticity depended on a concept of the human being 'in the making'. The *tabula rasa* or 'empty cup' concept of human nature came to the fore. The unconditioned human will became more important as a factor in the relationship between human beings and their environment than the human mind. In spite of the apparently predictable character of human action in a world enclosed by a natural process of cause and effect, the will could still exert its autonomy and impose its freedom to choose its own ends and means.

Out of this determination was born the voluntarist tradition of human moral discourse, some of whose effects we have already discussed. On the one hand, the transcendent was said not to exist. However, on the other, reason, contemplating the natural order, could not transcend itself and thus offer an explanation of how human beings, alone of all living things, could also contemplate themselves. Ever since, modern thinkers have been struggling to find a convincing way out of a room that apparently has no doors and no windows. As a consequence the human will and inner experience have been pitted against secular reason:

> By the last quarter of the eighteenth century, Enlightenment ideas were close to having become a sort of new intellectual orthodoxy amongst the cultivated elites of Europe. This orthodoxy was also starting to give way to an emergent 'pre-Romanticism' which

---

[1]  A. Bloom, op.cit., p. 196.
[2]  Ibid., p. 196.

placed greater emphasis on sentiment and feeling, as opposed to reason and scepticism.[3]

The refusal of an authority based on a source of knowledge, rationally accessible, though not rationally created, coming from outside of time and space into human history and culture, has produced a number of insoluble problems for human living. The substitution of belief in the doctrine of the closed natural order for belief in the doctrine of divine revelation[4] has been a high price to pay for the freedom to remain autonomous, as we shall see.

## The disintegration of the self

The most profound difficulty which modern people face is that of reestablishing a unity of being which does justice to the whole experience of life. What is needed is a theory which can not only offer a verifiable account of the processes at work in the worlds of biology, physics, chemistry and mathematics, but can also explain the moral sensibilities ingrained in human experience, the necessity to discover a sense of purpose that gives meaning to human achievements, the longing for community, expressed in contemporary society by the search for enduring relationships, and can also afford a satisfactory account of the existence of reflective intelligence among living beings and a sense of awe and thanksgiving for the sheer wonder and givenness of the universe.

According to Robert Nozick[5], something has intrinsic value to the degree to which it is organically unified. In wanting

---

[3] S Hall and B. Gieben, op.cit., p. 26.

[4] I deliberately use the words 'belief' and 'doctrine' to demonstrate the symmetrical nature and status of each tenet, as based on an assumption of faith which is not demonstrable to reason as indisputable fact. The modern rejection of revelation as the communication from a non-visible world of a message about the ultimate boundaries of existence is no more empirically based than its acceptance. Both are equally based on a faith-commitment as to the balance of probability for or against the notion.

[5] *The Examined Life: Philosophical Meditations.* New York. Simon and Schuster. 1989.

ourselves to be of value and our lives and activities to have value, we want them to exhibit a high degree of organic unity. This is possible, he argues, only on the basis of possessing certain knowledge about whatever is in question; specifically, its inherent character, its relational nature, what constitutes its fulfilment and what is its directional potential. In other words, the integration of the self depends upon solving the question of what he calls 'being's operating intention'. More simply expressed, we need to know what are we *for?*

There would seem to be only two possible ways of answering this question. Either we accept a conclusion which is given to us from beyond what we could possibly discover for ourselves, or we create our own answers. In the latter case, because reason contemplating the natural order – the world of empirical data – on its own, cannot create either values or meaning, these have to be plucked out of the air, so to speak, by some other means.

In the normal course of events people live on the basis of an inherited set of values, pragmatically justified, without seeing any need to give them a solid intellectual foundation: for example, business operates best on the basis of trust and honesty; people work better when they are made to feel a sense of worth. However, in cases where expediency quite clearly conflicts with a coherent set of moral norms (as, for example, in choosing to end a pregnancy, to live together without getting married, to lower wages by imposing new contracts, or to conceal income from the tax authorities), the norms are taken as no more than rough guides to be adjusted as circumstances seem to dictate.

Perhaps the supermarket approach to moral dictates is not a feature only of modern societies, but has always characterized people's approach to conduct. It might be argued that very few people have ever tried to live consistently on the basis of a commitment to a particular ethical code; we are all prone to rationalizing the exceptions that we make to recognized standards (for example, over the amount of time we spend in caring for others). Some, however, are not satisfied with an *ad hoc* approach to living and seek a more obviously unified and coherent pattern. This has given rise to theories of justice, equality, the pursuit of happiness and other ethical beliefs, all of which nevertheless suffer from any proper grounding either in a natural human essence or in a consistent teleology. Supposing that an isolated, self-regarding individualism could be said to demand, at the least, the minimal *negative* ethical criterion that others be not harmed by my actions, on what possible basis can the optimum *positive* ethical criterion of serving the needs of others be established?

When exclusion from the meaning of things becomes too hard to bear, when autonomy leads inexorably to anomie, when self-created goals become mutually self-defeating and end up in self-recrimination, when the emotions and the will can no longer cope with a world the intellect has failed to understand, some people turn to various forms of mystical experience to try to discover the coherence and significance of their own lives and that of the wider world of which they are a part. However, in so far as they do not overcome a mind/body, reason/will or matter/spirit dualism, mysticisms of all sorts have shown a perpetual propensity to lose touch with reality.

The empiricist reduction of the human being has dissolved the unity in diversity of God-humanity-cosmos. What takes its place, as in the case of the so-called heightened consciousness induced by the taking of certain types of drug, is a conflation of at least two of the three elements: God and humanity *or* humanity and the cosmos *or* God and the cosmos. Sometimes all three are merged in forms of pantheism. The price to be paid for experimenting with drugs (and excessive alcohol) will almost certainly be addiction (a severe case of the loss of freedom) and will quite certainly be diminished responsibility and an impaired intellect. The price to be paid for pantheism is the loss of the personal in life and a gradual lessening of the distinction between reality and illusion. A monistic unity of all being does not allow for a genuine interpersonal communication: i.e. for a real 'I-Thou' relationship, not with 'being-itself', but with the one external Source of all being. Neither on naturalistic nor pantheistic assumptions can there be *Anybody* there in an eternal sense, nor can we be sure that there is *anyone* there in our temporal world.

Some have tried to relieve the existential tension of nothingness, caused by the acceptance of a dualistic world-view, by resorting to the creative potential of language, particularly that of the poets. However, language alone, lacking any ultimate and stable reference-point beyond itself, cannot create meaning either: language merely classifies, but without revealing. A deconstructionist approach to texts, whereby the reader may take for himself or herself any meaning that the configuration of words might suggest, simply ends in the self-enclosed world of solipsistic isolation:

> To fall back on the rhetoric of infinitized 'freeplay' is to ignore the plain fact that texts cannot be made to mean just anything; that conflicts arise precisely where divergent, incommensurable readings each find warrant in 'the words on the page'.[6]

Freedom may mean that everyone can now tell and enact their own story, unencumbered by the dogmatism of the meta-narratives which demand a special hermeneutical privilege. However, the consequence is that there is no knowing whether any of these personal stories are significant beyond the significance that one is actually free to recount them. They become detached from history, culture and community – in other words, from the past. Anything deemed to have permanent validity becomes a burdensome restriction on the liberty to create endlessly new worlds.

Hermeneutical libertarianism marks the end of the road of absolute freedom from authority. That there is no ultimate way of distinguishing between the appearance of things and objective reality may be a nice philosophical debating point for some, who nevertheless do so distinguish in their ordinary lives; but for others it means insanity, a total disjunction between subjective experience and a world of fixed contours and boundaries.

Yet others have simply accepted the logic that dichotomy leads to disintegration and from there to nothingness and have embraced some form of the Buddhist metaphysic in which there is no permanent state of personal consciousness – as it has been expressed figuratively, 'we never bathe in the same water twice'.

---

[6] C. Norris, *Deconstruction and the Interests of Theory*. London. Pinter Publishers. 1988, p. 190. 'As a mode of textual theory and analysis, contemporary deconstruction subverts almost everything in the tradition, putting in question received ideas of the sign and language, the text, the context, the author, the reader, the role of history, the work of interpretation and the forms of critical writing' (V.B. Leitch, *Deconstructive Criticism: an Advanced Introduction*. London. Hutchinson. 1983, p. x).

This is one way of overcoming the division between subject and object that has been created by the dissolution of the unity between the particulars studied by science and the universal truths given by God. However, if there is no fixed and continuous centre to the individual's life, then all there is to life is silence.[7] The modern mind may feel this to be an unacceptably extreme consequence of dichotomy. Stopping short of this place, on the other hand, may signal either an unwillingness to be consistent to one's premisses or a lack of courage, or both.

**The relativity of perspectives**

In current British educational theory and practice it is deemed illegitimate to emphasize any particular foundation for morals or any one particular set of values over others. If that approach seems to be contradicted by a statutory preference given to the Christian religion as a basis for right living, it is easily offset both by the current confusion as to whose version of Christianity should prevail and the cultural priority given to context over principle and precedent. As a result, Christian ethics is easily dressed up as a kind of minimal, humanist consensus about being a good citizen in a multi-cultural and multi-faith society.

An even stronger force for the toning down of one explicit set of moral values is the teachers' fear that they may be accused of indoctrinating the young people they teach. Indoctrination is the inculcation of particular beliefs 'in a manner which, intentionally or not, precludes people thinking about it freely. Any teacher in the classroom who uses his or her powers of persuasion to make pupils adopt particular beliefs and values in a way which undermines their capacity to reflect upon these matters is guilty of such indoctrination.'[8] Indoctrination 'is

---

[7] 'There is no permanent and unchanging soul or ground of being in man or the universe'; 'apparent entities such as the mind are merely changing collections of evanescent events – a direct intuition of this is the experience of emptiness', J.R. Hinnels, *A Handbook of Living Religions*. Harmondsworth. Penguin. 1991, pp. 289, 294; cf. also J.A. Kirk, *Loosing the Chains: Religion as opium and liberation*. London. Hodder and Stoughton. 1992, pp. 77–9.

[8] B. Watson, 'Education and the Gospel' in H. Montefiore, op.cit., pp. 130–1.

inconsistent with the liberal and academic approaches to education, in which pupils are encouraged to think for themselves. It is also inappropriate for the utilitarian approach, for today's world . . . requires people who are not programmed but prepared to be flexible and creative.'[9]

Such a view seems to be incontestable. To attempt to force personal preferences upon pupils is to treat them without a proper respect, as means and not as ends in themselves. There is, however, a methodological problem and a hidden agenda in this line of reasoning. The methodological problem lies in the apparently commendable phrases, 'to think for themselves', or 'to make up their own minds'. How is anyone to make up his or her own mind simply on the basis of the presentation of (ideally) unbiased raw data or on the basis of a multiplicity of conflicting opinions? Presumably a teacher is not allowed, under pain of being found guilty of indoctrination, to present his or her own standpoint, because it has come as the result of a process of reflection not yet open to the pupil so that the teacher would have an unfair advantage in discussion.

In real life, if not in educational theory, people do not make up their own minds without consciously or unconsciously submitting to the superior wisdom or knowledge of another. There is likely to be a resonance between the person and a particular belief, which will have come about more by intuition than by some artificial, dispassionate weighing of the pros and cons of many disparate beliefs. In the real world the pupil is likely to hold beliefs on the basis of values taught and discussed at home or held by peers or taken in from the media (including text books). In each of these cases a certain amount of 'indoctrination' will be taking place.

At the same time, paradoxically, there are certain matters about which the pupil is not allowed by the educational system to come to his or her own opinion – for example, to state categorically that the only right sexual lifestyle is one, permanent, monogamous relationship with a person of the opposite sex. In a relativistic age, such a position would be considered far too dogmatic. So, sex education has a responsibility to emphasize that pupils are at liberty to choose a

---

[9] Ibid., p. 130.

number of different options, according to how they feel about relationships. It is advisable that they do not engage in sexual activities, unless there is a firm commitment to staying together as partners, and it is essential that they practise 'safe sex'. Apart from this all pupils have a duty to be tolerant of other people's lifestyles. Logically speaking, this approach simply conceals an alternative dogma based on an alternative set of absolutes and, therefore, by any other name, is also indoctrination.

The hidden agenda lying behind the commitment to a policy of apparent open-mindedness is concealed in what is not said. Brenda Watson recognizes this disguised form of indoctrination, which results in 'closed minds and restricted sympathies' as happening through omission:

> Pupils cannot think about what is never presented to them. It is largely in this way that indoctrination into a secularist approach to life takes place in Western societies.[10]

Thus, for example, any radical alternative to the 'enlightened' self-interest that oils the wheels of the consumer society will not be presented. Whatever the disclaimers, the very goal of contemporary education itself has to be that of fashioning people capable of competing in the highly aggressive world of business and industry. It is education for survival. The pupils will not be encouraged to make up their own minds about this matter: they will be presented, not with any meaningful alternatives, but with the assurance that this is the real world and there is no alternative. John Milbank argues that the very notion of an education 'into free choice' is already an education into the supremacy of the values of liberal capitalism.[11]

---

[10] Ibid., p. 131.

[11] Op.cit., p. 197. '(To) encourage students to make up their own minds . . . is simply to ensure that they will be good conformist consumers in a capitalist economy by assuming now that ideas are but another product that you get to choose on the basis of your arbitrary likes and dislikes' (S. Hauerwas, op.cit., p. 98). Some will argue that recent discussion of environmental issues is an exception to this rather overstated general rule. However, there is a world of difference between those who argue for a zero growth or even negative growth economy, on grounds of sustainability, and those who, under mounting pressure from the general public, are willing to make some 'green' adjustments to manufacturing processes. The former are still largely considered to be economically eccentric, if not illiterate.

This excursus into the undoubtedly well-meaning, but nevertheless ultimately hypocritical, current approach to educating the young illustrates the dilemma of a society which has lost touch with the notion of truth and yet cannot exist without it. Modern societies experience an enormously powerful emotional pull towards ascribing only a relative value to all beliefs and actions, whilst at the same time having to admit that on reflection such a society cannot function coherently. On the wall of the classroom is inscribed, as it were, the motto 'no absolutes' (like a 'no smoking' sign); but, whilst teachers and pupils are keeping guard to see that no absolutes ever cross the threshold of the classroom, these are already present and unrecognized (through the teacher's training, in TV programmes for schools and in the text-books) in the subtle form of the absolute rejection of absolutes. Open-mindedness stops well short of being open to the possibility that certain beliefs and actions are invariably true and right and others false and wrong.

The relative nature of all human values is the one truth that most people would subscribe to. There are a number of reasons for this. Firstly, there is the fear that any claim to final truth is also a claim to the right to impose it, if necessary by force, on others. Such a fear is not without its historical grounds, seeing that modern Western societies have emerged out of absolutist political regimes, sanctioned by authoritarian religious groups, and the twentieth century has witnessed the first ever totalitarian societies, based on the systematic imposition on the whole fabric of society of uncompromising ideologies. Whether on the basis of an assumed mandate given to the leaders of the church by Jesus Christ or that of the historically assured revolution of the proletariat or of a supposed racial superiority, absolutist world-views have wreaked havoc with millions of ordinary human lives.

Secondly, even where the claims to truth do not issue in the physical coercion of the minds and lives of others, they still represent an implicit (spiritual or emotional) violence. To claim that one possesses a truth which another (implicitly or explicitly) does not have is to call that person's integrity into question. It is to presume a position of superiority, an additional understanding or knowledge of existence which is either denied to the other or which the other is (by inference) too stupid to see.

It masks a judgemental and condemnatory attitude towards the other, and consequently violates their dignity.

Thirdly, claims to truth do not allow for that sensitive listening to people from different histories and cultural traditions that genuinely enables the expanding of horizons and the learning of new insights. Truth claims tend to reflect closed minds, minds that will not budge whatever evidence is brought to bear. They may simply be a means of insulating the fearful against the dread of doubt and uncertainty in a confusing world. How can we ever know that we have sufficiently considered all sides of an issue to such an extent that only one conclusion can be drawn? To pretend to have done so is both pretentious and arrogant.

Fourthly, claims to truth are claims to certainty, which given the contingent nature of human existence is not an open option. The most one ought to claim is truth as provisional, always open to modification and revision in the light of more adequate understandings of the meaning of life. And if we accept that our views can only be provisionally true, then we must grant that the views of others could *possibly* be true. The claim to indubitable beliefs is said to lead to epistemological exclusivism, the front for every kind of fundamentalism.[12]

These arguments and others for the relative nature of all human understanding have been powerfully stated in modern times and are widely accepted as a correct assessment of the possibilities inherent in knowing. And yet, contrary to what would seem to be the case, relativism does not enhance but is an obstacle to genuine freedom.[13] The major reason for this is that if there are no fundamental differences a proper, substantial choice between beliefs and goals is impossible. Relativism tends to reduce all stances to mere subjective judgements, inevitably biased by the historical and cultural location of the individual or community who upholds them.

---

[12] Cf. M. Volf, 'Provisional Certitude: The Unique Christ and the Challenge of Modernity' in B. Nicholls (ed.), *The Unique Christ in our Pluralist World*. Exeter. Paternoster Press. 1994.

[13] I have already argued at some length against both the dangers of relativism, and the impossibility of sustaining it either in theory or practice: cf. J.A. Kirk, op.cit., pp. 51–66 and 165–176. Here I will approach the problem from the perspective of the meaning of freedom.

Indeed, curiously, relativism maintains that the tainting influence of one's own background is the only absolute certainty. However, if relativism is true – i.e. if all beliefs and values are relative to time and place and cannot, therefore, function as universal standards by which all other beliefs are measured – one could not know that all beliefs are determined by geographical and temporal location, except as an *a priori* dogmatic assumption. Relativism, for some illogical reason, becomes the one non-controversial exception to its own rule.

Relativism denies real choice, therefore, by saying that choice is unimportant given the fact that no choice has any more transcendent value than any other. It is only when there is a set of mutually exclusive beliefs that choice becomes real, for then important decisions have to be made between rival ways of looking at the world. Relativism encourages intellectual laziness and a paralysis of the will. It assumes that the effort required to try to persuade people to change their beliefs is a waste of time:

> The term 'value', meaning the radical subjectivity of all belief about good and evil, serves the easygoing quest for comfortable self-preservation. Value relativism can be taken to be a great release from the perpetual tyranny of good and evil, with their cargo of shame and guilt. One need not feel bad or uncomfortable with oneself when just a little value adjustment is necessary.[14]

Of course, not everything is permitted. There is a limit to the beliefs and actions that any community can tolerate. It is true that freedom does entail a citizen's right to have their opinions heard and debated. It is also true that in many matters a person's choices are rightly a matter of indifference to the general public. All people, without exception, should have the liberty to reach their own conclusions and act on them, although society may have to decide whether in some cases the action dangerously infringes the integrity of another person or group of people and therefore has to be curtailed. Sometimes, as in the case of literary or press freedom over against the freedom not to be defamed or slandered, there is a nice balance to be kept. In such cases, society has to decide through its legislating representatives where the balance lies. Any form of legitimate non-toleration is clearly an argument against relativism.

---

[14] A. Bloom, op.cit., p. 142.

J.R. Lucas argues that 'social exclusiveness will flourish in an atmosphere of official permissiveness'.[15] If some people exercise their freedom in ways which are profoundly repugnant to others, but not in ways which demand official sanction by the state, the only recourse is to non-association or to some form of exclusion. The more permissive the society the more likely that it fragments into mutually-excluding groups. Society then has to decide between the relative merits of permissiveness and a sense of community identity. If either of these two values were entirely relative, logically there would be no cause for concern.

## Bureaucracy

The all-pervading, intrusive, involvement of state employees in the affairs of ordinary people has been the subject of literary nightmares, most conspicuously in the novels of Franz Kafka. The struggle of the lone individual against the inscrutable face of the public managers is also the stuff of tabloid drama. The lack of accountability of civil service mandarins and the secrecy surrounding the decision-making processes of government departments erupt from time to time into the arena of public debate.

Many instances of the power of the state to deny the freedom of movement of ordinary citizens could be given. The extreme difficulty of achieving compensation for operational errors in the armed services or the health service spring to mind. The legal technicalities that have to be gone through in order to demonstrate in a court of law 'beyond reasonable doubt' that participation in the testing of atomic weapons in the 1950s has produced leukaemia thirty or forty years later is one case in point. The exorbitant legal costs of bringing a civil case against the Ministry of Defence or the difficulty of securing legal aid – itself dependent on a bureaucratic decision of bureaucracy – to be represented by experts in the legal profession has deterred many from exercising the democratic right of holding government accountable for loss of life, limb or earning ability. The same is true of cases against the Department of Health for

---

[15] *Freedom and Grace*, op.cit., pp. 107–8.

permitting the manufacture and distribution of drugs that subsequently have been shown to have highly detrimental side-effects, or against health authorities for operations that have gone wrong due to the errors of judgement or defective skills of medical practitioners.

The growth in the complexity of modern societies, not least in the global interdependence of their economies and the rapid transmission of information, has given rise to a new coterie of experts – the consultants. Government, through the creation of quangos (quasi non-governmental organizations), has come to rely on the advice of self-styled specialists in areas of economic control and management, the environment, urban regeneration, housing policy, education, health care and trade. They are largely hidden people, operating on the edge of the bureaucratic system, writing their papers and memos or simply informing the decision-makers 'off the record' of the latest and best opinion in a given field.

Bureaucracy becomes more complex and more remote in instances of interstate cooperation or union. The case of the European Union illustrates graphically the way that bureaucracy, by seeking to balance incompatible political ends across states, ends up by restricting freedoms and curtailing innovation. The more bizarre cases (such as the alleged ban on the sale of curved cucumbers) hit the headlines, but many other instances of bureaucratic restriction on trade (for example, the limiting of wine production in certain areas of Europe or the restriction placed on the use of trade names) affect people's freedom of commerce and enterprise.

In a modern state the power of the Treasury to decide the levels and direction of spending has become ever greater. The commanding opinion that the economic policy of a government must be sure to gain the confidence of the business community, expressed through share prices and exchange rates, greatly restricts freedom for policy change. It is noticeable that the room for economic manoeuvre has become ever tighter and the economic policies of different political parties have been forced closer together. The first priority is achieving low inflation through tight control on spending and borrowing, which in turn is to be secured partly by limiting pay rises and cutting jobs in the public sector.

Increased productivity, but not necessarily the expansion of jobs, is also seen as a high priority for a modern economy. Current economic wisdom, therefore, has the effect of decreasing long-term employment and increasing the work-load of those who still hold jobs. Were it not for the deeply held moral conviction that society as a whole has a responsibility for guaranteeing a certain minimum standard of living for all who are willing and able to work (but with no access to a job), there is no doubt that the economic system as such, being entirely impersonal, would be altogether indifferent to the plight of the jobless. Some political commentators go so far as to suggest that the state will take to itself whatever power is necessary to ensure that the market remains 'free'.[16]

Economic factors have led the state to attempt to define moral ends for its citizens. Lifestyles which may prove costly to the Treasury are declared to be anti-social and may not, therefore, attract fiscal support. However, here government may be much less than consistent. To take a few examples: on the one hand, the break-up of families, which leads to the need for family support and priority housing and is said to promote teenage vagrancy, becomes a major moral issue. The choice to lead an unsettled life of travelling is disallowed through restriction of access to temporary camp sites and the bureaucratic obstacles to securing social benefits. Pressure on the funding of the health service may well bring discrimination against people who have chosen a deliberately unhealthy lifestyle, particularly smokers, drug addicts and, quite possibly in the future, those who do not take any significant exercise.

On the other hand, no government yet has begun to tackle seriously the economic, health and environmental problems caused by the motor car. Car-ownership and use is on an ever upward expanding curve. Attempts to limit use through indirect taxation (tax on car sales, the licence fee and petrol) have proved totally ineffective and, in any case, often hit the wrong target. Meanwhile the road network expands, sites of outstanding natural beauty and scientific importance are buried beneath concrete, traffic-pollution and its known debilitating effects (like

---

[16] Cf. A. Belsey, 'The New Right, Social Order and Civil Liberties' in R. Levitas, op.cit., p. 192.

asthma) continue to increase. Official attitudes to different lifestyles remain arbitrary: smoking is socially outlawed, whilst over-drinking and over-eating have not yet been similarly stigmatized.

## Economic determinism

The capitalist economic system justifies itself above all by asserting its ability to maximize the freedom of the individual as entrepreneur and consumer in the market and guarantee the freedom of the individual as citizen in the political system. However, it has rightly been criticized for turning economic processes into an ideological tool for restricting change. Capitalism's functioning is ideological, 'to the extent that it conceals from view *other* social possibilities'.[17]

Capitalism presents itself as a cohesive and harmonious way of ensuring that resources are distributed efficiently. It has often been likened to a game in which all may play and, as long as they abide by the rules, gain enjoyment and profit, although clearly those with superior skills or a modicum of good fortune will profit the most. Society, as the referee, is there to interpret and uphold the rules, but not to decide the outcome of the game in advance. Thus it will ensure that breaking or bending the rules through fraud, exploitative practices, monopoly and restrictions on trade are severely penalized.[18] The important factor is that, although some will do better than others in the system, all will benefit to some degree. It is intended to be the opposite of a zero sum game.

The major critique, associated mainly with the name of Marx, is that the ideal actually conceals a very different reality. A capitalist system in its practical working is conflictual at its core. There is said to be an intrinsic conflict of interests between those who sell their labour-power and those who own capital. Capitalism is thus seen to be a typical ideology, in that it conceals the real nature of social and economic relationships. The bearers

---

[17] Milbank, op.cit., p. 194.
[18] Cf. B. Griffiths, op.cit., p. 75. Some would say that society is also willing to change the rules, if and when the 'top professionals' are in danger of losing!

of the capitalist ideology, according to Marxist theory, are the bourgeois class who have managed to obtain the tacit consent of the whole of society, including those who are clearly disadvantaged by the system, to their interpretation of economic realities.

According to the French Marxist philosopher, Althusser, ideology is not merely the illusory representation of reality, but a means through which people live out their lives; it is a generally accepted way of viewing wealth creation, resource distribution, job opportunities and work. The ideology also consists in the way the concept of freedom is manipulated, so that alternative interpretations are effectively marginalized. The freedom that people have is to submit ('freely') to the dominant interpretation of reality.[19]

Another strategy adopted by apologists for capitalism is to argue that no other alternative for organizing economic relations exists. To return to the metaphor of the game: to change the rules would mean totally paralysing the contest. It would be like a game of football in which every encounter by two people on the ball was penalized by a yellow or red card. The game would come to a standstill, there would be no outcome. In this sense, capitalism has had remarkable success in delegitimizing all forms of socialism as alternatives or, perhaps even more subtly, in forcing socialists so to rethink their political ideas that these have become remarkably similar to the dominant ideology.[20]

In the light of the weaknesses of the system, some of which we have already highlighted, its ideological success is truly remarkable. Even though highly undesirable effects of the system are generally admitted, such as the realities that material rewards do not necessarily correspond to merit or obligation,[21] that all human relations are seen as commercial transactions in which the gift of personalized relationships are deliberately cut to a minimum[22] and that fierce competition, though natural to human life, drives many to bankruptcy and subsequently to

---

[19] Cf. D. McClellan, op.cit., pp. 31–2.
[20] Cf. R. Levitas, 'Introduction: Ideology and the New Right' in R. Levitas, op.cit., p. 17.
[21] B. Griffiths, op.cit., p. 77.
[22] Cf. Dykema in C.R. Strain, op.cit., p. 53.

marriage break-up,[23] few people today imagine that modern life would be thinkable under any other system.

One of the most significant successes of the ideology has been its ability to sidestep or elude altogether the more profound questions, for which the system has no easy answers. Thus, for example, its prominent claim to be the most efficient way of conducting economic life has managed to evade a serious discussion of the meaning in real life of efficiency. This evasion has been achieved (perhaps through appearing to be based on a serious scientific method) by reducing the terms of the debate to quantitatively measured efficiency: material output set against material input, the ever-expanding quantity of goods and services that are available at an appropriate price. If, however, one were to ask seriously about the human goals of efficiency and about quality of life, and measure these against the inefficiency of a system that makes some people virtually unemployable in their early forties and causes untold damage to human health and the environment through pollution and the over-exploitation of non-renewable resources, one would come to different conclusions. Efficiency is always relative to the end in view.

The ability of capitalist ideology to stifle a truly open debate is perhaps the most important facet of the system that needs explaining. It is as if the whole population of advanced industrialized societies has acquiesced in the supposition that no other organization of economic life is thinkable. Imagination has either been curtailed or reduced to the utopic and impractical. Aligned with this is the uncomfortable suspicion that the educated and articulate sectors of society, who could mount at least an intellectual challenge, have been bought by the prosperity which is available to them, whilst the marginally educated, who have most to lose by the system, are not powerful enough to confront it in any significant way.

## Scientific determinism

In an enclosed universe in which the sciences strive to give a full account of human existence in terms of prior material

---

[23]  J. Collier, in H. Montefiore, op.cit., p. 119.

causes, there has to be some fear that we human beings are no more than highly sophisticated machines. Having become used to the idea that, in comparison with other mammals, our distinguishing feature is our superior intellect, we may be dismayed by the idea that arguably the greatest chess player of all time, Gary Kasparov, has now been defeated by a computer chess program. As chess requires the most pure form of mental agility, has not such a computer proved itself superior to human beings?

Part of the reason for the fear is the tendency to regard a more complexly evolved brain as the main differentiating mark of human beings in comparison with animals. If, however, a machine can now manage much more complex mental functions at much greater speeds than human beings, what remains of our exalted place in the material scheme of things? If, following Descartes, the essence of humanness is found in the thinking subject, then being becomes simplified and susceptible to a reductionist explanation:

> Mind is nothing but the collocation of atomistic perceptions, none of which says anything about the substantiality of the person. There is no 'inner' being in which all perceptions persist.[24]

The behaviourist school of psychology has all but dissolved human freedom by suggesting that our actions are nothing more than naturally selected reflex responses designed to avoid adverse conditions.[25] Everything we do is the result of a sophisticated system of programming over which we have no final control and which we cannot alter. Thus, even when we spontaneously or impulsively change our minds and course of action, this is only due to a long chain of brain-cell stimuli that indicates that the choice could not have been different. What to a casual outside observer appears to be an instance of exuberant freedom to be or act differently, is wholly explicable to the scientific analyst in terms of implicitly predictable prior causes.

---

[24] I. Barbour, op.cit., p. 137.
[25] Cf. R. Gross, *Themes, Issues and Debates in Psychology*. London. Hodder and Stoughton. 1995, Chapters 5 and 12; B. Schwartz and S.J. Robbins, *Psychology of Learning and Behaviour*. New York. W.W. Norton. 1995.

However, the idea that human activity is inevitable, given a particular genetic make-up, comes about as the result of a terminological confusion:

> The idea of a cause as meaning that something is *forced* to happen is surely confused and anthropomorphic. The scientific idea of a force, as used in physics, is not the idea of a dramatized power struggle – of compulsion prevailing over a will or driving a helpless being . . . – but simply a generalization about regular sequences of events . . . The question about determinism is much more about the language we choose to use . . . than about how the world really is.[26]

Lucas also points out that there is considerable confusion in the way that we use the term, cause. By cause we may mean 'the antecedent sufficient condition' of an action. In this sense causes will be followed inevitably by their effects. On the other hand, we may mean 'the most important member of the set of conditions that are conjointly sufficient'. In the latter case no inevitability is involved, for a person's own decision then becomes an essential part of the antecedent sufficient condition of his own actions.[27] In other words, human action is only limited to a certain extent by the component parts that go into our genetic make-up or environmental background; the sustained effort of a highly motivated will can bring about different effects.

There is also a popular misconception about the nature of scientific laws, which comes about by giving to the notion of law personal attributes and making it the agent of certain activities, as in the sentence: 'The laws of physics preclude the possibility of miracles.' Scientific laws are not immutable, quasi-personal forces that take on a life of their own. Strictly speaking, they are created by human beings who are seeking to order and coordinate their observations. So they describe and clarify the conjectural outcome of a set of experiments. If further experimentation discovers that the laws are insufficient they are changed. Thus nothing is 'governed' by a law, but may be explicable in relation to other matters in terms of a law. This

---

[26] M. Midgley, 'Strange contest: science versus religion' in H. Montefiore, op.cit., p. 49.
[27] *Freedom and Grace*, op.cit., pp. 5–6; cf. also the discussion in P.F. Strawson, *Freedom and Resentment and Other Essays*. London. Methuen and Co. 1974, pp. 1–25.

allows scientific work to be entirely open-ended.[28] Thus, in the case of miracles, the most that could be said is that, based on experience so far, it is probable that, if there is sound observational data to confirm some events as miracles, they are exceptional and not normal occurrences.

It is surely the sheer fact of human existence, in what otherwise appears to be a machine-like universe, that is impossible to explain either on the basis of pure chance or absolute necessity. Human beings, in the nature of the case, stand outside the experimental work that they are conducting. They not only observe but they are conscious of their activity of observation. There are, therefore, excellent grounds for considering it inconceivable that the many different operations of the human mind – abstract thought, logical reasoning, self-consciousness, recollection, deciding between options, setting goals and the means of achieving them – could ever have arisen by random selection from an impersonal beginning. Random mutations, even after 15 billion years, would not produce the unique person, conscious that he or she does not have to act on the basis of involuntary impulses. The human being stands outside the machine:

> As Gödel's theorem puts it, no algorithm, or computer programme, that demonstrates a mathematical proof can also prove its own validity, a crucial indispensable link between machines and minds.[29]

Reason does not stand as the end-product of a chain of biological processes stretching back to the beginning of the cosmos, for then there would be nothing to account for its ability to order and understand itself. Determinism is possible only if we discount completely the capacity that human beings have to observe themselves. In attempting to find a unified theory explicable of all phenomenon, scientists will constantly come up against the enigma that the universe is comprehensible rather than being incomprehensible:

---

[28] Karl Popper in his celebrated book, *Conjectures and Refutations*, advocated this kind of open-ended approach to scientific knowledge, indeed to all forms of knowledge, in which any hypothesis should be tested against carefully controlled experimental procedures.

[29] L. Sanneh, op.cit., p. 174.

Science does not explain the mathematical intelligibility of the physical world, for it is part of science's founding faith that this is so . . . The physical universe seems shot through with signs of mind.[30]

The best explanation for what we observe about ourselves observing, or perceive about ourselves as participants in the scientific enterprise, is that mind or consciousness has existed from the beginning and is not an entity that inexplicably has emerged late in the process without any sufficient antecedent cause.[31]

---

[30] J. Polkinghorne, *Reason and Reality*. London. SPCK. 1991, p. 76.
[31] Cf. V.H. Fiddes, op.cit., p. 76.

# Eight

# Muslim Understandings of Freedom

## Islam's encounter with the secular West

Up to this point, we have dealt with modern, secular views of freedom and introduced religious ideas and values only in so far as they have contributed to or been opposed by the secular. We turn now to look at the convictions about freedom of two major faiths: Islam and Christianity. Though both of them are marked to differing degrees by their respective brushes with modern culture, they still offer significant alternative ways of looking at the world to make the comparison a valuable exercise.

As far as the West is concerned, Christianity is an obvious choice. The history of its ebbs and flows has been so intertwined with the general history of Europe that it is difficult, if not impossible, to disentangle the two. Indeed, both the concept and the experience of freedom as we know them today would most probably not have come about, were it not for certain beliefs, intrinsic to Christian faith, coming to the fore at an appropriate historical conjunction.

The selection of Islam is not so easy to justify. Arising in the Arabian peninsula and spreading along North Africa and throughout the Fertile Crescent, north into Central Asia and east to the Indian sub-continent and the Indonesian archipelago, it has not penetrated in any significant sense into the heartlands of the European continent. Moreover, at exactly the time that modern societies were in the process of emerging in Europe, Islam as an intellectual and spiritual force was in decline.[1] At the present time, as we shall see, the relationship between the two is characterized, at the very best, by mutual suspicion.

Nevertheless, Islam has been influential in Europe in many indirect ways. Of particular note was the flowering of a remarkable Islamic civilization in southern Spain; Islamic architecture, sculpture, poetry and philosophy (particularly that of Averroes (d.1198)) have all left their impress on the rest of Europe. Simultaneously two of the greatest religious philosophers of all time, Avicenna (d.1037) and Ghazzali (d.1111), were expounding their beliefs in Baghdad. Through translations from Arabic to Latin, these men and others reintroduced the thought of the Greeks into Europe and gave to the West some of the foundations of modern science.

Hichem Djait[2] argues that for 1000 years, from the end of the Magyar invasions until 1914, Islam formed a protective screen between Europe and the waves of violence that came down from the steppes of Central Asia: 'It was Islam that absorbed the deadly poison of the Mongol hordes; Islam that later stopped Tamerlane.'

Fortuitously, he argues, Islam was instrumental in securing for Europe an unprecedented period of peace from outside invasions, thus enabling the kind of stability which is needed if notable advances in civilization are to occur.[3] Conversely, the end of the middle period of the flowering of Islamic thought and culture coincided with the sack of Baghdad in 1258 by Hulegu Khan (sixteen years before the death of Thomas Aquinas).

There are other more contemporary reasons for including Islam in a comparative study. They are obvious and do not need much expanding. Firstly, significant communities of Muslims now live in many European nations. They are not visitors, but residents and nationals. If Western democracy is anything near the ideal that is often presented, their participation as full

---

[1] Cf. A. Ahmed, *Postmodernism and Islam: predicament and promise*. London. Routledge. 1992, pp. 84–6.

[2] *Europe and Islam*. Berkeley. University of California Press. 1985, p. 110.

[3] In one sense he is right. Has he not forgotten, however, that Islam itself in the presence of the Ottoman Turks was also an invading force from the East?

citizens will be important for the future well-being of these societies. Secondly, Islam is regarded by many Western observers as a strong force (although often negative) in global geo-politics. With the collapse of Communism as a serious political contender to the hegemony of the West,[4] Islam is seen as the only potential external alternative to the triumph of modernism. Whether or not this perception has much validity, the views of Islam are clearly of vital importance in the West today.

Islam and modernity have an uneasy relationship. Our concern initially is to look at the ways in which the former responds to the latter. It has to be said that, by and large, the attitude is contrary. There is almost a knee-jerk reaction to the whole idea of the secular, even amongst intellectuals who live in the West and do not base their interpretation of it on second-hand sources. Thus Akbar Ahmed equates the secular automatically with godlessness: '"Secular" and "Muslim" are by definition incompatible words, as any dictionary will confirm. There can be no Muslim without God . . . '.[5]

Elsewhere, in a striking confession of faith in the irreconcilable nature of the two perspectives on life, which follows a (secular) challenge to him to accept the human origin of his religion, he says: 'For those who believe in Islam, the choice is between being Muslim and being nothing: there is no other choice.'[6]

The relationship between the world of Islam and Europe has generally been fraught with difficulties. The challenge of secularization represents the third major encounter between the two: the first happened at the time of the Crusades and the

---

[4] For various reasons, which are not the subject matter of this study, China, though still outwardly professing communism, does not pose the kind of threat that the Soviet Union was perceived to offer. Principally, this seems to be because economic modernization is fast bringing it into the all-embracing sphere of the world capitalist order.

[5] *Postmodernism*. op.cit., p. 173. It is clear from the context that Ahmed is using secular in its modern sense of a world free from the controlling influence of those who believe in God, not in its original sense, meaning the mundane world. An informed Christian would not necessarily make the same equation, distinguishing between the secular, secularization, secularity and secularism. Probably only the latter term and the convictions which lie behind it would be viewed negatively.

[6] Ibid., p. 42.

second began with the British conquest of India and Napoleon's expedition to Egypt. The first two were military confrontations and involved a struggle for political power in certain regions of the world, hitherto dominated by Muslims. The third is an economic and cultural struggle in which, once again, the West seems to be the stronger force:

> Islam is gradually losing control, as did the Christian Church some time ago, over the daily life of secularised believers . . . The secular age . . . is more hospitable to rational philosophy than to dogmatic theology.[7]

For Islam the culture of modernity, which, unlike an armed struggle, cannot be confronted head on, is much more insidiously perilous than the colonial intervention. For more than one reason it strikes at the very heart of the faith. Kenneth Cragg, a sympathetic Christian interpreter of Islam, puts his finger on one of the central problems:

> Traditionally Islam has been a very self-assured faith. Heart-searching and mind-querying have not normally been thought congenial or even thought necessary in Muslim history. The call for the complete Islamization of knowledge has never been in doubt of itself.[8]

Now, the self-sufficiency of Islam is being exposed. Its tight-knit system of life and belief is being pulled apart as never before. Its categorical authority over the life of the community (the *ummah*) is being challenged, if not massively at an intellectual level, certainly at the level of lifestyle and commitment. The contemporary meeting between the two cultures has bred in Islam a severe sense of insecurity over the West's technological leadership and general cultural and economic hegemony:

> Muslims since the nineteenth century especially have been defensive about charges that their cultures, or the Shari'a, was 'pre-modern' or impossible to reconcile with modernity.[9]

---

[7] Shabbir Akhtar, *A Faith for All Seasons*. London. Bellew Publishing. 1990, pp. 16–17.
[8] 'The Riddle of Man and the Silence of God: A Christian Perception of Muslim Response', *International Bulletin of Missionary Research*, Vol. 17,4, October 1993, p. 161; also W. Montgomery Watt, *Islamic Fundamentalism and Modernity*. London. Routledge. 1988, pp. 1–23.
[9] A. Mazrui, op.cit., p. 218.

Muslims have generally adopted one of three responses to this challenge. Firstly, whilst accepting largely the technological improvements brought by modern science, they have embraced an attitude of resistance to 'Westernization'. This latter is seen as a matter of self-surrender, so that any attempt at inculturating Western values into Islamic history is interpreted as an admission of inferiority, which strikes at the soul of the faith, revealed by the very God whom the West has rejected.[10]

Secondly, they have sought to exploit the weak elements in modern culture – its fragmentation, its lack of a secure family base, its moral confusion, its endemic racism – contrasting favourably the Islamic sense of cultural integration, moral integrity and racial harmony:

> The inner suffering of the West comes from the fact that its culture has been devoured by modernity . . . [Modernity is at] once beneficial and poisonous, [and in any case heavy with fate] . . . In the West, in a world where God has been expelled, the conflict between culture and modernity has brought alienation.[11]

Inherent in this stance is the hope that in the long term, when the internal contradictions of Western culture become no longer sustainable, the West, having already implicitly turned its back on Christianity, will adopt Islam as its natural and rational religion instead.

Thirdly, there are those (admittedly a minority) who wish to maintain the essentials of Islam but, at the same time, bring it into a dialogical rather than confrontational relationship to modernity. The key concept which they use is that of reinterpretation. The first stage in this process is liberation from the 'dogma' of *taqlid* – 'the unquestioning and rigid adherence to one of the four schools of Sunni *fiqh* (Islamic jurisprudence) developed in the post-classical period of Islamic history'.[12] The second (positive) stage is to recognize that the roots of historical development and change are already in place in Islam's foundation document, the Qur'an. There is a necessary

---

[10] Cf. B. Tibi, *The Crisis of Modern Islam: A Preindustrial Culture in the Scientific-Technological Age.* Salt Lake City. University of Utah Press. 1988, p. 90.

[11] H. Djait, op.cit., p. 172.

[12] Anon., 'Muslim Modernists: the Torch-bearers of Progressive Islam', *Islamic Quarterly*, 31, 1987, p. 194.

distinction to be drawn between 'essential' and 'symbolic' verses in the Qur'an: the former constitute the irreducible minimum of the Islamic creed, whilst the latter are open to more than one interpretation and, therefore, permit deductions, appropriate to other ages and circumstances, different from those of Arabia in the early seventh century.[13]

Between the groups, an interesting and significant diversity of language is being used. Conservatives or Traditionalists tend to speak of the *revitalization* or *renaissance* of Islam, assuming a lost pristine purity (usually located in the times of the first four, 'rightly guided' caliphs) which has to be recovered. According to this perspective, after the rapid rise and flourishing of Islam in its first 40 years of existence and ever since the Umayyad dynasty took power (661), there has been a steady decline. Modernists, on the other hand, speak of *reformulation*. Fazlur Rahman calls for a radically new vision of Islam:

> Muslims must decide what exactly is to be conserved, what is essential and relevant for the erection of an Islamic future, what is fundamentally Islamic and what is purely 'historical' . . . The need to cultivate a sound historical thinking about Islam is the first . . . prerequisite of any successful process of the reformulation of Islam.[14]

The question still very much before Muslims, and the implications of which they have not yet properly addressed, is whether you can have the changes introduced by economic and technological development without far-reaching social changes as well. It is, for example, the thesis of Bassam Tibi that Islam will only remain fundamentally unaltered to the degree that it is practised within an essentially pre-industrial society.[15] If it is to become a religion of the modern world, which Kenneth Cragg believes will happen either by choice or by default, it must decide how it is going to convince a specifically post-modern generation that it is the one religion divinely suited to human nature (cf. Qur'an 30.30).

---

[13] Cf. A. Ahmad, *Islamic Modernism in India and Pakistan, 1857-1964*. London. Oxford University Press. 1967, p. 45.
[14] B. Tibi, op.cit., p. 142.
[15] Ibid., pp. 131ff.

## The present political reality of Islam

Many Islamic societies are still coming to terms with the end of the colonial experience and discovering what their role should be within the global political and economic realities of the end of the twentieth century. It is clear, from the fact that 'almost without exception the forty-four Muslim nations . . . are run by different varieties of dictatorship',[16] that the ideals of liberal democracy have not caught on amongst the political elite. This is not the whole story, of course. Some nations have struggled to implement a political system in which there is a recognized, constitutional opposition to government and periodic popular elections. Where these have failed, sections of the population have risked their own liberties in protest against censorship and corruption.

Western commentators on Islam are inclined to think that a rigid interpretation of Islamic history and law tends towards an absolutist form of government. This is not necessarily true. Media attention focuses on the arbitrary powers exercised in countries like Iraq, Libya and Indonesia and on the various attempts to introduce at least modified forms of shari'a law in nations like the Sudan and Malaysia. However, there has been a long discussion, mainly centring on South East Asia, of democratic forms of government according to fundamental Islamic principles.

Whatever constitution Islamic nations have, or may have in the future, there is no doubt that the last 50 years or so have seen a remarkable revitalization and repoliticization of Islam:

> Islam . . . is, when militant, powered by revivalist radicalism: it seeks to regain its ancient vigour and distinctiveness . . . The Ayatollahs of Iran have opted for a return to the historic point of deflection, a move backwards to transcend the diversion perpetrated by the Western cultural hijackers . . . The quest is for a cultural re-entry into the original universe of Islam, as well as a cultural exit out of the Western diversionary maze.[17]

---

[16] A. Ahmed, *Discovering Islam: making sense of Muslim history and society*. London. Routledge. 1988, p. 221.
[17] A. Mazrui, op.cit., p. 243–4.

Yvonne Haddad argues that the major characteristic of the Islamic revival has been the breakdown of the monopoly on religion of the *ulama* class, those educated in traditional Islamic sciences. There has been a 'laicization' of Islam, in which their role as sole educators, adjudicators and legislators has been assumed by a new elite class – university graduates, often trained in the West. The status of the *ulama* has declined, as most gifted people now enter secular professions. Along with the decline of the influence of the *ulama* has gone a kind of 'privatization of Islam' in which 'reinterpreting the faith for modern life has become very much a personal concern'. This is also affected by the fact that nowadays literacy is acquired through the public school system not the traditional *kuttab* (Qur'anic school). As a result of the shift (modernization?) in the educational system, there is an intense debate going on throughout society about the meaning of Islam in the contemporary world:

> The current dialogue is . . . not over the choice between Islam and secularism, but over the decision as to which, or whose, Islam is to be the framework for the revitalized Islamic society of the future.[18]

According to Bassam Tibi, the repoliticization of Islam has sprung from an acute crisis brought by secular ideologies, which have not themselves been able to fulfil their visionary promises. It is also a reaction to the perceived collapse of Islam from the grandeur which, as the true way of God, it ought always to have. It also fulfils a function, therefore, of 'absorbing disappointment' as well as bringing needed change.[19]

Repoliticization has been resisted in some Muslim countries – most notably Egypt, Syria and Pakistan. There 'the secular . . . and the religious intelligentsia are engaged in cultural class warfare', which is a struggle both for control of the state and the general collective consciousness of the masses.[20] In each of these

---

[18] 'Muslim Revivalist Thought in the Arab World: an overview', *The Muslim World*, LXXVI, 3–4, 1986, pp. 162–6.

[19] Op.cit., pp. 50–54.

[20] M. Fischer and M. Abedi, *Debating Muslims: Cultural Dialogues in Postmodernity and Tradition*. Wisconsin. University of Wisconsin Press. 1990, p. 385; also G.A. Parwiz in A. Ahmed and G.E. von Grunebaum (eds), *Muslim Self-Statement in India and Pakistan (1857-1968)*. Wiesbaden. Harrassowitz. 1970, p. 227.

countries there is a considerable non-Muslim minority, whose plea for cultural and religious diversity, equality and freedom has attracted international attention.

## Political and economic debate within Islam

Apart from the reception of the Qur'an, the most momentous event in the life of Muhammad was his migration (*hijra*) from Makka to Madina in 622, the event which marks the beginning of the Islamic era: 'In Madinah he arrived (at the invitation of its inhabitants) as ruler, laying the foundations of a nascent state and religion. He now began to establish his community.'[21]

The founder of Islam became head of state: he had to establish a system of law and a judicial order and defend the city against the determination of the Quraysh in Makka to crush what they saw as a rebellion. Ever since, as Islam grew as a religious and political force and became an empire and then various empires, the precepts of the Qur'an and the *sunna* (the customs of Muhammad) has been translated into legislation to direct the life of social communities.

Islam has gloried in the fact that it is a faith that informs the whole of life, down to the smallest details, and does not allow religion to become a separate compartment of life; indeed, there is no word in Arabic for religion, denoting a sphere of life separate from other aspects of existence. This is an undoubted strength, in that it gives to the faith both coherence and integrity. Potentially, the indissoluble link between faith and political power is also a weakness, in that the faith will be measured by the perceived success, or otherwise, of its political outcome: for example, a harsh, authoritarian regime is judged to be but the natural outcome of the faith it espouses. Moreover, it cannot easily hide behind an intrinsic separation between the state and the religious community, for, as Bassam Tibi puts it, 'Islam is organic not ecclesiastical'[22] (by this he means that there is no separate religious community within the state, the former and the latter form an organic whole). Ali Mazrui puts the matter

---

[21] A. Ahmed, *Discovering Islam*, p. 20.
[22] Op.cit., p. 132.

differently when he says that in both orthodox Judaism and Islam there is a pull towards a kind of divine 'unitarism' linking heaven and earth, which together form one kingdom under God. As a result, theocracy (or nomocracy – rule under the law of God) is the natural political system for Islam.

However, to declare a unitary existence in which religion and socio-political life occupy the same space in a human community does not solve the problem of the relationship between belief and action. Rather, it considerably sharpens the many dilemmas implicit in the interpretation and transposition of a faith given once for all in one set of circumstances to other widely differing conditions. The politics of difference within the Islamic world shows that the Qur'an and *sunna* do not provide 'a catalogue of simple rules that provide unambiguous guidance for all aspects of life'.[23]

Akbar Ahmed has identified three main groupings within contemporary Islam, differing according to how they tackle the predicament of interpretation and application: traditionalists, radicals and modernists.[24] He admits that the categorization is fluid and needs clarification. For our purposes there are, according to his descriptions, only two real alternatives when it comes to the implementation of Islamic precepts in contemporary life, for his 'modernists' are only nominal Muslims, having been born into the community but largely repudiated its tenets under the influence of either Western liberalism or Marxism. Moreover, those he describes as traditionalists – people like Sayyed Ahmad Khan, Muhammad Iqbal, Hossein Nasr, Fazlur Rahman – others have called modernists.[25] Whether radicals, traditionalists or modernists, the fundamental question of dispute and discussion is exactly the same as that which has been at the root of political and civil change in Western societies since the sixteenth century: namely, the legitimation of political sovereignty and its accountability.

The radicals, among whom one would have to include Khomeini, Shabbir Akhtar, Parvez Manzoor and most notoriously (in Britain) Kalim Siddiqui, the creator of an

---

23 M. Fischer and M. Abedi, op.cit., p. 387.
24 *Postmodernism and Islam*, op.cit., pp. 158–167.
25 Cf. A. Ahmad, op.cit., pp. 53, 154, 227.

(unofficial) Muslim parliament, are largely contemptuous of all attempts to accommodate some principles from the Western liberal tradition into Islamic political theory and practice. They tend to assume that shari'a in a form received from the earliest Islamic jurists, the four 'masters of Islamic law', Hanifa, Malik, Shafi and Ibn Hanbal, has an abiding, trans-temporal quality that allows it to be implemented in a more or less direct form in any society. For them 'the gates of *ijtihad*, independent judgement, (are) henceforth closed'.[26] Rulers in Islamic nations, therefore, have an obligation to put into effect the ancient regulations of shari'a concerning forms of punishment, the economy, the place of women in society, the status of other faith communities and so on.

The traditionalists/modernists, on the other hand, precisely believe that the 'gates of *ijtihad*' should remain open, and this for two main reasons. Firstly, situations have changed to such a degree in the contemporary world from that experienced in the Arabian peninsula fourteen centuries ago, that legal provisions have to be reformulated to take account of the intervening historical processes. Secondly, due to the fact that Islam does not have a clerical or priestly class with the authority to impose an unequivocal body of teaching, there is no one with the requisite status to produce a singular set of laws binding on all at all times and in all places. However much imams, jurists and scholars may be revered for their piety, knowledge and leadership, their views have no infallible status. To claim otherwise has often been a cover for a struggle for political power or influence.

The difference of opinion between the two groups is not necessarily centred on whether or not shari'a should be implemented, but on *which* shari'a and under *what conditions* it should be made effective.[27] If it is true that 'sovereignty to all intents and purposes belongs to shari'a', the locus of all political authority is the community of believers who, ideally, elect the ruler(s) and obey them only in so far as they do not violate shari'a. This means that, in practice, sovereignty belongs to the community, which through the principle of *ijma* (consensus)

26 A. Ahmed, *Discovering Islam*, op.cit., p. 48; also M. Fakhry, *Ethical Theories in Islam*. Leiden. Brill. 1991, p. 12.
27 Cf. M.H. Kamali, 'The Limits of Power in an Islamic State', *Islamic Studies*, 28/4, 1989, pp. 323–52.

moderates the making of law. According to this view, the community is primordial and precedes the state:

> The state is only the political dimension of the collective endeavour of the Muslims.[28]

The implications of this understanding are far-reaching. Shari'a is designed to constitute a comprehensive defence mechanism against oppression and arbitrary rule (akin to the Reformation view of the *lex rex*). It was never intended to be an instrument of authority in the hands of any particular government, because it exists independently of the state. The citizen is granted the freedom to question and monitor government activity by constructive criticism and ultimately by refusal to obey a government which transgresses the law (as is suggested in Qur'an 9.71; 3.104, 110; 22.41).[29] Though there would certainly be discussion about the precise content of law, this perspective and mode of operation is not far removed from that of Western-style democracies. It is not surprising, therefore, that many Muslims have argued that democracy is perfectly compatible with the most basic principles of Islam.[30]

## The Islamic world-view

Before embarking on a study of the actual beliefs of Islam regarding the meaning of freedom, it is necessary to set the discussion within the context of Islam's consciousness of itself as a distinct and original religion. Apart from the strong identity between faith and life, which we have already mentioned,[31] there are two other basic convictions which go to make up what might be called 'normative' Islam.

---

[28] H. Turabi, 'Principles of Governance, Freedom and Responsibility in Islam', *The American Journal of Islamic Social Sciences*, 4/1, 1987, p. 3.

[29] M.H. Kamali, op.cit., pp. 326–36.

[30] Cf. A. Ahmad, op.cit., pp. 264–70.

[31] Though faith in God is a vitally important part of a person's life, it should not be identified with mere belief, for it implies complete submission to the ways of God in which there can be no separate sphere of faith which is not bound up completely with life lived before God.

Firstly, there is the absolute conviction that knowledge of the will of God has been finally and completely communicated to the whole of humanity through Muhammad in the 114 *suras* of Al-Qur'an ('The Reading' or 'The Recitation'), received as a revelation between the years 610 and 632. Muslims insist on the miraculous nature of the gift of the Qur'an, based on the fact that Muhammad was allegedly illiterate and therefore could not have 'read' or written the words that came to him in his visions. The supernatural nature of the collection is further affirmed on the basis of the magnificence and perfection of its language and the utter uniqueness of its content. The *hadith* or sayings of Muhammad, not directly communicated from God, are also held in high regard as a supplementary source of wisdom and guidance, but are on an inferior level to the Qur'an.

Secondly, the prophetic revelations contained in the Qur'an are said to recapitulate, complement and bring to completion all the prophetic messages that God has, from time to time, communicated in different places to other peoples. In this sense Muhammad is 'the seal of the prophets'. The Islamic view of religion is diametrically opposed to the view, fashionable a century or so ago, that monotheism was the climax of an ascending process from original primitive polytheistic beliefs, through which humankind gradually came to have a clearer understanding of the nature of the deity. On the contrary, monotheism was the original religion, revealed to Adam, which then, in diverse ways in a descending process, became corrupt. Throughout history God sent prophets to teach the true path of righteousness and correct all the false ideas and practices which marked the age of *jahiliyya* (age of ignorance), particularly the animistic practices and idolatry practised in Makka in the early seventh century. These teachings have been preserved in fragmentary and partially corrupted form in the law, prophets and gospel of the Bible, but are now manifest in written form in all their perfection and finality in the Qur'an: 'There are no revised versions, no "neo-Islamic" doctrines or trends.'[32]

---

[32] S. Akhtar, op.cit., p. 189. Muslims believe that the prophets brought to their communities a pure revelation of monotheistic beliefs, which the latter then corrupted to a greater or lesser degree.

The result of this line of reasoning is that Islam is proclaimed as the primordial faith of all people. All religious expressions which do not match up to the revelation of God are inadequate approximations to the basic 'monotheistic proclivity of human nature', to humanity's 'inherently theistic tendency'.[33] As a consequence of natural inclination to serve God, Islam affirms the primacy of 'being' over 'becoming' or 'coming-into-being', for 'the object of the vision is clear, established, permanent and unchanging'.[34] Further, it follows from this that there is a natural harmony in the universe which has been established by God, and that people are free to operate within the boundaries set out in the revelation, so that they may be everything that God has intended:

> *Din* [the life of piety] is aimed at making the banks firm, in order to prevent the overflowing of the river.[35]

Even more than the Qur'an, which is after all a vehicle, Islam centres on God as the one true reality. It is fundamentally important that God is one, as the basic confession (*shahada*) of Islam stresses, for if there were more than one God, there would be disorder and chaos in the universe and disunity among the peoples. The unity of God also implies a unity of knowledge; there is no bifurcation between secular and religious sciences. Finally, the uncompromising assertion of *tawhid* (oneness of God) frees the human intellect to discover the truth by itself; it is not dependent on the authority of those who would set themselves up as intermediaries between God and humankind:

> (A) personal relationship with God and the emphasis on the individual efforts and struggles to seek and act according to objective truths whether revelational, historical, natural, or logical, is very evident in the Quranic world-view.[36]

The individual's relationship to God is constituted by *amana* (trust, in the sense of being entrusted with a high calling). Human beings have been made into trustees of God to care for

---

[33] Ibid., p. 198.

[34] *Islamic Quarterly*, 30, 1986, p. 66.

[35] G.A. Parwiz, p. 227.

[36] W.M. Nor Wan Daud, *The Concept of Knowledge in Islam and its Implications for Education in a Developing Country.* London. Mansell. 1989, p. 13.

the world and give an account of their lives on the day of judgement. Islam rejects the specifically Christian notion of the human will being biased towards evil through an original act of rebellion against God, holding that human beings have an equal capacity for good and evil, depending on whether they listen to the voice of God or not. Human freedom, intellect and other faculties are not to be used for self-gratification, but as forms of worship. The harmony and purpose of nature includes the intrinsic spiritual dimension of human beings as creatures of God. Not to recognize and nourish the spiritual, therefore, brings the disharmony, malaise and meaninglessness which is such a feature of secular societies:

> *Ibada* or worship . . . is a . . . comprehensive concept frequently joined to other key ethical terms like *shukr* (thankfulness) and *taqwa* (God-consciousness). *Taqwa* is the moral torch that man needs to make an objective evaluation of his thoughts and actions as well as his environment.[37]

Islam is fundamentally a way of life in which a human being, with the help of the fellow-members of the *dar-al-Islam* (the abode of Islam or peace), strives for an upright life:

> The term that expresses the moral and religious spirit of the Qur'an better than any other is *al-birr*, which I translate as righteousness. It occurs . . . in a number of verses in which the nearest attempt is made in the Qur'an to formulate an Islamic creed (e.g. sura 2.177).[38]

The great proportion of divine injunctions relating to human affairs are found in suras 2–5, revealed at Madina: for example, the requirements of evidence, the laws of inheritance, different kinds of punishment and matrimonial affairs.[39] It will be

---

[37] Ibid., p. 23.

[38] M. Fakhry, op.cit., p. 13. 'Righteous is he who believes in Allah and the Last Day and the angels and the Scripture and the prophets; and gives his wealth, for love of Him, to kinsfolk and to orphans and the needy and the wayfarer and to those who ask and to set slaves free; and observes proper worship and pays the poor-due (*zakah*). And those who keep their treaty when they make one, and the patient in tribulation and adversity and time of stress. Such are they who are sincere. Such are the God-fearing' (sura 2.177).

[39] Cf. A.R. Cornelius, 'The Concept of Justice in Islam' in S.M. Haider (ed.), *Islamic Concept of Human Rights*. Lahore. Book House. 1978, pp. 271–9.

obvious, both from the heavy stress on the givenness of divine guidance and the absoluteness of God and the creaturely status of human beings, whose being is realized in submission to the will of God, that Islam rejects a utilitarian basis for ethics.[40]

## The nature of freedom

As one would expect with a religion so focused on the transcendence of God freedom is linked in Islam with submission to the greatness and absolute goodness of God's will: by definition one can be truly free only when following the way of God. The individual's relationship to God is defined by two words, '*abd* (slave) and *rabb* (sovereign lord). Therefore, freedom from a recognition of God as God is not an ideal to be strived for but a disaster to be avoided.[41] A story is told about a Sufi leader, Luqman as-Sarakhsi, who asked for freedom from the service of God. The freedom he was granted was insanity.[42]

Of course, submission to God, if it is to be more than a mere formality, demands a certain degree of freedom. Human beings are responsible for their actions. In a sense their freedom is circumscribed within the framework of the call that each has to fulfil God's divine mandate that they should be a *kalifa*, a deputy of God in the world. Men and women are the sublimest part of the created order, nevertheless they remain creatures. They discover the meaning of freedom in recognizing and fulfilling their status as creatures, given the responsibility to search out the secrets of the natural order and harness its resources and power to enhance their God-given dignity. According to the Qur'an, God invested human beings with a threefold uniqueness: to be chosen by God, to be his representative on earth and to take the risk of being a trustee of a free personality.[43]

---

[40] Cf. I.O. Oloyede, 'Secularism and Religion: Conflict and Compromise (An Islamic Perspective)', *Islam and the Modern Age*, 18, 1987, p. 34.

[41] Cf. W. Montgomery Watt, *Islam and Christianity Today: a contribution to dialogue*. London. Routledge and Kegan Paul. 1983, pp. 125–7.

[42] Cf. F. Rosenthal, *The Muslim Concept of Freedom*. Leiden. Brill. 1960, p.5.

[43] Cf. A. Ahmad, op.cit. pp. 143–52. 'We offered the trust unto the heavens and the earth and the hills, but they shrank from bearing it and were afraid of it. And man assumed it' (sura 33.72).

In the light of the dilemma of freedom, the linguistic background to the term is somewhat paradoxical. The Arabic word for free is *hurr*. In its origins it was often used for the 'freeman' in contrast to *'abd*, the 'slave'. However, we have already noted that the truly free person is the one who is the slave of God. The word, therefore, came to mean freedom from the slavery of uncontrollable inner desires. In his Qur'an dictionary, ar-Raghib al-Isfahani (1100) 'distinguished two kinds of *hurriyah* (freedom), the one referring to the person who is not subject to any authority, and the other to the person who is not dominated by such ugly qualities as greed and the desire for worldly possessions'.

Fakhr-ad-din ar-Razi (1209) defines freedom in similar terms: 'Linguistically, "freedom" is used to indicate something that is opposed to slavery. It is well known that desires enslave.'

In Sufi tradition, *hurriyah* means a complete relief of the mind from any attachment other than that to God:

> When a human being arrives at . . . freedom, . . . he does not follow the command of his own soul. Rather, he becomes the owner of his soul . . . He no longer feels that divine worship is a troublesome obligation. He sees in it his joy and relaxation, and he joyfully performs it (at-Tahanawi).[44]

The core meaning of freedom within the Islamic world-view can be summed up as follows:

> The liberal emphasis on freedom from restraint is alien to Islam. Freedom in Islam is not the ability to act, but the ability to become.[45]

One may note the strong sense of a call to fulfil a destiny that has already been marked out by a compassionate Creator. Human beings are not automata, and therefore they have freedom to turn away from God's purposes. They can, and do, envisage obedience to God as restraint. However, in the act of breaking free from God's rule, they render themselves incapable

---

44 Rosenthal, op.cit., pp. 24, 27 and 28. Other significant Arabic words are: *qudra* (capability), *istita'a* (capacity), *tahrir* (emancipation or manumission), *ikhtiyar* (choice), *irada* (will), cf. M. Fakhry, op.cit., pp. 19–20.
45 A.A. Said, 'Human Rights in Islamic Perspectives' in A. Pollis and P. Schwab, *Human Rights: Cultural and Ideological Perspectives*. New York. Praeger. 1979.

of reaching their true end. If freedom is necessary to make responsibility meaningful, then in an Islamic perspective the primary responsibility is to God. Indeed, the verb *yus'alu*, from which the term, *responsibility*, comes, should be rendered 'liable to question', i.e. *answerable* for doing or believing that which is either good or reprehensible (sura 21.23). Each person will be held accountable in the day of judgement for the way he or she has used or abused his or her freedom.

The strong emphasis in Islam on the essential equality of all people, deriving from their status as *kalifa*, has a strong bearing on the notion of civil freedoms. Irrespective of a person's birth, under Islam anyone should be able to attain whatever social position is within the reach of his or her ability. Hence, equality means adequate opportunities for all. If there are distinctions of status and wealth, they must in principle be attainable by all, and they must be required by common welfare. Rank should correspond to merit. Thus, 'equality is a symbol of man's revolt against chance, fortuitous disparity, unjust power and crystallized privilege'.[46] This emphasis on equality raises the question of human rights in Islamic perspective.


## Human rights[47]

The notions of a universal declaration of human rights, human rights charters and codes of practice undoubtedly have their origins in the West in the context of the kind of social and religious forces that we have described elsewhere. As part of a

---

[46] S.M. Haider, op.cit., p. 217.

[47] An excellent survey of the main issues of human rights as these affect Muslims (and Christians) is presented in J. Schwartlander and H. Bielefeldt, *Christians and Muslims Facing the Challenge of Human Rights* (Bonn. German Bishops Conference. 1992 (ET, 1994)). Here are discussed in more detail than I have space for the same questions I mention: religious liberty and the freedom to convert, the rights and status of women, the role and intention of the shari'a, the basis in faith for human rights, the distinction between religion and politics. The potential conflict between the modern 'ethics of freedom' and traditional Islamic (and, to a much lesser extent, Christian) ways of approaching human life are unambiguously stated and debated. Whilst the document is sympathetic (and I would judge fair) to Islam, it presents a Western, Christian perspective.

world community, in which an emphasis on human rights has become a weapon of political diplomacy and economic relations, Islam has responded with its own understanding.

As one would expect from the perspective of a world-view dominated by a consciousness of human responsibility to God, human rights are not seen as an intrinsic dimension of some innate faculty, said to inhere in a man or woman as a self-enclosed and self-referring individual. Rather they are understood as the consequence of human obligations both to God and to the human community. It is for this reason that Islam does not perceive the rights of the individual as absolutely sacrosanct. They are respected only in relation to the concomitant responsibilities that are a constituent part of belonging to a community that sustains and nourishes the individual. Rights and liabilities are coextensive. Whilst the human conscience may recognize individual moral rights, social opinion recognizes social rights. Rights can be recognized only when they promote the common good of all members of society.[48]

According to A.R. Cornelius, the Islamic way of thinking gives prime importance to human communities. Rights, therefore, are consonant only with the maintenance and cohesion, progress and health of the community. Obligations to the community rank higher than the welfare of its individual members. It does not make sense, Cornelius argues, to be able to enjoy all the rights of a citizen of a particular nation, and yet at the same time to have the liberty to bring that nation into disrepute within the international community. He notes that human rights are often used as a powerful instrument in international politics in which one nation seeks to subordinate another to its concepts of freedom.[49]

Nevertheless, in an increasingly pluralist world, Muslims are coming to terms with their situation as minorities in many countries, and therefore are inclined to adopt views of human rights and freedoms not dissimilar to those expressed in the Universal Declaration. Thus, according to the *Universal*

---

[48] Cf. F. Malick, 'The Islamic Concept of Human Rights' in S.M. Haider, op.cit., pp. 49–50.
[49] 'The Islamic Concept of Human Rights' in ibid., pp. 250–66.

*Declaration of Human Rights in Islam* (Article 3), a free society is one in which 'the freedom of the human being is the very meaning of his life, where he is born free and carries out his personal destiny in liberty, free from repression, tyranny, humiliation and slavery'.[50] Hidayat Hussain maintains that the Qur'an and *sunna* spell out the fundamental right to enjoy the freedoms of conscience, contract, expression and association, the protection of life and property and to be treated only in accord with sacred law.[51] The civil rights and the personal status of minorities has been set out in the Qur'an (e.g. sura 2.256, 4.42, 5.43, 5.47, 109.6).

In spite of many assurances to the contrary, some Islamic views on human rights are suspect in certain sectors of the West. There have been three areas, in particular, where neither the theory nor the practice of freedom of action seem to measure up to the standards which a modern democracy has come to expect: the status of women, freedom of speech and religious freedom. We will look at each in turn.

## The status of women

There is no question about the intensity of debate within contemporary Islam concerning the role of women in modern society and their relationship to men. Two attitudes are in dispute between themselves. On the one hand, the traditional or customary view, whilst allowing an equal dignity to women as that given to men, believes that their subordination is given in the very constitution of human life. Men, it is argued, are

---

[50] Quoted in 'Universal Declaration of Human Rights in Islam', *Islamochristiana*, 9, 1983, 103–20. The Declaration was drawn up by an international panel of Islamic jurists.

[51] 'Due Process of Law – Process of Shari'ah' in S.M. Haider, op.cit., p. 244. According to I.R. Al Faruqi, human rights may be conveniently arranged into nine clusters, associated with birth, childhood, adulthood, economic activity, political activity, social activity, international activity and death. Thus, to give a few examples: a person's worth is not a matter of birth; children are entitled to the love and care of parents and to free education; discrimination on the basis of religion, race, colour, language, ethnicity, descent, geography or history is a threat to the unity and transcendence of God; all humans are entitled to marry and raise a family; there is the right of refuge in a Muslim state – 'Islam and Human Rights', *Islamic Quarterly*, 27, 1983, pp. 14–20.

physically stronger, and therefore should be the protectors of women. Moreover, they are more rational and less emotional than the female sex, and therefore should be entrusted with the decisions of the state and business. Women, on the other hand, being by instinct nourishers and comforters, are ideally suited to a role as leaders within the family, where they are entrusted with all the most important decisions regarding the welfare of the children and the management of the household.[52]

This conventional view is based on what appears to be the natural interpretation of sura 4.34:

> Men are in charge of women, because Allah hath made the one to excel the other, and because they spend of their property (for the support of women). So good women are the obedient . . .

From this and other verses, in the course of time, a whole code of practice has been deduced in the realms of divorce, inheritance, witnessess in the law courts and public prayers, which put woman in an inferior and disadvantageous position to that of men.

On the other hand, many Muslim commentators dispute the traditional interpretation of this and other Qur'anic verses. Some say that the verse was never intended to teach the subordination of women. Quite the contrary, it could mean that women have precedence over men, because they are the ones who manage the economy of the family.[53] Others take the verse as referring only to local and temporal conditions, prevalent in Arabia at the time,[54] and therefore not susceptible to being read as an everlasting norm.

---

[52] Cf. A. Ahmad, op.cit., p. 72. 'In traditional Islam women enjoy a secondary status, because she is looked upon and treated as the weaker sex (*zaifah*) who is emotional, irrational, unpredictable, irresponsible, indecisive, risk-aversive and mischievous and therefore is in need of man's constant supervision, protection and domination', H.R. Kusha, 'Minority Status of Women in Islam: A Debate between Traditional and Modern Islam', *Journal of the Institute of Minority Affairs*, 11, 1990, p. 58.

[53] It is often pointed out that Khadijah, the first wife of Muhammad, was a successful business women who exercised a certain role of leadership and prominence within the marriage.

[54] Thus, for example, Parwiz, op.cit., p. 223; Amir Ali in A. Ahmad, op.cit., pp. 89, 95; S. Saeed, 'The Legal Status of Muslim Women', *The Islamic Quarterly*, 24–5, 1980–1, p. 14.

The latter would argue that the Qur'an never intended the movement of women to be restricted, that it does not define different work or roles for men and women,[55] that the segregation and veiling of women was a later interpretation forced upon texts of the Qur'an (such as sura 24.30–31 and 33.53), which do not advocate anything more than due modesty of dress and the right of privacy. They would also stress, in an apparent allusion to what it is believed Christianity teaches, that women are neither blamed for sin (Islam rejects the notion of original sin) nor created as an afterthought to men.[56]

Thus, the argument for real freedom and equality for women is based first on an interpretation of the Qur'an which distinguishes between universally binding laws and those temporary regulations which were formulated to meet specific situations of the time, secondly on a rejection of customary law and, thirdly, on the customs of Muhammad himself in his own impeccable treatment of the dignity and sacredness of women. In the light of these considerations, polygamy, though allowed under strict conditions in the Qur'an, today has to be seen as an unjust and anachronistic institution, arranged marriages as tyrannical impositions, the veil as a restriction of liberty forced upon the innocent party and privileges (for example, in the laws on inheritance) given to the male members of a family as subversive of the Qur'anic insistence on the unity of all human beings.[57]

Whatever the strengths and weaknesses, in Islamic terms, of the arguments of those Muslims in favour and those against traditional attitudes towards women, a similar debate is going on to that which has been conducted in the West for the last forty or so years. It may be true that 'the Muslim woman is still wavering restlessly between two sets of values. She admires the freedom and individualism of the Westerner, yet her deep-seated tradition tells her that there is something fine about her own culture which should be preserved and cherished. She wants the

[55] Cf. A. Wadud-Muhsin, 'Understanding the Implicit Qur'anic Parameters to the Role of Women in the Modern Context', *Islamic Quarterly*, 36, 1992, p. 128.
[56] Cf. H.R. Kusha, op.cit., p. 62.
[57] Cf. A. Ahmad, pp. 73–6; A.W. Ata, 'The Impact of Westernizing and other Factors on the Changing State of Muslim Women', *Islamic Quarterly*, 30, 1986, pp. 237–47.

best of both worlds at once' . . . but in the long run she will have
to face up to the implications of what she really wants.[58] It is
also true that in most Muslim communities the actual position of
women is quite inferior to that of men.[59]

### Freedom of speech

The intense and often vitriolic controversy that was sparked
off by the publication of Salman Rushdie's novel, *The Satanic
Verses*, shows acutely the kind of dilemma Muslims face as they
confront modern views of freedom. Both the book itself and the
reaction that it produced pinpoint an enormous discrepancy
between two sets of assumptions as to what should be permitted
in contemporary societies.

Different people perceived the controversy as involving
different issues. For those who defended the writing, publishing,
release and untrammelled sale of the book, there is no question
that authors, as long as they do not contravene any law, have an
indisputable right to write whatever content and in whatever
vein and medium that they choose. Indeed, some would go
further and say that, even if certain laws might have been broken
(such as those on obscenity or blasphemy), sometimes it is the
duty of an author to 'publish and be damned', since in a more
tolerant, less prurient and less overtly religious age the laws
invoked might well be anachronistic. Moreover, the attempt by
one particular (minority) community to have a book banned
displays a lamentable lack of awareness of and sensitivity to the
consciousness of Western society in its long struggle to
institutionalize guaranteed freedoms in the face of religious and
political tyrannies. To follow this attempt by a resort to force
(burning, intimidation, incitement to murder) demonstrates an
incredible lack of judgement both about the willingness of
Western people to fight in defence of their freedoms and about
the immense harm that would be done to the image of Islam as
a result.

---

58  Ibid., p.243.
59  Cf. the data collected by A. Ahmed, *Discovering Islam*, op.cit., pp. 184–95.
Ahmed believes the plight of women in contemporary Islam is due to a
generalized reaction to the colonial era, which brought about the collapse of
the careful symmetry of traditional societies and, with it, a great sense of
insecurity. He does not, however, substantiate this opinion.

Those who were incensed by the overt message of parts of the book, by the hidden symbolism of other parts, by the apparent reasons for writing it and by the way it was received by the Western public, felt that the legitimate sensibilities of a believing community had been trampled upon, as if they had no right to exist. Two different controversies were going on simultaneously: the one between Islam and the West, and the other between Islam and Rushdie. In the latter case, Rushdie's crime was not only a religious one, as the West might interpret it (i.e. the defamation of the founder of a world religion), but a profoundly cultural one (the betrayal of his community). He was guilty not only of apostasy, in the sense of calling into question the reliability of God's revelation and the integrity of Muhammad, but of treason – he had betrayed the community (*umma*).

Many Muslims interpreted the publication of the book as a kind of conspiracy by the West to discredit their faith. They did not believe the plea that censorship would have been impossible, seeing that there are grounds of public taste and decency which, from time to time, have led to the censoring of the Western press and broadcasting media. Muslims in Britain would have been more mollified if Christians had joined forces with them to condemn both Rushdie's book and Scorsese's film, *The Last Temptation of Christ*, which was showing at the time of the publication, or if they had been willing to lobby for an extension of the law of blasphemy to cover the vilification of other religions besides Christianity.

Muslims saw Rushdie being praised by the hostile critics of Islam and then lavishly rewarded through the payment of enormous royalties. They saw him as a hybrid, born in the Indian subcontinent, Muslim by birth and upbringing, but Western by education, by speech, by marriage and by the circle of friends he moved in. For those living in Britain there were additional issues that, at the time of publication, were fermenting on the surface: the refusal of the British government to fund Muslim schools; the local community or poll tax (subsequently abolished), which was interpreted as a head count, and therefore an attempt to monitor, if not control, immigrant communities; racial discrimination and racially motivated violence, particularly against those of a Pakistani and Bangladeshi background. These contributed to the sense of scandal and betrayal, so that, according to one observer, in many respects the book 'has more to do with the social relations beyond the text than with the content of the text'.[60] Another writer points out that: 'For the majority of Asian immigrants life is a constant struggle to cling to their own cultures.'[61] Meanwhile, Western commentators accused governments in Iran, Pakistan and India (in particular) of fuelling the controversy for their own political gain.

Whatever may be the theory about human rights that anyone espouses in the cool of the seminar room or study, in the heat of a particularly difficult matter there are strongly conflicting loyalties at work. Thus, for example, Ali Mazrui admits to being torn between being a believer in Islam and in an open society, and struggles in his own mind with the question as to whether the banning of the *The Satanic Verses* would be any more legitimate than any other censorship.[62]

Another issue, wider than the controversy about the legitimacy, or otherwise, of censorship in those particular circumstances, is the freedom of minority groups in a plural society to propagate openly views they hold to be true, even when these may lead to civil unrest. For Muslims to believe in private is not enough, for it belongs to the essence of their beliefs that they necessitate public expression.

### Religious toleration

Those who live outside the *dar al-Islam* (the abode of Islam), particularly if they are Jewish or Christian believers, would like to believe that Islam holds to a non-coercive interpretation of religious commitment. It is not difficult to find the appropriate Qur'anic verses which seem to stress that compulsion is incompatible with religious belief: the most well-known is the short sentence, 'There is no compulsion in religion' (sura 2.256). The Qur'an also allows in human beings the capacity to resist God's call, which is the very criterion of true freedom of belief

---

[60] M. Fischer and M. Abedi, op.cit., p. 396.
[61] A. Ahmed, *Postmodernism and Islam*, op.cit., p. 128.
[62] Op.cit., p. 83.

(suras 5.51, 10.99 and 88.21–2, among others, have been interpreted in this way). There is a ready theological foundation for religious liberty in the divinely ordered nature of human beings. From a Qur'anic perspective, 'human rights are rooted in what every man is by nature, and this is by virtue of God's plan and creation'.[63]

Muslims have often protested that, under the regulations for the *dhimmis* (protected minorities under Islamic rule), people of other religious persuasions have complete freedom of belief and worship. According to one interpretation, the different beliefs held by separate faith communities has more to do with the accidents of history and geography than with a wilful refusal to believe the message that Muslims believe God sent to Muhammad for all humankind.[64] Though in the Qur'an polytheists are repudiated and repeatedly warned to turn from their idolatry, those who have attained to a belief in one God are commended and given assurance that 'their reward is with their Lord, and there shall no fear come upon them neither shall they grieve' (sura 2.62; also suras 2.111, 113, 136, 5.69). They are perceived to be very close to believers in Allah – 'the nearest of them in affection' (sura. 5.82) – who recognize the truth 'revealed to the messenger (i.e. Muhammad)' (sura 5. 83–4). The continuing (peaceful) coexistence of more than one religious community (in this case, Christians) seems to be implied in sura 5.48, where the believers in different Scriptures are told to 'vie with one another in good works'.

Yet there are good reasons for non-Muslims to be profoundly suspicious of the Muslim attitude to religious liberty. Alongside the Qur'anic verses which show respect to the 'people of the Scriptures' (Jews and Christians), there are others which are much more harsh: thus Jews, and particularly Christians (because of their alleged tritheism), are accused of being 'rebellious', of being 'wilfully blind and deaf' and are warned that 'a painful doom will fall on those of them who disbelieve' (sura 5.70–3; also 3.85, 9.29–30) for having falsified (hidden) the testimony which they have received from Allah (sura 2.140,

---

[63] Mohamed Talbi, 'Religious Liberty: a Muslim Perspective', *Islamochristiana*, 11, 1985, p. 102.
[64] Cf. A. Ahmad, op.cit., p. 93.

5.18). True believers are admonished not to follow the creed of either Jew or Christian, for 'then would you have from Allah no protecting friend nor helper' (sura 2.120), and are warned not to 'take the Jews and Christians for friends' (sura 5.51).

On the surface, at least, the Qur'an seems to be somewhat intolerant in its attitude to people who profess beliefs other than those which have come through 'the messenger'. It may be that many of these verses have to be interpreted against the background of a new, fragile community seeking to establish its own identity and secure its survival against the immense opposition mounted by those who certainly did not themselves believe in an easy religious pluralism. In a later age, once the faith had taken solid root in a culture among a people, Muslims could have afforded to be more magnanimous. Thus, in some periods of Islamic rule, the status of *dhimmis* allowed Christians and Jews a certain freedom to practise their respective faiths.[65] Yet, when it has suited Muslim authorities to persecute religious minorities, there is enough 'ammunition' in the Qur'an to support their strategies. Severe discrimination is not only a matter of the past (as Talbi admits[66]), but unfortunately all too common in a number of countries today, where Muslims are in control of the political apparatus.[67]

Whatever may be the balance of the case both historically and in the contemporary world, there is one case where it would seem that orthodox Muslims are adamant in their refusal to countenance religious toleration – the case of the so-called 'apostate'. According to traditional theology, although

---

[65] Although in previous times Muslims may have been more tolerant of other faiths than Christians – for example, they did not create a mechanism of persecution like the Inquisition – here we are talking of modern views and the actual reality of either discrimination or freedom of action.

[66] Op.cit., p. 107.

[67] A. Ahmed an-Naim maintains that 'discrimination on grounds of religion or belief is fundamental to traditional shariah law', and that 'even the best *dhimmah* system would violate religious freedom'. He advocates that 'the [Qur'anic] verses of compulsion and discrimination against non-Muslims' should be abrogated, in the sense of denying them legal efficacy in modern Islamic law: 'Religious Freedom in Egypt: Under the Shadow of the Islamic Dhimma System' in L. Swidler (ed.), *Religious Liberty and Human Rights in Nations and in Religions*. Philadelphia. Ecumenical Press, Temple University. 1986.

conversion to Islam is to be 'without compulsion', it is to all intents and purposes impossible to leave Islam once one is inside. Conversion to another religion (transference to the *dar al-harb*, the abode of war) from Islam is treated as treason and the apostate is liable to the death penalty.[68] Whether, or not, the death penalty is actually carried out (sometimes outside the law by religious zealots), all kinds of social pressures are applied to those who conscientiously wish to join another faith community.[69]

There shouldn't be any doubt, at this juncture of human history, that real freedom to convert, without social pressures or civil penalties, is the litmus test of genuine religious liberty. Once that is conceded, freedom of religious worship, assembly, institutions (like schools), buildings and legal protection by the state against any kind of intimidation falls into place. Oloyede, interestingly, allows that today a truly secular state is a necessity to guarantee substantitive equality and freedom for the adherents of all religions.[70]

Though in many instances espousing traditional Muslim views, it is to the credit of Shabbir Akhtar that he allows that religious freedom effectively presupposes the need to countenance desertion from a society based on Scripture and that 'heresy and even apostasy are morally more acceptable than any hypocritical attachment to orthodox opinion out of the fear of public sanctions'. Though he stresses that Islam is profoundly opposed to heresy and apostasy and cannot 'naturally tolerate leakage from the vessel of belief', nevertheless he acknowledges that these possibilities must be allowed for by what he calls 'modern integrity' – presumably the modern view of freedom in

---

[68] According to Talbi (op.cit. pp. 109–11), such a severe penalty is dependent on a *hadith*, which is not *mutawatir* (i.e. 'transmitted by several links of reliable witnesses who guarantee it'), and is not specified (nor is any other legal penalty) anywhere in the Qur'an. In all cases punishment for the apostate is left to God's judgement and the afterlife. Nevertheless, members of the community are warned that for their salvation they should not depart from their faith.

[69] A distinction is often made between these and 'secret believers', who may have changed their beliefs but without actually having submitted to an outward sign (like baptism) which is interpreted as a repudiation of their loyalty to the community.

[70] Op.cit., pp. 33–4.

which, in matters judged to pertain to private conviction, the liberty of the individual has priority over the prerogatives of the community.[71]

---

[71] Op.cit., pp. 21–2.

# Nine

# Christian Understandings of Freedom

## The Christian encounter with secular culture

Like Islam, Christianity continues to face the challenge of a secular mind-set which is now spreading inexorably across the globe. Unlike Islam, it has itself been an integral part of that world which gave rise to societies in their distinctively modern form. So powerfully disruptive has been the transition from a feudal to a modern society that all religions, to differing degrees, have been pushed on to the defensive. Their common reaction has been to fluctuate between an attitude of accommodation and one of resistance,[1] and within each religion (as we have already seen in the case of Islam) different positions are taken between the two ends.

Within the Christian tradition, those called 'liberal Protestants' and 'modernists' in the Catholic tradition have been the ones most willing to adjust the historic faith to modern

---

[1] Cf. A. Gilbert, op.cit., p. 140.

canons of thought.[2] The crucial 'surrender' has been in the areas of nature and history:

> God was banished from the world of nature and history in order to secure for man's scientific conquest an unembarrassed right of way, and for faith a sanctuary.[3]

In practice this has meant accepting the Kantian radical split between the phenomenal and noumenal worlds, a bifurcation of reality into nature and spirit. On the one hand, the Old and New Testaments of the Bible, which hitherto had been thought to provide the normative foundation for the knowledge of God and of his intentions for the world, were considered to be quite unreliable in the areas of historical reporting and the natural world. On the other hand, nevertheless, it was suggested that the Scriptures still contained a residue of 'truth' in the area of spiritual, moral and emotional life.

Two great problems have arisen directly out of the acceptance of this dichotomy: locating this residue and relating it to the public world of science and politics. The unbroken uniformity of nature apparently makes it impossible to conceive of God making an objective linguistic communication to human beings or actively engaging in the natural world. Liberal Christians constantly affirm that we must not think of the language of God's speaking and acting in a literal, but in a purely metaphorical or figurative sense. The consequences for belief of denying and reinterpreting that which the biblical authors took for granted was real about God and the world have been devastating: the universe has become a closed box and faith has been situated within the inner recesses of the human self. Religion has become a matter primarily of subjective experience; the Bible is

---

[2] This process is undoubtedly part of a debate within the Christian tradition which goes back at least to the controversy within the early church over the circumcision of Gentiles. Adaptation, contextualization, indigenization, syncretism are concepts used to explore the complex relationship between the given nature of revelation and tradition and the changing realities of cultural experience. The topic is too vast to enter into here. I am seeking to make a basic distinction between changes to the language, forms, customs and concepts of Christian faith which illuminate and which enable genuine communication and understanding to take place within different cultures, and those which produce a disparate core interpretation of the substance of the faith.

[3] I. Barbour, op.cit., p. 256.

perceived as containing an interesting record of the (admittedly profound) faith experience of other people in other times, similar in character to that registered in other religious Scriptures.[4]

At the same time, the liberal Christian tradition granted to the public world the autonomy from religious discourse it was demanding. Indeed, the newly fashioned faith was used as an instrument to guarantee the complete independence of the secular, which was to be free forever to pursue its own research and come to its own conclusions without any recourse to the message of revelation. At last, scientific and human disciplines could make sense of the world they investigated without having to appeal to Christian theology for confirmation.[5]

Even ethical theory, which in the European experience had always been closely allied to belief in the Christian God,[6] was now cut adrift from its former moorings in a supernatural reality.[7] To attempt to sustain the absolute, inalienable nature of certain rights, without the Christian foundation, the myth of a natural constitution for human beings was invented. But, because the myth was an act of sheer belief, sustained more by the need to find a substitute for the Christian ethic than by any convincing evidence, the new-found rights were easily set aside by authoritarian powers of the right and the left. These were able to argue that any specific rights which did not fit the particular visions of the future which the government espoused,

---

[4] In the mid-twentieth century there was a sustained effort in 'dialectical' or 'crisis' theology, inspired by Karl Barth, to make God's word into a reality outside and addressing human subjectivity. However, without a firm foundation for perceiving revelation as a wholly reliable communication from God coming into time and space from outside, this attempt withered and died. For many people from a liberal Christian background, religious experience today is no longer couched necessarily in Christian language, but in the language of many faiths.

[5] Cf. J. Milbank, op.cit., p. 208.

[6] For example, Locke's doctrine of natural rights is fully intelligible only in the context of a conception of natural law as an expression of the divine nature and ordained by God, cf. J. Gray, op.cit., pp. 12, 23.

[7] I think this is now true not only in respect of (a) an objective moral law communicated to specially chosen people by a personal, communicating God or of (b) the natural law of a creator inscribed in the workings of nature and accessible to reflective human reason, but also of (c) the subjective moral law that is called conscience and which, in former times, was held to be the 'still, small voice' of God in the innermost soul.

corresponded only to historically conditioned social perceptions, not to any imaginary permanent human essence.

The notion of a given truth, which confronts us independently of situation, desire, need or effectiveness, has all but completely vanished beyond the horizon of human consciousness. If the Creator-God is outside the system of knowing that the modern world has accepted as the only valid or ultimately reliable one, human beings are alone and are compelled to recreate their own world with whatever resources lie to hand. Christianity may have a hand in this, because it has shaped the Western world in numerous ways (and the liberal Christian strives particularly hard to show the usefulness and relevance of certain carefully selected elements of the tradition[8]), but it certainly has no monopoly on valid insights into the human condition, many of which may equally well now come from committed humanists or members of other faith communities.

Preference for the autonomy of reason over the integrity of revelation has had a profound effect on the course of human history. No longer is it possible to assume that one framework for life possesses universal validity:

> If religion is essentially to do with private experience, it becomes ineffable and non-identifiable . . . Then it cannot be shown to be a universal constant.[9]

Reason on its own operates in the realm of matters that can be scientifically investigated and quantified. It gathers an enormous variety of particular data, like a fruit picker on a farm in the height of summer. But it has no means of moving from such particulars to a cogent, coherent system of belief and moral action.

The liberal Protestant and modernist Catholic venture began by using the notion of a self-authenticating, rational, critical scholarship to undermine the credibility of the Bible. It sought to capture the Bible and remove it from its context in the Christian community, in order to be able to tell the whole human community what it really means when stripped of its

---

[8] Cf. L. Sanneh, op.cit., pp. 208–9; J. Milbank, op.cit., p. 15; Lesslie Newbigin, op.cit., p. 80.
[9] J. Milbank, op.cit., p. 127.

'unacceptable' mythical elements. In the process, it has rendered the Bible inoffensive,[10] a mere reflection of the latest and best Western liberal thinking.

Since the Bible has now been thoroughly domesticated, people are able to take from the text anything which seems to them particularly inspiring, comforting or fitting for their needs. Much modern theology has taken upon itself the task of (to coin a phrase) 'sprinkling holy water' on anything that is new in modern culture. The faith has been split into myriad portions designed for a consumer-led and user-friendly market. And the agent who has performed this modern miracle is Hermes, the winged messenger of the gods. Through his currently fashionable skill (hermeneutics) we are offered interpretations to suit everyone's inclinations. The text becomes marvellously elastic in the hands of those who begin from the premise that the meaning of a text is located, not in the intention of its author, but in the impact it makes upon the readers as they seek to make sense of their world of experience.[11]

Other Christians, described as conservatives or traditionalists,[12] have attempted, in various ways and to differing degrees, to resist the fundamental assumptions of modern secular thought. Some enormously regret the passing of an age, when the teaching of the church was given solemn credence in the affairs of both individuals and the state. They see in religion a necessary counter-balance to a society and culture always in flux. It has a role to preserve those beliefs, customs and values in the inherited tradition which are wise and valuable. It provides a link with the past which gives continuity, and therefore stability, to human history. They criticize, therefore, the *hubris* which imagines that what is contemporary is necessarily superior to what has passed.

---

[10] Cf. A. Bloom, op.cit., p. 374.

[11] Cf. K. Vanhoozer, 'The World Well-Staged? Theology, Culture and Hermeneutics' in D. Carson and J. Woodbridge, op.cit.; M. Moriarty, op.cit.; A. Bennet, op.cit., Chapters 1 and 2..

[12] They represent the majority of Christians worldwide 'on the ground', for Christians of a liberal persuasion are located mainly among the intellectual elite of the various churches of which they form a part.

Their 'philosophy' of history is likely to include the notion of a former 'golden age' (the Apostolic Church, the high Middle Ages, the Reformation, the age of Catholic spirituality, the modern missionary movement or even, though recently somewhat ridiculed, the age of Victorian values), when faith was both much purer and taken far more seriously than it is today. They also tend to find the cause of most modern ills in some cataclysmic event of the 'modern age' such as Luther's rebellion against the authority of Rome, the Counter-Reformation and Inquisition, the divorce between science and theistic belief, the rise of the *vox populi* in the French Revolution, the Enlightenment's freeing of human thought from the authority of God, the liberating of economics from ethical discussion or the rise of Marxism. Their approach to the Bible is likely to be dogmatic and inflexible, using methods of interpretation which defend cherished beliefs and assumptions against the threatening challenge of change.

There are yet other Christians who are neither wholly accommodators nor resisters. On the one hand, they believe that the destructive forces unleashed in the contemporary world are in large part due to the assumptions which are peculiar to modernity: thus, in the area of human existence, there is a profound loss of the concepts of meaning, identity and purpose which hitherto have elevated and ennobled human dignity; in the area of knowledge, there is a cacophony of discordant and confusing sounds which, in the implicit absence of any certain knowledge of the truth, breeds indifference and violence; in the area of moral values, people have had to become a law to themselves, but as a result have no way of coping adequately with the guilt, shame and inconsistency they feel.

These Christians want to insist that the modern age, despite all the prophecies to the contrary, has not yet finished with the question of truth. They believe that those who, for whatever reason, hold that truth is no longer a possible subject for debate and resolution will constantly find that the absence of truth creates for themselves and society a void (like a black hole) which devours everything within its range, and will therefore need to re-open the question. In other words, they are hopeful that some crucial aspects of modern consciousness will eventually be seen to be untenable, because they are self-contradictory, self-defeating and self-immolating.

On the other hand, they recognize that the past is not where a person is called to live, even were it to be possible. History is much more ambiguous than any notion of a lost innocence can possibly allow. Every period of history has its own inheritance of things both good and bad. There are many things that we enjoy today, unknown to our forebears, which Christians can accept as gifts of a providential God who seeks the welfare of his creatures. It is true that some may be used for destructive ends, but may serve creative and healing ends as well. They recognize that some changes in thinking and living, fiercely resisted by Christians in the past, are entirely acceptable and beneficial. There is much that is corrupt and harmful in contemporary life; it is, however, a moot point whether one could ever say that on balance our society is any more evil than those that have gone before. With regard to understanding and communicating the message of the Bible they recognize that particular interpretations are not necessarily free from unexamined assumptions, prejudices and ideological commitments of one kind or another. In responding to the many challenges of secular assumptions they are typically neither liberals nor conservatives, neither mainly accommodators nor mainly resisters.

A strong case can be made for reading human history in terms of cycles of renewal and decline, or rather of a mixture of the two in which one or other of the poles may come to predominate for a time and then be replaced by the other. The evidence today suggests that the balance is being tipped towards a decline of authentically human values. However, this is always a slow and relative process, in the sense that there has not been an obvious peak from which the descent is taking place, and it is modified by signs that point in the opposite direction. A major piece of evidence, either for renewal or decline, is how any generation understands and deals with the reality of freedom.

## The Christian world-view

We have not space to do justice to the many intricate problems which surround a comprehensive discussion of the distinctively Christian way of perceiving existence, or the roots and sources

of that view.[13] I can only state in broad outline what I take to be
the consensus of most Christian communities, when they have
been challenged to define their views as ecclesial bodies on such
matters as the authority of the Bible, the nature of God and
God's relationship to the world, the meaning and scope of
salvation, the moral life and alternative world-views.[14]

The Christian faith is centred on a living relationship to God,
understood in a manner consonant with the entire message of
the New Testament, which has originated in the unique story of
Jesus of Nazareth, whom Christians confess to be the one
specially anointed by God to bring salvation to the world. The
message claims that this life, as narrated in the four Gospels, and
lived out in the rest of the New Testament, is normative for the
rightness, or otherwise, of all other stories, so that 'everything

---

[13] My own approach to the reality of a world-view, to the relationship between
both history and faith and between the meaning of God and Jesus of Nazareth
and to the study of the documents of the New Testament, is in broad agreement
with that proposed by N.T. Wright, in *The New Testament and the People of God*.
London. SPCK. 1992, Chapters 1–5, 16. In particular, I appreciate his
willingness to call into question many of the methodological blind-allies into
which biblical scholarship has wandered, owing to its inability or
unwillingness to examine critically many of its dubious assumptions. My views
on the place of Christianity among the religions of the world has been set out
in J.A. Kirk, *Loosing the Chains: religion as opium and liberation*. London.
Hodder and Stoughton. 1992.

[14] I am aware, of course, that substantial differences remain between
Christians on some important matters – not least that of the locus of authority
for Christian belief and action. Nevertheless, the last thirty years has shown a
remarkable convergence between different Christian traditions on a wide
range of issues, as witnessed in bilateral talks between separate world
confessional movements, in multilateral talks within the World Council of
Churches and in conversations between representatives of the conciliar
movement and evangelical Christians. In terms of our discussion of a Christian
understanding of freedom, I estimate there would not be any wide divergence
on either the basis or content of the discussion.

It is also worth bearing in mind that the controversial views of some church
leaders and academics, so prominent in the media, hardly ever represent the
opinions of more than a small minority of church members. A necessary
distinction has to be made between the views of individuals, whatever their
personal status or the plausibility of their opinions, and the considered view of
the church, speaking through its proper channels (i.e. episcopal conferences,
synods or general assemblies).

which subsequently happens is nothing but the acceptance or the rejection of Christ'.[15] In order to understand the meaning of these claims, which one would expect to be fiercely disputed by all who do not call themselves Christians, they will be set out in a little more detail.

Though Christians share with Jews and Muslims belief in one personal divine being who created all that exists, there is no disguising the differences between their respective perceptions:

> Judaism claimed that Christianity, by putting Jesus in the middle of its doctrine of god, had irreparably damaged that doctrine. Christianity claimed that mainline Judaism, in clinging to the idea of national privilege and not recognizing the righteous saving act of her own god in the death and resurrection of Jesus, had stepped aside from the covenant. Both religions claimed that they were giving the true meaning to the word 'god', in line with prior scriptural revelation, and that the other was not.[16]

The Christian view of God is not only shaped *by* Jesus of Nazareth, in the sense that he put forward a profound and distinctive teaching, it is that Jesus *is* 'part of God' – a conviction which scandalizes Jews and Muslims with their 'mathematically precise' understanding of God's unity. However, in a Christian world-view the trinitarian account of God is not negotiable, simply because God is wholly present in Jesus in a way which demonstrates the nature and appearance of God as no other means of communication could.[17] Thus, the 'way of Jesus Christ' is, without any addition or subtraction, the way of God.

Christians are drawn to confess that all we can or need to know about God is in principle contained in this one human-divine story, and that therefore there is no abstract, universal knowledge of God, of which the Christ is but one manifestation among others. Such a 'cosmic God' is a fiction of the imagination of those who would see all religious beliefs as expressions of the human experience of the same divine reality,

---

15  J. Milbank, op.cit., p. 383.
16  N.T. Wright, op.cit., p. 474.
17  J. Moltmann in particular has explored in depth the significance for an understanding of God of the passion of Christ. A summary of his view can be found in J. Moltmann, op.cit., pp. 172–81.

a phantom figure who inhabits the shadows of the fantasy world of the religious pluralist. There is no substance there. About such a being one would always have to be agnostic, for there is not enough substance or evidence to convict it of not existing.

There should be no embarrassment about the accusation that the Christian view of God is arrogant, because apparently exclusive: Christians affirm that what they know about God has been freely given to them, that it does not depend in any way upon their superior wisdom or mode of life, that it is knowledge which they do not 'own', freely available to the whole of humanity without exception or prejudice, and in no way implying an assured knowledge of where 'God is not'.

So, for a Christian world-view, truth-claims are fundamental. The message about Jesus (the gospel) could not be 'good news', unless it was 'true news'.[18] This avowal of truth is, perhaps, a revolutionary creed in the modern world, used to considering that all beliefs are relative to particular histories, cultures and subjective judgements. However, only a little reflection shows that acceptance of the relativity of all views is itself a truth-claim which, if it is to be substantiated, has to appeal to some absolute vantage-point. *The proper alternative to the claim to truth is not relativism but agnosticism*, a refusal to make any statement about the way the world is. This may be a possible intellectual position, but it is not one by which a person is able to live on a daily basis. The Christian claim is, then, that a non-Christian cannot live consistently with his or her non-Christian world-view. Though unconsciously and quite innocently, sooner or later non-Christians, in order to live coherently, will have to borrow elements from the Christian world-view, even if they repudiate its fundamental convictions.

It must be said that it is part of the Christian world-view that its understanding of reality has to be open to discussion and ultimately to verification or refutation. It takes the risk of staking everything on there being a fundamental congruence between reality as experienced by every human being and the Christian interpretation of that reality. To put this another way, Christians, without wanting to suggest simplistic answers to complex issues or to claim that they have the whole truth, or a monopoly on the

---

[18] L. Newbigin, *Truth to Tell*, op.cit., p. 52.

truth, do believe that in principle there is a perfect correlation between their world-view and the world as it is. This means, among other things, that human beings will perform to their highest ability, will be all that they are meant to be, will understand themselves fully, only when they follow in the way of Jesus, seeing life through his eyes. From a Christian point of view this undoubtedly has fundamental significance for the meaning of freedom.

## Perspectives on freedom

### (i) The structure of creation

As one would expect from a faith whose Scripture begins with the words, 'In the beginning God created the heavens and the earth' (Gen.1.1), Christians believe that the universe manifests an essential, underlying order. This order is manifested in the first place in a set of relationships which exist between the Creator, human beings, who stand at the apex of creation, and the rest of the natural world. There is a mutual interaction between the relationships and the order, such that the harmony of one is dependent on the harmony of the other. Both the order and the relationships are given in the act of creation itself. Indeed, classical Christian theology has spoken of 'the orders of creation' (e.g. the family, work, political life, artistic endeavour, technological innovation) as existing prior to any human decision. They are gifts that come as part of the very warp and woof of life itself.[19]

From this fundamental understanding of the structure of life comes the idea of a natural law by which the whole of the created order, and in particular human beings and societies, function. The law, according to Christian 'natural theology', is discernible in part by all human beings through their disciplined research into and reflection upon the workings of nature and through their own conscience. It reflects the maker's way of regulating the created object, so that it operates in the best

---

[19] Cf. R.H. Preston, op.cit., p. 76.

fashion possible. Whenever the law is broken, the book of instructions, as it were, is being either ignored or rewritten and the result is *dis*order and *dys*function.

In fact, the universe has a marvellous, intricate design[20] and structure; it will run smoothly in so far as each part is in the right relationship to all the other parts. The key to the notion of natural law is 'fine tuning', not in the sense that the universe, and even less human beings, are to be understood wholly in mechanistic terms, but in the sense that both the whole and its parts work to perfection only when certain conditions are in place. For the sake of human beings, the order is moral: i.e. there are right and wrong ways of behaving and acting in accordance with or contradiction to the given order. This has implications for what used to be called 'situational ethics', and today is better known as 'contextual ethics', which is based on the belief that the proper course of action depends on a given set of circumstances and not on fixed principles. From a Christian perspective on creation this view breaks down into an anarchic improvisation, because it does not respect the given order:

> Preferring to assume that the universe is still waste and void, awaiting the cry of the human voice, 'Let there be . . . ', we have no idea what is to follow![21]

It follows that there is an inevitable causal nexus in the moral life, sometimes expressed in the saying, 'People reap what they sow.' Right human relations, which depend upon respect for the other, trust, the willingness to serve the other's needs, absence of fear, jealousy and authoritarianism, cannot emerge out of

---

[20] Recent research into the state of the universe at its earliest moment of existence following the 'big bang' have shown that life as we know it would not have been possible if the physical variants had deviated by even an infinitely small amount. Many people, surveying the amazing nature of the evidence, have formulated what has come to be called the 'anthropic principle' which states that 'a physical world which is fruitful in evolving complexity out of simplicity, to the degree that an almost homogeneous ball of energy becomes, after fifteen billion years, a home for self-conscious beings, is not in scientific terms 'any old world', but rather one which is very special in the finely tuned balance of its law and circumstance', J. Polkinghorne, op.cit., p. 77. Cf. also I. Barbour, op.cit., pp. 135–6 and S. Hawking, *A Brief History of Time*, p. 121.
[21] O. O'Donovan, op.cit., p. 25.

arrogance, suspicion, selfishness, anxiety, rivalry and the will to dominate.

From the perspective of a created order autonomy and freedom are very different things. 'Autonomy' conceives the world as formless and malleable, without any binding reality that would constrain us in any way. It follows that imagination (as expressed in some forms of art, for example) is free to use the material world in whatever way it may fancy. Reality becomes whatever takes our whim; ultimately it is mere fantasy, dream, invention. Whatever we create out of the depths of our inner self is good, true and beautiful, because its reality is confirmed in the creative act itself. 'Freedom' conceives the world as possessing a meaning which is already inherent within it, but which, nevertheless, allows immense scope for exploring and giving a diversity of expression to the underlying form.

Here are two ways, probably irreconcilable, of encountering the world. For the first, existence, if it came as an already given reality, would be experienced as a prison from which we need liberating. For the second, a given reality is the necessary precondition of genuine freedom, since in the absence of some necessary boundaries chaos and confusion reign and they are, and always have been, destructive forces.

### (ii) The existence of evil

The preceding discussion finds graphic expression in the second account of creation in Genesis. The story tells how God put the man and the woman whom he had formed into a lush garden. It contained all kinds of trees to grow, both ornamental ('pleasing to the eye') and edible ('good for food'). God gave one word of warning:

> You are free to eat of any tree in the garden, but you must not eat
> from the tree of the knowledge of good and evil, for when you eat
> of it you will surely die (Gen. 2:16–17).

To speculate about why God forbade the man and the woman to eat the fruit of one particular tree would be to miss the point, at least within the context of our discussion. God has simply confirmed the principle that freedom is set within the ultimate bounds of a moral order. They have immense freedom. They are 'free to eat of *any* tree in the garden.' This is not imprisonment, restriction or petty-mindedness. The man and the woman may sample and experiment as far as they are able to wander. Moreover, God endows the man with freedom to name all the animals as he wishes. 'Whatever the man called each living creature, that was its name' (Gen. 2:19).

As we have seen, this freedom was not without limits. There was one boundary beyond which the pair might not trespass. Their well-being depended upon exercising their considerable freedom within this limitation. Erich Fromm is right, therefore, to point out that sinfulness arose directly from the original misuse of freedom.[22] By going beyond the limit, the first human pair broke the harmony of the created order and the result was a tragic disruption of the harmony of relationships. And so, according to the Christian interpretation of the world, it has been ever since.

Here we find a fundamental disagreement between secular and Christian views of evil. For the former, evil is basically imperfection. It occurs when external conditions cause disruptions in the psyche (the centre of the mechanical operations of the human person). From these arise the kinds of neuroses, psychoses and aberrations described in psychiatric medicine. For the Christians, evil is the result of a perverse will. It happens as the result of a personal choice to disregard the order of creation and break relationships.[23] It may be partly caused or exacerbated by external conditions, but those do not constitute the main explanation of its existence.

The alternative accounts can be seen, to take one example, in the differing approaches to the exploitation of work. Marxists, for example, describe the workings of the capitalist mode of production as an alienation of human beings from one another and from their own creative impulses. They depict how this works through the expropriation of the 'surplus value' of human labour by the capitalist owning class, creating a conflict at the very heart of human society. Once the external conditions are changed (either by revolutionary means or by the eventual internal collapse of capitalism), human beings will live in a non-alienated relationship to one another.

---

22 op.cit., p. 27.
23 Cf. J. Milbank, op.cit., p. 125.

Christians would not necessarily disagree with this analysis of the way capitalist economics are set up, although they would want to debate the enormously more complex question of ownership in today's world. But they would ask some more radical questions about the way the mode of production is organized. Why do some want to exploit others? Why do some wish to pursue and hold on to power, even when it means that others suffer through their action? Why, if the apparently true nature of reality were exposed, would they not be willing to share their power equitably with all?

A Marxist might reply that this is the necessary stage of economic development through which humanity has to go, in order to transcend exploitation once for all. If that is so, then words like exploitation and alienation have to be divested of any moral content or connotation, for they are simply technical economic terms which explain an internally determined process. On this view, the relationship between workers and owners of capital is a purely historical-mechanistic one. If, on the other hand, the reply to the question is that the subjection of one human being to another by force has always been part of the real world, then the Christian understanding of evil has been conceded. On a Christian understanding of evil in human affairs the Marxist analysis is hopelessly naive.

One way in which Christians have tried to understand the persistent, deep-rooted nature of sinfulness in human beings is in terms of idolatry. By this is meant something much more radical than honouring or reverencing external objects: idolatry is the choice to abandon, in whole or in part, the order of things created by God, and to seek to live in a world of one's own construction. Paul uses the word *exchange* to describe the process:

> they exchanged the truth of God for a lie, and worshipped and served created things rather than the Creator (Rom. 1:25).

Idolatry arises out of dissatisfaction with having to live on the basis of someone else's (God's) truth and entails the creation of myths (i.e. interpretations of the meaning and purpose of life) by which to nourish the deviant life which has been chosen instead.[24]

---

[24] Cf. E.P. Sanders, op.cit., p. 105.

One may observe the 'exchange' of Romans 1:25 in the way in which societies respect some moral principles and neglect, or repudiate, others. There is a confusion in our human encounter with the real world, for to the extent that we are not willing to accept the basic structures which have been given, we do not know what is real and what illusion. One possible result is the invention of a false moral order, as if it were part of the structure of creation. This has certainly been done in former times in the name of Christianity, e.g. in the assertion of the inviolability of a hierarchical mode of being (the natural right of some to rule), in the presumed subservience of women to men, or in notions of racial supremacy. Moral arguments from a created order are particularly vulnerable to the danger of being used to sanction whatever *status quo* happens to suit those who employ the argument. For this reason, when true to itself, Christianity has balanced this structural emphasis with another which stresses God's transforming will. Arguments from creation are balanced by the (equally real) future prospect of a new creation in which all things are remade.

The existence of evil in the terms in which we have described it creates a tremendous problem for freedom. Oliver O'Donovan sees it as a tearing apart of the human will and human reason:

> In the will's convulsive embracing of evil the reason must find a point of rest. It cannot rest in the reality of chaos which the will has embraced, but must create for itself a new order, a fantastic order without objective reality or substance, formed around the new orientation of the will, a parodistic imitation of reality which it calls 'my' good . . . From then on reason is enslaved to this new orientation of the subject, obligated to form representations which justify it . . . In the free exercise of the will to sin, man deprives himself of his freedom, for he cuts off his cognitive access to the created order.[25]

This is a sober account of the human predicament, as the Christian faith sees it, once human beings abuse their freedom by choosing to cross forbidden frontiers. Later, we will explore some particular instances of this abuse and the consequences it brings.

---

[25] Op.cit., pp. 111–12.

## (iii) Liberation into true freedom

The nature of freedom depends on the nature of the slavery, or other constraint, from which one seeks to be liberated. The Old and New Testaments recognize that there are external forms of captivity from which it is right that human beings should be freed, such as exploitation by others, starvation and forms of physical restraint (e.g. Ps. 146:7; Isa. 61:1). The liberation of the Hebrew people from slave-labour under the Egyptian ruling aristocracy is a prime example of this kind of freedom. It has been taken as the model of God's constant and resolute intention that some people should not be subjected to a brutal assault on their human dignity by others. The memory of the Exodus became the major foundation for a series of laws designed both to institutionalize certain freedoms in the nation of Israel and to frustrate the curtailment of individuals' freedoms, as a result of adverse circumstances (poor harvests, the early death of a breadwinner) or the manipulation of economic power (mainly through loans and debt repayments).

However, vitally important though these freedoms were and are, the Scriptures consider that freedom from idolatry, in the terms we have discussed, is even more basic. A conversation between Jesus and some of his fellow-Jews goes to the heart of the matter:

> If you hold to my teaching, you are really my disciples. Then you will know the truth, and the truth will set you free . . . If the Son sets you free, you will be free indeed (John 8:31–8).

The debate is about the origin, achievement and consequences of freedom. The Jews argued that their ethnic ancestry and identity gave them the guarantee of freedom, in the sense of not being enslaved by anybody (v. 33). By this they meant both external coercion and oppression and internal colonization by alien philosophies and religious traditions (Judaism taught that the study of the Law makes a man free – cf. *Pirke Aboth* 3.5). Nevertheless, the two parties were not discussing abstract philosophical principles. In the context, Jesus' life was under threat because of the message he was delivering. He accused the Jews of being enslaved by lies, because they had deliberately turned their back on the real truth that came from God. They were locked into their own version of the truth which did not match the ultimate truth, embodied in Jesus.[26] Rather than acknowledge that ultimate truth, they sought to eliminate it, and the inevitable result was that they put themselves under the authority of a distorted interpretation of reality.

The discourse illustrates two profound realities about freedom. In the first place, freedom cannot be built on lies (a more powerful and accurate word than error). Freedom is dependent upon having an accurate and undistorted view of human life in the world. Unfortunately, Jesus' opponents had built their world-view on the inviolability of their culture and ethnic identity. In the second place, as the distinction between truth and untruth becomes ever more blurred, freedom becomes increasingly less of a possibility. This can be seen to occur when individuals or even a whole culture becomes insensitive to the truth. What happens is that 'unbelief has become an attitude of life in self-enclosure, a hardening or stubbornness'.[27] 'The flaw is not with the communicator, but with those whose values and prejudices make them constitutionally unable to "hear"'.[28]

In the light of contemporary debate about language and whether it reflects or creates reality, it is fascinating that language occupies a central place in this discussion of whether a person is either free or enslaved. The question is not about the language or its use that is at fault, but whether there is an ultimate truth which language either reveals or obscures. It is not only contemporary minds that struggle with issues of language, for the problem is much the same as in the time of Jesus: whether the mind is able to listen to the voice of the 'outsider' (Jesus of Nazareth), or whether it remains imprisoned within a closed circle of its own assumptions and prejudices. The predicament for many of Jesus' audience was their inability to recognize the truth when it stood before them, because they had already come to accept as valid another (religious) way of

---

[26] 'Jesus is the truth, because he embodies the supreme revelation of God – he himself 'narrates' God (John 1:18), says and does exclusively what the Father gives him to say and do (John 5:19ff; 8:29), indeed he is properly called "God"(John 1:1,18; 20:28)' D.A. Carson, *The Gospel according to John*. Leicester. IVP. 1991, p. 491.

[27] G.R. Beasley-Murray, *John* (Word Biblical Commentary, Vol. 36). Milton Keynes. Word (UK) Ltd., 1991, p. 135.

[28] D.A. Carson, op.cit., p. 353.

looking at reality. In the fierce conviction that they were being faithful to what God *had* revealed, they were unable to respond to what God *was* revealing.

When the first Christians took the message of freedom in Jesus Christ to the peoples of the Roman empire, and beyond, they encountered similar difficulties. Their message provoked a clash of world-views, which they interpreted as in part a conflict between differing beliefs about the meaning of freedom. It was to Gentile Christians in the province of Galatia in Asia Minor, that Paul wrote, 'It is for freedom that Christ has set us free. Stand firm, then, and do not let yourselves be burdened again by a yoke of slavery' (Gal. 5:1). He had heard that itinerant religious evangelists were persuading the new Christians to return to beliefs and practices which had formerly denied them a proper freedom. The specific requirement was the strict observance of the law, understood as complying with the meticulous regulations required by belonging to a particular community. These, Paul argued, had ceased to have any value in terms of the new message they had accepted (Paul refers particularly to circumcision, ceremonial observances and rules regarding 'clean' and 'unclean' categories.)

The problem, Paul said, was not with the Law, which both Paul and his opponents acknowledged as having its origin with God, but with making its observance the principle by which one seeks to live. As the main axiom for orientating one's life, the keeping of laws brings bondage, not freedom. A life centred on correct action is ultimately a self-centred life, for it leads to continued preoccupation with the question of whether the demands of the law have been fulfilled, whether one has 'done enough'. It becomes a self-regarding life, a life of internal self-scrutiny. Ultimately, if carried to excess, it generates obsessive and burdensome scrupulosity.

There are further problems about prescribing law as a response to human dilemmas. Invoking law as a remedy highlights an unresolved paradox in contemporary societies. On the one hand, law is seen as an externally imposed means of regulating or restricting personal freedoms; this is why there is so much pressure for increasing 'deregulation', e.g. in economic life and medical procedures.[29] On the other hand, law is rightly seen as necessary to curb the abuse of freedom (increasingly in corrupt business practices and violence against the vulnerable and minorities). In the latter case, in the absence of a genuine freedom, too much expectation is invested in the ability of the law to produce a more righteous society. Law is necessary as a consequence of human sin, but it also exacerbates the problem by both showing the extent of sin (the range of laws and regulations demonstrates the reality that people cannot be trusted to act with moral integrity) and tempting people into breaking the law. So, law becomes simultaneously vilified and condoned.

We see a 'modern' response to this dilemma when people who lack a firm knowledge of the truth seek to resolve the paradox by arbitrarily selecting those laws which they personally believe are necessary. The measures that one person sees as an absolute necessity to help stem the rush of the swine towards the abyss of the further disintegration and dehumanizing of life are seen by another as an illegitimate restriction on personal choice. Depending, then, on individual self-interest, the law is regarded either as a vital agent in the struggle against violence and deceit or alternatively as an unacceptable impediment to the enjoyment of individual rights. See below for more examples of the way the paradox works in our actual world.

Paul's message was that 'Christ is the end of the law' (Rom. 10:4). He brought the good news that 'what the law was powerless to do in that it was weakened by [our] sinful nature, God did by sending his own Son . . . to be a sin offering' (Rom. 8:3). In place of law as a means of achieving a morally upright life, the Gospel declares another principle: that of a life of trust, centred on God who offers that freedom from self-righteousness and self-concern which are needed if men and women are to respond to all of God's demands. If the fundamental predicament which humanity lives, keeping it in thrall to a false

---

[29] The article by Simon Jenkins, 'A Plot against the Family?', *The Times*, Wednesday, June 6, 1994, p. 16, is fairly typical of those who do not believe the government has any mandate to intervene to control the new techniques of human fertilization. It is a predictable presentation of a utilitarian ethic, in which the '(private) 'happiness' of an infertile couple (heterosexual or homosexual), or even a single woman, becomes the only consideration.

world, is that of idolatry and untruth, the solution is to be freed from this spurious life and brought into a new way of perceiving and living our human existence. For the New Testament there are two kingdoms, which between them control every member of the human race. One causes its subjects to be morally and spiritually blind, the other opens their eyes to the true nature of reality (cf. Col. 1:12–14; Acts 26:18; 1 Cor. 6:9–11; Eph. 5:5, 8–11).

According to this view, freedom is the fruit of conversion – a radical transformation of the way one is oriented as a person, either towards the truth as it is revealed in Christ or towards the false assumptions of a world unconscious of any need to be accountable to its Creator. The change is made possible by God himself who, in the death and the conquest of death by Jesus Christ, has taken upon himself all the consequences of our epistemological futilities, existential confusions and moral blindnesses and broken their power to keep us enslaved to an unreal world.

### (iv) The necessity of community

We have already seen how modern concepts and experiences of freedom lead to the break-up of genuine community life. The stress on the rights of individuals rather than on responsibilities to various communities is a central feature of modern societies. Individualism is incompatible with genuine community, for a community can function only when its members, to a greater or lesser extent, resist a life which seeks first its own fulfilment or pleasure. If 'freedom' is taken to mean the right or ability to choose one's own way of life, without the restrictions imposed by obligations to others, then Christians are not called to such freedom; their calling is to be the servant of all.[30] But even more, they are called to practise the freedom they have in Jesus Christ by being part of the creation of a new type of society.

Contrary to the belief of many in the West, it is not possible to be a Christian on one's own. The idea of faith as an internal, personal matter which one may exercise if one is so inclined without any necessary relationship to the faith of others is a contradiction of Christianity. It drives to one extreme the

---

[30] Cf. S. Hauerwas, op.cit., p. 129.

Protestant emphasis on personal response as a necessary part of genuine faith in God. It is reinforced by the cultural insistence that the individual is the locus of belief and action and by the notion that faith has more to do with the territory into which one was born than with a voluntary community to which one chooses to belong.

For the Christian faith, however, God's purpose is not so much the salvation of isolated individuals as the reconstitution of authentic human community, broken by the abuse of freedom. The church is intended to be the first-fruits of a new society, where people use their gifts and talents for the benefit of all. Baptism, which is the sign and symbol of the beginning of the Christian life, is always baptism into the 'body of Christ', a corporate entity in which each part is dependent on the proper functioning of all the others.

Acceptance of the Christian faith entails, therefore, acceptance of the community, the church. This may seem a contradiction of freedom, in that, although in its institutional form the church is a voluntary society (one may choose to join or not), in its theological understanding it is a society to which one has to belong to be a follower of Christ at all. Moreover, there is no justification for driving a wedge between the actual visible institution and some imaginary invisible reality of which one is a member merely by thinking about it.

Again, the notion of a non-voluntary community appears to be a severe contradiction of modern concepts of freedom in that we are used to thinking of freedom in terms of becoming part of a group of people (such as a club) to whom we naturally relate because they are 'our kind of people'. The church, on the other hand, comprises all sorts of people to whom we may not be related either biologically, culturally or in terms of any other affinity at all. The church is a community of people called by God to belong to Jesus Christ and be his followers (1 Cor. 1:9). It includes 'all sorts and conditions' of people who, precisely, may not be 'my type'.

The church thus points to the paradox of freedom. In a state of naked individuality, in which the measure of freedom is the ability to stand on our own feet, owing nothing to anyone, we are not free. We become free when we learn, often with many tears and struggles, to be an integral part of a community in which all kinds of barriers are being broken down and broken relationships mended. The church's calling is to be a family in which reconciliation and forgiveness takes place, in which we learn not to be self-assertive, but to look first to the interests of others, and allow ourselves to be served by them.

This is the ideal. We are speaking of a community in which the personal abilities of each member are recognized and allowed to flourish for the edification of all. The reality, however, is often different. The church can be a profoundly unfree place by virtue of the fact that some use it to achieve their own selfish ambitions, live out their fantasies or externalize their irrational anxieties. The church too often suffers from the emotional and intellectual inadequacies of its leaders and the passivity of some . members who use it, not necessarily in a conscious way, as a refuge from the demands of daily living.

Nevertheless, the church stands as a permanent reminder that freedom should not be equated with the pursuit of the satisfaction of one's own desires or the rejection of responsibilities to others, and that owning one's place in the community is not a restriction on freedom, but part of fulfilling the destiny for which one has been created. As long as our culture insists that freedom and the widening of personal choice are identical, those who are deceived by this cultural dream will find membership of the church too costly. On the other hand, people who have experienced the joy of responsibility freely assumed by a group of individuals dedicated to caring both for one another and for those outside know that belonging to such a group is a profoundly liberating experience.

**Some consequences of Christian understandings of freedom**

*(i) The answer to a meaningless existence*

If we inhabit a structured universe, which has been put in place and is sustained by a personal Creator, any attempt to reconstruct one's own universe, either by deliberate choice or by default, while at the same time having to live in the real world, is likely to result in a sense of futility and confusion. Most 'modern' people believe they inhabit a universe in which the human race has come about by the chance process of random selection from an impersonal beginning and in which their own individual being will be snuffed out at the moment of death, without any remainder or survival.[31]

Such a person will recognize diverse cultural and artistic achievements from the past, and probably to a lesser extent in the present, but will have no way of judging whether they are great or inconsequential, beautiful or ugly. He or she will be amazed at the ingenuity of the human mind in technological innovation and exploitation but will have no way of deciding whether the way this is used is positive or whether the new developments are important or insignificant. For in the universe of one's own imagination, there are no maps or signposts, except what one has devised for oneself. Values and meanings make sense only if they are part of a universe one shares with other human beings on the basis of a common conviction that it is really there and can be comprehended, at least in part, as it really is.

Unaided human reason based on a naturalistic philosophy, which has opted to 'take leave of God', has come to a dead end in its attempt to give a comprehensive account of the whole experience of life. Unfortunately, few people have the courage and honesty displayed by Bertrand Russell to admit that choosing one's own world offers no comfort:

> That Man is the product of causes which had no prevision of the end they were achieving, that his origin, his growth, his hopes and fears, his loves and his beliefs, are but the outcome of accidental collocations of atoms; that no fire, no heroism, no intensity of thought and feeling, can preserve an individual life beyond the grave; that all the labour of the ages, all the devotion, all the inspiration, all the noonday brightness of human genius, are destined to extinction in the vast death of the solar system . . . Only within the scaffolding of these truths, only on the firm

---

[31] Though this affirmation may seem to be contradicted by the persistent evidence from opinion polls that a high percentage of people believe in God, I do not think that the two sets of belief do necessarily cancel each other out in the popular imagination. The evidence may be circumstantial, but I think it is compelling enough to suggest that the notion of God is regarded by many as a 'safety-valve' or 'insurance' against the possibility of failure or tragedy. God represents security in an accident-prone world.

foundation of unyielding despair, can the soul's habitation henceforth be safely built.[32]

Albert Camus seeks to evade the ultimate question, 'What is the meaning of life?' by declaring it illegitimate. More modestly, he asks, 'What gives meaning to my life?' He believes one should answer this according to circumstances. Thus in his famous novel, *The Plague*, the meaning that the hero's life must have at that moment is fighting the disease and comforting its victims. This is his struggle against 'an order of the world shaped by death'. Of course, the ultimate question is not evaded, only postponed. Without knowing the contours of the real universe, one cannot tell whether or not the plague is the direct visitation of God upon the people (as Father Paneloux believed), in which case to fight it is to contend futilely against a particular providential ordering of things. The individual is left (Camus himself and the central character of the book, the doctor, Rieux) with an intuition (born perhaps of the memory of a Galilean carpenter who had compassion on the outcasts and marginalized people and healed the sick and dying) that this kind of suffering is unjust and an outrage, precisely because it involves the innocent. From there, in order to give some substance to the intuition, one struggles to find some rational basis for believing that one's action is meaningful. The best option Camus can find is that of acting 'as if' the battle against human suffering is a meaningful act and 'as if' this struggle can ultimately be won.

The 'as ifs' however rest on the telling of stories which may, but in the modern world probably will not, represent the real structure of creation. The abuse of freedom described above means that all that is left to human beings is the hope that the stories they invent will somehow produce significance. In the real world, contrary to what many people think, meaning is neither *discovered* (by the unaided use of human reason) nor *invented* (by imagination),[33] but *given* by the way the world is, a creative act of an infinite and personal Being whose ways are always truthful and good.

[32] *Mysticism and Logic and Other Essays*. London. Longmans, Green and Co., 1918, pp. 47–8.

[33] Cf., for example, A. Castell, *An Introduction to Modern Philosophy: Examining the Human Condition*. New York. Macmillan College, 1994, p. 737.

## (ii) The family – saved from extinction?

In the West today the effective interaction of the wider family, encompassing three generations and including the parents' siblings and their offspring, is, for practical purposes, a thing of the past. Indeed, the purpose, function and viability of the family even as a relatively self-contained unit of two parents and children is under intense debate and pressure. The issues are not merely theoretical or utopic, for the family has been undergoing sweeping changes in the last three decades of the twentieth century, as have attitudes and practices related to sexuality.

The causes of the transformation are, as one might expect, both social and cultural. Reliable methods of contraception have severed the act of sexual intercourse from the procreation of children. If contraception has failed, or not been practised, then termination of pregnancy may be had more or less on demand and, despite a vigorous pro-life campaign, the majority of the populations of Western liberal democracies now agree that abortion is, as a last resort, an acceptable, additional means of family planning.

Most women are in paid employment and therefore in a different relationship to the family than if they were able to concentrate exclusively on maintaining the home. They have a function as significant contributors (in times of high unemployment possibly the only contributors) to the family budget.[34] With a few exceptions, particularly among immigrant communities, modern economies are no longer based around family units of production. On the contrary, work opportunities usually separate members of families geographically from one another.

Attitudes to sexual relationships have become increasingly permissive. It is rare for either a man or a woman to come to their wedding night as virgins; many will already have been cohabiting with the person they eventually marry and possibly with others in succession. Some couples decide that marriage as

---

[34] It is a notable feature of modern societies that they do not recognize in economic terms the contribution of mothers to child-rearing. However, if, for example, parents (mothers in particular) never became involved in any way in their child's education, the repercussions on schools in terms of additional hours of teaching (and therefore labour costs) would be severe.

an institution no longer fits the needs of the late twentieth century. Splitting and regrouping is commonplace, supporting the conclusion that the West now permits (serial) polygamy and polyandry. Through divorce and remarriage children find themselves parts of different family groupings, having to relate to their separated biological parents and the step-parents and step-siblings of the new pairings. A swiftly increasing number of children now live in a home having only one parent. With the advent of new *in vitro* fertilization techniques (IVF), a child may be brought up by a couple neither of whom is its biological parent; it may not even know who the latter are, nor even who one of them is. It is also increasingly possible, though still statistically rare, that a child will be brought up by a couple of the same gender.

This pattern of life is unlikely to change substantially, except in the direction of increasingly looser bondings. A set of values which takes the rights and pursuit of happiness of the autonomous individual as the main focus for what is desirable is likely to encourage yet further experimentation in relationships. The traditional structure of the family will come under further stress as people accept that continual change is inevitable. This trend makes the customary position of the Christian faith (and indeed of other faiths) towards the family – sexual intercourse as restricted to marriage perceived as a life-long relationship between the same couple of different genders – seem absurdly antiquated. How can Christians possibly defend, let alone commend and promote, such an ideal, given the shift in social life and moral perceptions?

Christians would begin their response by referring to their view of the given structure of the world. Marriage is among the 'creation ordinances'. It is a gift to the creature by the Creator, in which alone each person who is called to create a new family, can find fulfilment as a mature human being.[35] This is the way God intended human beings to relate to one another, in order to bring into the world and nurture a new generation. Divorce is permissible only as a last resort, being a sign that human

---

[35] Singleness is considered an equal, though different, vocation. Growth to maturity does not depend on the particular calling, but on each being conducted within the right relationships.

relationships have gone profoundly wrong. On the basis of Scripture, Christians cannot accept the modern notion of 'no fault' divorces or the euphemism 'the irretrievable breakdown' of marriage, which suggests that marriages can be viewed like clapped-out cars that sooner or later come to the end of their useful life and are replaced.

When a marriage breaks up, something fundamentally tragic has happened as the result of the complex interworking of sinful natures. Guilt is certainly present. From a Christian perspective, the husband and wife have sinned against one another, against their children, in a sense against society too, since divorce has negative repercussions for the wider community, and against God who has given the gift of marriage. This does not mean that marriages should always be held together, whatever the circumstances. In cases, for example, of persistent violence, and after all attempts at mediation have failed, divorce may be the lesser of two evils.

For Christians sin and guilt are never the last word. As long as the participants in the separation admit that a tragedy has happened and that they must accept part of the blame, there can be real healing through forgiveness and acceptance. Those whose marriages remain intact also experience times of severe tension, often the result of sin in some form; so they have little cause either for complacency or the condemnation of others. Nevertheless, marriage is regarded as such a positive institution that some of the causes of its demise (such as boredom, incompatibility, preference for another person) should not be taken as serious reasons for bringing it to an end, but as destructive forces whose end will be increased misery and despair.

Marriage has been attacked, particularly among some feminists, simply on the basis that some marriages have proved to be exploitative and oppressive.[36] This makes sense only if marriage as such implies necessarily a relationship of domination and subservience. In fact the view is the result of a cynical attitude to life which assumes that people get involved in human relationships only for selfish ends, always seeing others

---

[36] Other 'feminists' reject the social structure of marriage itself, not just the way it has been habitually set up in the past.

as means to their own fulfilment or self-gratification. Tragically, many people use relationships in this way; though often this is done unconsciously as they invest too much of themselves in finding a partnership which 'works for them'.

If this were all there was to marriage, then genuine love would no longer be a reality in human experience and the age-old words of endearment, 'I love you' (which sound so much better in languages which employ the familiar second person singular), become a mere formula. No one wants to lose the real romanticism of 'falling in love'. Unhappily, however, the modern notion of love has roots that go little deeper than physical passion or emotional sentimentality, even though modern love quite often proves more durable than the image might warrant. It is not surprising that once the first flush of attraction has passed, such a relationship can easily wither. For Christians marriage is a lifelong covenant[37] between two equal people. Their love for one another, publicly signified and sealed in the marriage vows and in the exchange of rings, finds expression in a commitment to give themselves for each other through difficult, as well as easy, times. The idea of covenant also implies in Christian terminology an alliance between the couple and God, so that all that is done and said in the relationship is in the sight of and accountable to God.

Choosing to cohabit rather than get married is a pale reflection of what the marriage relationship could and should be.[38] Inevitably it signifies a weak commitment, because the mutual consent on which it is based is something into which the couple may have drifted without going through a similar process of decision-making associated with engagement and getting married. A limited time-span, possibly little more than a test period for sexual compatibility, is also likely if the couple tacitly accept that their relationship is a limited experiment which can be ended if it appears not to be working. The cohabitation option is also implicitly rooted in the fear, intrinsic to the tentative

---

[37] Within the 'catholic' tradition of Christianity, marriage is also regarded as a sacrament, i.e. a means of receiving God's grace which enables people to grow into maturity in Christ. Other Christian traditions are hesitant to use the same word for marriage (or the laying on of hands in healing or penitential contrition) as is used of the Lord's Supper and Baptism.

[38] Cf. J.R. Lucas, *Responsibility*, op.cit., pp. 247–48.

outward expression of the relationship (i.e. without a clear, public commitment to one another), that it may well fail; indeed, an argument often advanced against marriage is that divorce is so financially complicated and emotionally traumatic that marriage is not worth the risk.

The idea that cohabitation is a 'trial marriage', rather like a purchase that you may send back within a month with full refund guaranteed, if you are not satisfied, is a nonsense, if not a deceit. The reason is obvious: marriage cannot be tested until it is a lived experience. Cohabitation is a different kind of relationship, even when a couple intend permanence; it results in a quite different connection with the wider community, most particularly in relation to the families of the cohabitors.

The major argument for the Christian view of marriage – that it is a gift of God's love to creatures he cares about – carries little weight in contemporary society, even though it may be true. A further refinement of the argument, and one that can also be discussed on the basis of empirical evidence, is that, since it is God-given, it is the only context in which human beings, not destined to remain single, can grow to the mature, balanced and integrated persons they are intended to be. Conversely, the disintegration of marriage and the family and *laissez-faire* attitudes to human sexuality will hinder, damage or corrupt human development.

This argument, and the evidence supporting it, are strongly opposed. But it seems doubtful that the so-called 'sexual revolution', which has unleashed an obsession with the physical act in itself, has led to more warm, satisfying and joyful relationships than existed before. The view of freedom which has led to the liberation of sex from former constraints assumes a mechanistic relationship between bodily possession and pleasure. In fact, abandoning sexual modesty brings a fresh set of problems, as A. Bloom points out. Modesty made sexual intercourse

> central to a serious life and to enhance the delicate interplay
> between the sexes, which makes the acquiescence of will as
> important as possession of the body . . . Suppression of modesty

. . . dismantles the structure of involvement and attachment, *reducing sex to the thing-in-itself*.[39]

Evidence has been accumulating to suggest that the children of broken homes, who have been through the experience of the separation of their parents, are more prone to self-doubt, less likely to risk challenging received opinions, more vulnerable to unstable relationships in later life, more likely to swings of temperament between aggression and compliance and more easily distracted in their educational performance than children who come from families where there has been no separation.[40]

## Conclusion

A similar approach to freedom within the context of other fundamental aspects of human living may be made: i.e. that freedom becomes a full reality only when realized as variation and diversity within a basic given structure. This is true, for example, in the realm of economics:

> Current economic orthodoxy sees exchange as basic and gift as a peripheral afterthought. Christian economic thinking has to recognize that gift is a far more fundamental category, in terms both of God's blessings to humankind and our human economic organization . . . Maximization techniques, processes of summation, the handling of variables, econometrics and model-building all tend to be incapable of handling relationships between people and institutions. The problem has dominated the history of welfare economics, the dustbin in the discipline into which all the relational problems have been thrown . . . Stewardship in a biblical sense . . . means not just loving one's neighbour in immediate personal terms but also through a long-term strategic pattern of care.[41]

Here Alan Storkey recognizes that there is a particular pattern of life which is a gift of God's bounty to his creatures, and that that pattern centres on the enabling of proper human relationships. Modern economics, because it is founded on the

---

[39] A. Bloom, op.cit., p. 102 (my emphasis).
[40] Cf. N. Dennis and G. Erdos, *Families without Fatherhood*. London. Institute of Economic Affairs, Health and Welfare Unit. 1993, pp. 48–55.
[41] A. Storkey, op.cit., pp. 71, 72, 74.

priority of an abstract, impersonal system of monetary exchange, cannot reflect the freedom implicit in the pattern. Therefore, in diverse ways, contrary to the ideology, it inhibits the kind of community which is necessary for true freedom to flourish.[42]

The Christian concern for freedom is expressed in searching for and discovering the right balance between liberty *from* arbitrary authority and liberty *for* non-oppressive structures. The authenticity of such structures is measured by their ability to enable people to become what God, as revealed in Jesus Christ, created them to be.

---

[42] Cf. also J. Collier, op.cit., pp. 111–23 (See H. Montefiore, op.cit.); M. Schluter and D. Lee, *The 'R' Factor*. London. Hodder and Stoughton. 1993.

# Ten

# Whither Freedom?

## Reviewing the situation

Today freedom is one of the most supremely desired objectives and ideals for the majority of people, whatever their background. I know this is so, not only because I have studied the subject but through my own personal encounter with modern culture.[1] Ideas about freedom are expressed in an amazingly diverse language representing the many aspects of the subject. In particular I have noted the wide use of the vocabulary of 'rights', 'equality' and 'democracy'.

Some people doubt that the concept of *rights* has any longer the moral and political 'surplus value' that once was credited to it.[2] Many others, however, hold that it has a 'use value', at least

---

[1] Having travelled extensively in Africa and Asia and lived for 12 years in Argentina, with visits to most other parts of Latin America, I am also acquainted with a considerable number of other cultures. My experience confirms the thesis that freedom (liberation or emancipation) is the most sought-after good for most people.

[2] Cf., for example, R. Bellamy, 'Citizenship and rights' in R. Bellamy (ed.), op.cit., pp. 43–76. He argues that all theories of rights as the basis for a coherent view of citizenship founder on the intractable moral pluralism of modern societies: 'The world fails to evidence the moral regularity which even these minimalist theories of human rights need to be made coherent' (p. 62).

in monitoring and restraining all attempts to repress conscience and non-violent opposition to the undue concentration of power. It is increasingly recognized that secular reason cannot provide a satisfactory basis for the defence of people's individual rights. Nevertheless, if all forms of arbitrary power, particularly those directed against vulnerable groups in a nation, are to be eradicated, it is crucial that the essential dignity of every human being and the absolute requirement to respect it should be recognized as unqualified moral duties. Given the widespread moral confusion of modern societies, this defence of human rights can be founded on little more than pragmatic considerations: 'as if' the absolute worth of every individual were an established and agreed moral certainty. Sooner or later, the manifest contradiction between an unconditional, universal concern for the freedoms of individuals and the prevailing relativistic attitude towards diverse human cultures, whose practices often deny those freedoms, will have to be resolved.

There is probably even less agreement about the meaning and realization of *equality* for all. We are not speaking here so much of the freedoms guaranteed in the constitution and legal practice of a nation, where everyone is treated with equal impartiality by the law, but of those equalities that influence the individual economic situations of all citizens of a state or wider political entity. The dispute has to do both with the scope of equality (is the target simply equality of opportunity, or does it include an equalization of income through forms of wealth redistribution, minimum wages and policies of high employment?) and the balance between positive and negative liberties implied in discussions of economic justice. In part the debate is about the ground for moral values: those who stress equality and justice tend to assume a given, absolute norm which must be applied if a human community is to be righteous; those who stress economic freedom and the relative nature of equality tend to rely on a consequential ethic which derives from the observation that the greater the equality the greater the stagnation of a society.[3]

---

[3] The appeal to justice is by its very nature an appeal to some final, indisputable good that must be implemented. Justice is not open to being relativized by other goods. One of the fascinations of present moral debate in politics is to note that those 'on the left' appeal to absolutes in the realm of social policies, but disdain them in the realm of private values; while the

'*Democracy*' has a good feel about it. As long as we are not talking in too much detail about any particular manifestation of it, or trying to define it too closely, everyone is in favour of democracy, as they would be about an income tax rebate ! Democracy is the result of a number of historical factors that have combined to create an irresistible movement towards 'government of the people, by the people, for the people'. We noted the importance of the struggle for full religious liberty as implying a locus for authority more fundamental than that exercised by any political regime, namely the unmediated supremacy of individual conscience. Historically parallel to this demand came a gradual questioning of the legitimacy of all rule, which began with the incipient cultural assumption that no institution nor set of beliefs was immune from a process of radical appraisal. Eventually, the power of rulers was institutionally circumscribed by the separation of the functions of government into executive, legislative and judicial branches.

The slogan 'no taxation without representation' was both the cause and consequence of the rising economic and political influence of the middle-classes on the affairs of state. The onset of industrialization brought to the forefront of modern societies the primacy of economic considerations in the running of the state. The increase of wealth convinced those that had produced it that they had the right and responsibility to see how it was spent. Finally, the growing complexity of modern societies seemed to require an expanding bureaucracy which could no longer be filled with the retainers of the ruling class but needed a professional body of well-educated, publicly accountable employees.

Though modern democratic traditions arose in the context of Western European history, partly under the impact of Christian faith, we noted that there is in Islam a substantial, ancient principle which should encourage democratic institutions of government and thwart autocratic ones. This principle is the requirement laid on government to gain a consensus of the people through broad and sustained consultation. Although it is unfortunately true that Islamic societies have not been known in

opposite tends to be true of those 'on the right'. It seems that very few contend for the implementation of both social justice and high personal morality, before freedom.

practice for their democratic procedures, proper consultation implies proper representation, if it is not to degenerate into a mere formal exercise. In other words, the lack of a broad-based, democratically accountable political system can be said to betray fundamental Islamic principles.

With the collapse of Communist regimes, some political philosophers and commentators believe that Western liberal democracy is the last and final stage of human social evolution. John Robert, for example, states that every human society will have to incorporate into its own history the benefits of Western civilization:

> The story of western civilization is now the story of mankind, its influence so diffused that old oppositions and antitheses are now meaningless.[4]

However, it is Francis Fukuyama in his celebrated thesis about the end of history and the coming of the 'last man' who has most cogently argued this position.[5] As a matter of historical fact, he states, the Western democratic system has seen off all its rivals:

> As mankind approaches the end of the millennium, the twin crises of authoritarianism and socialist central planning have left only one competitor standing in the ring as an ideology of potentially universal validity: liberal democracy, the doctrine of individual freedom and popular sovereignty. Two hundred years after they first animated the French and American revolutions the principles of liberty and equality have proven not just durable but resurgent.[6]

Fukuyama argues that this is not a mere accident of history. Following Hegel, he advances a wide-ranging thesis that human societies are dialectically destined to work through the conflict between Master and Slave – the will to subjugate and the will to equality – resolving it finally in the constitutional conventions of democratic processes:

> Popular self-government abolishes the distinction between masters and slaves; everyone is entitled to at least some share in

---

4 *The Triumph of the West*. London. British Broadcasting Corporation. 1985, p. 431.
5 *The End of History and the Last Man*. London. Hamish Hamilton, 1992.
6 Ibid., p. 42.

the role of master. Mastery now takes the form of the promulgation of democratically determined laws, that is, sets of rules by which man self-consciously masters himself.[7]

For much the same reasons, Fukuyama's liberal democracy now takes the place of Marx's proletariat democracy. Both are based on supposed laws, internal to historical human processes, coming to inevitable fruition in the fullness of time. For Marx the resolution of social conflict marks the beginning of history proper; for Fukuyama it marks the end of history. However, those who live in nations possessing neither Western liberal democracy nor an economic system that properly rewards the labour of those who create wealth will not be impressed with the notion that history has ended, before their real history has arrived.

Fukuyama's thesis is a grand *tour de force*. History is by no means complete. Many chapters may remain to be written, and the outcome of the plot is not assured at all in the way he supposes. Indeed, he runs into the same impasse concerning human rights that we noted above:

> Rights spring directly from an understanding of what man is, but if there is no agreement on the nature of man or a belief that such an understanding is in principle impossible, then any attempt to define rights or to prevent the creation of new and possibly spurious ones will be unavailing . . . Today everybody *talks* about human dignity, but there is no consensus about why people possess it . . . The intellectual impasse in which modern relativism has left us . . . does not permit defense of liberal rights traditionally understood.[8]

So Fukuyama is aware of the 'moral impasse' we have identified! Now we have it straight (so to speak) from the horse's mouth! Fukuyama follows the logic of a culture which finds no adequate reasons for distinguishing the dignity of human beings from that of all other sentient beings. The result will be not only the exaltation of hitherto unimaginable rights for all non-human creation but the drastic diminution of special care for individual human beings:

---

[7] Ibid., p. 203.
[8] Ibid., pp. 296–8.

The liberal concept of an equal and universal humanity with a specifically human dignity will be attacked from both above and below: by those who assert that certain group identities are more important than the quality of being human, and by those who believe that being human constitutes nothing distinctive against the non-human.[9]

Perhaps, the title of Fukuyama's book should be more appropriately rephrased as *The Last History and the End of Man.*

Scepticism, relativism, eventually nihilism, have so eaten away the fabric of moral norms, like acid rain dissolving the sandstone splendour of British cathedrals, that the grandiose edifice of Western civilization appears to be crumbling to dust. As with the Marxists of a former generation, similarly facing substantial evidence of the breakdown of cohesive communities and the dangerous consequences that flow from this, one wonders whether Fukuyama's optimism is a kind of whistling in the wind of destructive change to keep up the spirits.[10] Nevertheless, on another, less comprehensively ideological reading of history, although there are good reasons to question optimistic interpretations of the present and future, there are also good grounds to be profoundly thankful for many of the transformations that have permeated society in the last quarter of a millennium.

## Real achievements

In many respects, the boundaries of freedoms have been widened in ways that are beneficial to human individuals and societies. Nothing that needs to be said about the negative consequences of some aspects of freedom or that is intended to qualify the uncritical enthusiasm which sometimes surrounds

---

9 Ibid., p. 298.

10 Fukuyama's final analogy of the wagons driving into town (pp. 338–9) is based on the dubious assumption that the final destiny of human history (its highest virtue and supreme goal) is the installation of liberal democracy across the whole globe, which will be advanced and guaranteed by universal economic development. His thesis of an inevitable process and the triumph of economic rationality and desire over the violent impulses of nationalism, racism and war is, unfortunately, nothing more than a pious aspiration.

the subject should obscure the gains that undoubtedly have been made. Every generation should both celebrate freedom afresh and also strengthen it where it is weak and reinforce it where it is securely established.

For freedom to be authentic a number of conditions have to be fulfilled. Thus, people must be able to take decisions for themselves without being under undue external pressure prescribing their decisions and actions. Freedom involves being willing and able to take risks, in the knowledge that the course chosen may turn out to be disadvantageous. It is of the essence of free choice that there is no guarantee that the hoped-for result will necessarily come to pass. Coercive action on the part of others (the state, family, friends) which seeks to bend another person's will in a particular direction implies a judgement that the risk of freedom is too great. Thus a person's freedom may be curtailed either by physical restraint, economic sanctions, the force of another's personality or by the threat of some kind of harm, because *A* has judged that *B* should not be allowed to take the risk of making what *A* thinks are wrong choices. A society is free in so far as it protects its inhabitants' potential for taking risks for themselves without being hindered by undesired external pressures.

It is in this connection that we can see why the censorship of literature, other art forms and the media should be minimal; for where there is room for genuine debate between differing views on a wide range of subjects, freedom of expression is itself a strong means of guaranteeing further civil liberties. Although no freedom of this kind is totally without qualification, a society needs to be watchful that limitations to freedom are not imposed by a particularly powerful group within the state, such as a political party, a business or commercial lobby or a professional or religious organization or even by a powerful press that denies a fair hearing and response from those it attacks or vilifies. The curtailment of freedom in any form should be agreed only following extended public debate and because it is in the interests of society as a whole and not of one pressure group within it. A society committed to freedom of expression will naturally engage in an ongoing discussion about the criteria involved in taking such decisions. The reality of risk we have referred to can be extended to a whole society or nation, where it promotes or allows freedoms that may well eventually undermine its own coherence.

Freedom also depends upon access to accurate data, in order that people may make informed choices. For me to be free from external restraint and pressures implies that I have the liberty or ability to take the action which I personally will for myself, simply because I will it. However, my freedom of choice may be circumscribed if I am ignorant of significant information bearing directly on the choice I want to make. Thus, if I have money to invest and I want to ensure that it goes to companies and industries that fulfil what have come to be called 'ethical criteria', then before I invest in any company I will need to know how they treat their labour force, what kind of environmental policy they have and if they have a reputation for business honesty. Lacking such information my personal freedom of manoeuvre in the stock market will be limited. Similarly, if faced with different possible medical treatments for one of my children, each apparently involving side-effects which could permanently damage the child's health, I would need to know as much as I could about all the likely effects, including those of non-treatment, if my final choice was to be as unrestricted as possible.

Freedom of action also depends upon having a coherent field within which to function. We noted earlier that the Greek philosophers believed that to know the purpose for which one was living in the world and to shape one's whole being towards attaining that end is more important than any number of formal freedoms. Christian and Muslim traditions of thinking concur (though for different reasons): they believe the world exists in a certain way because a divine being external to it has created it to a particular design and sustains it in fulfilment of that design. Not to discover, or deliberately to reject, the plan and the intent behind it means, on this view, confining freedom to choices and activities within a world we merely imagine to be the real one. Of course, for us today freedom does mean that we have this very possibility of living in a world we create for ourselves. Consequently, it is a mark of the modern practice of freedom that people are not pressed to define their aims in life according to someone else's formula or their beliefs according to someone else's world-view. Those who have strong convictions about the ultimate purpose of life have to be particularly careful not to abuse freedom by seeking ways of imposing their beliefs on others.

Nevertheless, without a solid external reference point that reveals the meaning behind the events, life is reduced to a ceaseless flux in which goals, moral commitments and human relationships may change arbitrarily from day to day. All that is left are the events in an endless kaleidoscope of changing patterns. This surely spells the loss of freedom, for freedom has to be related to what is *worth* choosing, and without a substantial end in view we do not know. Even the most libertarian can hardly believe that any and every action is as meaningful as every other.

Freedom is also dependent upon people acting out of a coherent and integrated inner self. Such an assertion is related to the last point. In the most extreme of cases a person whose personality is unstable and shifting, who has no sense of a firm centre to life, around which changes may happen in a discriminating way, is one for whom freedom is a random matter. One reason is that such a person will be open to the propaganda or suggestive manipulation of others. It is well known that bizarre cults with strong leadership thrive on the sensibilities of people considered, as we say, to be 'mixed-up'? What is the value of self-determination, in the absence of a 'lucid' self to determine things?

Freedom is more than the ability to stand apart from the meaning and values which have been inculcated in us by the set of relationships and culture in which we happen to live and to decide which, if any, we will accept for ourselves. It is more than overcoming, as far as we may, the contingencies of our particular histories. Freedom is the ability to engage with meanings, values and purposes that we set for ourselves after intelligent reflection according to an orderly set of criteria. To return to the language of the philosophers and the religious thinkers of the past, the alternative to adopting consistent, reflective goals is to act according to the sudden vagaries and impulsive passions of the moment. Such a situation implies being dominated by forces over which we do not have proper control: in other words, not to be free. Freedom means being able to choose whether we travel upstream or downstream.

Always to be carried downstream, however invigorating the sensation of flowing with the current and however arresting the scenery on both sides of the bank, is not to be free.

It will be clear from the discussion so far of the conditions necessary for full freedom that I believe an account of freedom couched in negative terms only is insufficient. In addition, the heritage of thought and resulting policy programmes which have given rise to social justice and egalitarian concerns in the socialist or social democratic tradition have to be accepted as one essential facet of freedom. It is too easy, though common, to opt for a negative definition of freedom as the only legitimate one, and then argue on that basis that all other so-called freedoms are really the restriction of basic freedoms. Such a procedure clearly begs the question from the outset. The positive definition argues from a different set of assumptions, namely that some positive freedoms take precedence over some negative ones, which then, partially or wholly, have to be set aside. The basic question is not which definition of freedom is the most valid, but which freedoms are to be permitted in which circumstances.

The socialist case, it seems to me, is also based on the argument that there is more to the restraint of freedom than the overt action of government or other individuals. There are social, economic and cultural structures and attitudes which narrow and confine people's opportunities to make decisions about their lives. These influences, which are not necessarily embodied in overt actions or laws, also have to be addressed, if freedom is to be expanded. A contemporary example is the 'freedom' of women with young children (especially if they are lone parents) to hold a regular, full-time job, with prospects of advancement in it. As long as they do not have access to child-minding facilities, their situation is fraught with difficulties. Establishing their freedom to engage on equal terms with others who do not have the same commitments has led to the call for government-funded nursery places to be universally available. The argument is based on the self-evident rightness of equality of opportunity in the job market. However, it takes government action to level the playing-field.

The socialist case breaks down, however, if every conceivable equality of opportunity is demanded as an incontestable right.

Firstly, there is a limit to how much welfare provision any society can afford. Secondly, lack of opportunity may be due to specific choices which individuals have made, which have disadvantaged them in comparison with others. It is not obvious that the state has a responsibility always to redress the balance by counteracting the effects of people's (presumably) free choices. It is argued that this is true for women who have children, on the supposition that they were 'free' not to have them, but have exercised a choice to forego certain freedoms in order to satisfy other goals – if one eats a cake one no longer has it. On the other hand, it could be argued that in this case the state has a special responsibility to women, because the nursery provision made will, in terms of social and intellectual development, eventually benefit the state itself. This reasoning is less true, perhaps, in the case of housing families that have split apart or young people who have simply decided to leave their homes, without having adequate alternative accommodation to go to. In both cases it may be appropriate, on grounds of compassion, to ensure that they have appropriate accommodation at the state's expense, but there should be no statutory obligation where individuals could have foreseen the consequences of their choices.

In other words, equality of opportunity is a matter of looking at different cases on their merit. The right to make demands on the state seems to be at its strongest in cases where people have been disadvantaged in the past, either by the direct action of a particular government or by its deliberate inaction. The socialist vision of freedom is most persuasive, when it can demonstrate that specific injurious practices in the past have adversely affected people's present opportunities to gain access to resources, such as adequate education, medical facilities, living accommodation, credit for starting a business or other means of livelihood, to such an extent that it is now appropriate to offer them.

An unregulated market, so greatly valued by the liberal economic tradition, has no power to redress just causes of grievance. In such cases, freedom is best served by a government's using its legislative or fiscal power to restore to hitherto marginalized people(s) the opportunity to make real choices about their own future. Such action could be construed as infringing the freedom of others, only if one were to argue that all possible freedoms were of equal and unquestioned legitimacy and immediately realizable.

The question of whether it is justifiable to limit people's freedom to do as they like is a matter of intense debate in a society which prides itself on its tolerant attitude to people's private moral views and its advocacy of deregulation in the public square. To this topic we now turn.

## Ambiguities in the meaning and practice of freedom

We can all think immediately of circumstances in which it is perfectly justifiable to remove people's freedoms. Imprisoning people who have violated other people's physical integrity is, perhaps, the most obvious example. There are other forms of punishment which also curtail freedom. Even the greatest advocate of libertarian economic views, who believes that taxation is one of the most iniquitous of modern institutions, because it deprives people of enjoying the full fruit of their work, usually has no difficulty in accepting that it is right to fine people who are convicted of 'insider dealing' or embezzling funds or to confiscate the profits made from child-prostitution or drug-dealing. Though the context is wholly different, a fine or confiscation affect the exercise of freedom in the same way as taxation.

Other cases are less clear-cut. Some people may have to be restrained, not because they have committed an actual crime, but because they are a potential threat to society. People with some forms of mental disturbance would fit into this category. Whether they are literally locked away in a psychiatric hospital or whether they are strongly sedated, their normal freedom of action has been restricted. Children, who are in the custody of their parents, guardians or, in exceptional cases of violence or neglect, the court are deprived of some specific freedoms. In most societies they are not free not to go to school (as long as there is an educational system in place for them), nor to drive a motor vehicle. A very important aspect of bringing up children is educating them into and trusting them with increased freedoms, as they grow older. This already presupposes their gradual release from confinement and restriction – 'I want you home by ten (eleven, twelve) o'clock tonight.'

What about the freedom to kill oneself? Modern societies are becoming more hesitant about whether individuals should be free to commit suicide, or not. This question highlights the secular predicament of freedom. On one side is the strong individualistic tradition which emphasizes the right to choose one's own destiny and to be in control of one's own body and deplores other people's assumed duty to stick their nose into one's private affairs. On the other is the notion still generally agreed that threats or attempts to commit suicide signal an abnormal situation, in which a person is temporally acting out of a disturbed mind and distraught emotions, and therefore not making a free decision on the basis of who he or she really is. The individualistic tradition argues that a person may have the right to take their own life, particularly if he or she seems to have weighed up the options with some care. This is part of the argument of those who defend the right to voluntary euthanasia.[11] The alternative assumption is that to intend suicide (or of assisted death) is itself evidence that a person is not behaving like someone in control of his or her own free choice.

So, in practical terms how should one respond to a note threatening suicide or on seeing someone about to jump from the fifteenth floor of a building? Instinctively, most people would resort to physical restraint (by removing the sleeping pills, firearm or piece of rope, or by grabbing them from behind). Failing this, they would seek to persuade the person to change their decision. But why? Possibly on consequentialist grounds: the ending of that person's life will entail hardship and misery for others: after his wife's recent death, he has to care for five children between the ages of three and ten; following the emigration of her brother to New Zealand, she is the only member of the family left to look after an ailing mother; he has

---

[11] Most arguments for the legalization of euthanasia assume a set of circumstances in which a person is (a) suffering from a terminal illness, (b) has undergone all known treatments without any reversal of the pathogen, (c) is in constant, acute physical pain, (d) is obliged to have permanent nursing assistance, (e) is, on the best medical prognosis available, likely to die within a short time. In other words, euthanasia is not advocated on trivial or irresponsible grounds. Nevertheless, it raises the critical questions of who has the authority to end life prematurely and by what criteria could this decision ever be more right than the one to continue it, until it ends itself (i.e until the body has reached a point of irreversible disintegration).

recently set up in business with one other partner, she has the gifts and experience on the sales side, whilst he is the one with financial and accounting abilities.

This line of reasoning against suicide seems perfectly natural and generally conclusive. However, it clearly acknowledges that in practice there are quite strong limitations on choice and freedom of action. Perhaps it takes an extreme case, like suicide, to point up the difficulties surrounding the common notion of freedom as liberty of action from controls extraneous to the will of the individual. The example of suicide demonstrates that the right to determine one's own life is balanced by the responsibilities one incurs simply by being a human being in relationship to others. Of course, one can tip the balance towards the right of choice and there is no sanction against the dead. But deep down most people realize that there are many occasions when responsibilities to others outweigh the right to one's own independent action. This belief is strong and is not derived simply from cultural norms or enlightened self-interest.

Interestingly, within a Christian (and Muslim) world-view suicide is seen in a wholly different light. Taking one's own life is not an option under any circumstances, for the simple reason that anyone who takes seriously the implications of being, first and foremost, a creature (rather than, say, an autonomous citizen) accepts that their life is not their own to dispose of. Christians (and Muslims) recognize that an individual life is not the property of any individual, as if they were free to determine and order it as they see fit. They believe, rather, that their entire being, physical, mental, and emotional, is held on trust from the One who made it and makes it possible: the Creator is the freehold landlord, whilst we are the leaseholders entrusted to look after the property of another. According to this view, the most fundamental human freedom is the decision to collaborate unconditionally with the legitimate owner.

Such a belief inevitably conflicts with a secularized culture. It seems to set the clock back to an age when all kinds of constraints were imposed on liberty on the grounds that the one divine Being required conformity to regulations and practices and that it was the duty of the state to enforce these. So the discussion about the meaning of freedom oscillates between two false poles. One is the belief (presumption, creed and operating conviction) that the individual is born into the world to be an agent free from the controlling influence or direction of any other agent, an independent, self-determining and self-governing being.[12] The other is the assumption that to compromise this belief to the least degree is to place oneself, without qualification, under the authority of a body one is not able to influence.

This basic contemporary misunderstanding of the nature of freedom explains why most people do not see its exercise as a paradox, which cannot be resolved by trying to have all or nothing. When truest to its own core beliefs, Christianity (and Islam) regard the dichotomy between the two poles as false. On the one hand, no person is free in practice from the constraint of living in a series of different communities which themselves have the right to impose demands irrespective of an individual's personal wishes.[13] Moreover, although this is less immediately obvious, we are not free either from the constraint of living in a world which has a certain given order to it. One is free, of course, to rebel against the constraints. However, such freedom is no more than licence to demonstrate against the nature of reality, but not to alter it fundamentally. On the other hand, submission to the controlling guidance of God does not entail any necessary submission to any human institution nor the necessary following of a particular way of life stipulated by human authority. That is why a contemporary Christian (and a modernizing Muslim) is able to affirm, in agreement with the secular view of freedom, that any attempt to compel people to believe or act in particular ways is a denial, not an entailment, of faith.

Yet, whether one is a believer in God or not, achieving genuine freedom (and here is the paradox) does require a self-imposed discipline. One is never so free as when one recognizes and abides by the proper limits to freedom inherent in the human condition. In a continuing debate about freedom, questions

---

[12] One of the principal axioms of humanist thought is that life has to be taken as 'a given', but not as given in the sense that there is a giver (or givers) to whom we owe gratitude and to whom we are accountable.

[13] Clearly these demands are themselves limited, for communities may well be unjustifiably oppressive of an individual's legitimate need to act as a free moral agent in conflict with the will of the majority.

about exactly where those limits lie and which have to be self-imposed and which imposed by the community as a whole should be explored much more carefully. Such a debate would continue to range across all the areas that we have discussed: economics, democratic politics, human rights, access to information, communication, the arts, health and healing, education, women's concerns, sexual activities, scientific research, technology, bureaucracy and others besides. There are certain criteria which can guide us in our pursuit of authentic versions of freedom. Whereas secular, Muslim and Christian views will coincide at some points (were it not so, there could be no discussion between them), at others there will be sharp differences of vision and perspective. I have written this book out of the conviction that, although there are substantial divergences, even conflicts on occasion, the debate is important and worthwhile. As a Christian, I also believe that the Christian world-view ultimately offers the only entirely adequate account of the way we experience and may interpret the world. I close, therefore, with a short review of the marks of what I understand to be an authentically Christian approach to freedom, and the consequences that flow from it.

## Choices

Freedom cannot be understood as a theoretical concept, abstracted from the conditions of living in the real world. Its meaning is defined in relation to people carrying on their daily business within their own particular set of circumstances (ancestors, upbringing, education, culture, economic opportunities, ethnic identity, national situation). Freedom is shaped not only by the conditions into which we were placed by our birth, childhood and youth, but more particularly by the choices we have made for ourselves during our development into early adulthood and beyond. A person who decided while young to give up learning a musical instrument cannot expect to be an accomplished musician later in life. A person who stopped studying foreign languages at school, at the earliest opportunity, cannot expect to converse with people of other nationalities in their language. Because we do not take opportunities at the appropriate time, most of us forfeit freedoms in the future.

There may be plausible or implausible reasons offered for such choices. But the responsibility for making them rests largely with the person concerned. While we may take account of special circumstances, we also believe that people are accountable for the decisions they make. It follows from this that determinism (the view that any 'choice I make is fixed, in whole or in part, by previous events, decisions, or conditions'[14]) is a theoretical construct, which is clearly contradicted by the way each person actually conducts his or her life: 'People arguing for or against freedom know what they are arguing about only because they experience freedom.'[15]

It is in principle impossible to demonstrate that the factors which are said to determine choice and action (whether environmental, historical, psychological or physical) actually do so. Even if one knew what they were, one could take steps to break free from them. If I was fearful of crowds, I could take measures to overcome the fear. If I took an instant dislike to someone with whom I worked, I could grow to like that person by trying to understand him or her or by examining my own preferences or prejudices. The very idea of being determined causes individuals to demonstrate in practice that they, and not some biological or social process, are in control of their own choice.

Determinism is given some credibility by the notion of cause and effect derived from scientifically controlled observation. On the basis of the examination of a constant sequence of events in the natural world, some scientists and others have concluded that, given sufficient knowledge of all hitherto antecedent events in a person's life and physical make-up, it would be possible in principle to forecast exactly what decisions that person will take in the future. But this assumption is mistaken; it is based on the erroneous assumption that the next step in a sequence of events is always caused by what preceded it. There is in human affairs no easy and obvious correlation between events that happen at different times. When a person is faced with a major decision, he or she will take into account a number of antecedent factors that

[14]  R. Billington, *Living Philosophy: An Introduction to Moral Thought*. London. Routledge. 1988, p. 229.
[15]  Ibid., p. 228.

have brought him or her to this point. They will try to weigh up the different consequences of different options. They will invoke the moral sensibility of their conscience. But neither they, nor even less someone on the outside, will know exactly what comparative weight to give to all the elements in the decision-making process. They may well rely in the last resort on an intuition derived from a cumulative personal experience quite impossible to break down into numerous constituent parts, all of which have combined to determine the action decided upon. To the person who takes it, the final decision may seem like the toss of a coin, equally likely to come up 'heads' or 'tails'.

Our experience of the reality of choice and of moral responsibility demonstrates that freedom is not an illusion. So far, a thoroughly secular person and a theist can agree. However, they part company, when the theist (Christian, not Muslim) argues that there is another reality at work in human life which, whilst not determining a person's actions and choices, predisposes them in a general direction. The theological name given to this fact of life is 'original sin', 'evil inclination' or 'corrupted will'.

The doctrine is disputed not only by secular thought but also by every other religious tradition, including the other monotheistic faiths (though the truth of the belief is not settled by numbers). The most commonly held view is that everyone is born into the world with a potential for good or evil. By their own exertions, guided by God's law or the instructions of Allah or the light of reason and experience, or through meditation and spiritual exercises (or a combination of some or all of these), people *can* walk in the ways of goodness and righteousness, but they *may* choose the path of error and delinquency instead. Christianity is the only world-view which affirms that human nature is intrinsically biased towards evil from the beginning. In the colourful words of Eliphaz the Temanite: 'Man is born to trouble as surely as sparks fly upward' (Job 5:7).

This remarkable divergence prompts two questions. Why is Christianity seemingly out of step with all other systems of thought? What difference does the belief make to the practice of freedom?

Christians base their belief on a double foundation: the revelation to the whole human race contained in the Scriptures of the Old and New Testaments; and the accumulated and indisputable testimony of human history and personal experience. In the previous chapter we have seen how the Bible views the origin of evil: it has sprung from the idolatrous decision of the progenitors of the human race to abuse their freedom by disbelieving God's word, opposing their will to God's and ultimately creating an environment of their own imagination. This process is continued in every person's individual decision, by commission or omission, to reject God's rightful claim to the undivided dedication of his or her life to God's purposes in creating the world.

The way evil works in human lives and societies is powerfully presented in the first section of Paul's letter to the church in Rome. Humanity as a whole has chosen to believe its own account of truth and go its own way, rather than to believe God's depiction of the world and the place of human beings in it. Though there may be some justifiable reasons for being hesitant about believing in God – the most powerful being the existence of indiscriminate and undeserved suffering and the attitudes and lifestyle of some people who do believe – ultimately there is no valid excuse. The Bible, like the honest contemporary seeker, takes account of the difference between doubt felt as agony by a person who longs to believe, but finds real intellectual or moral problems, and doubt as either a pretext for uninhibited self-determination or as an evasion of the deep questions of life.

The Christian explanation of the problem of evil which begins from a message written down two thousand or more years ago is likely to leave the average modern person quite indifferent. Most people are in the habit of not basing their opinions and decisions on something as remote from contemporary life as a story or stories recounted two millennia ago in a context so far-removed and alien from their own. Thus there is a ready-made credibility barrier, which is hard for the agnostic to consider surmounting. This barrier is raised further by the common misapprehension, based on a popular but superficial reading of history, that Christianity is a way of life that the Western world has tried and found defective and inadequate. Christianity has not, however, been properly tried, except in what have generally been distorted forms.

The reason that Christians nevertheless continue to advocate their world-view is that they believe it perfectly matches everyone's ultimate experience of life in its various aspects. The world-view stands, in one sense, as a hypothesis. The crucial question concerns the evidence for or against it. The difference between believing in the Christian view and scepticism is whether one is persuaded, or not.

Christians do not deny the existence of much generosity, uprightness, truth and beauty in the world. But they reject any romantic notion about the essential goodness of human nature. The message they have accepted as true has prepared them to take evil with the utmost seriousness, without inventing excuses or smoothing away the jagged edges. Christians are often accused of being obsessed with sin, guilt and evil. They are also accused of using their understanding to manipulate people into believing and then make them dependent on the church to overcome the effects of sin. These accusations may sometimes be justified. However, some bad practice does not automatically invalidate the doctrine itself. What counts is the power of the Christian world-view to explain both the nature and extent of evil and the failure of alternative explanations to do justice to the whole of reality.

In order to see whether there are sufficient clues to substantiate their interpretation of human experience Christians may focus on a number of different pieces of evidence. The first piece of evidence might be the uninhibited behaviour of small children. We say this one has a mind of her own, or that one is throwing a temper tantrum. What is evident is the determination of children to get their own way and have their desires satisfied. If thwarted by an adult, they may well scream, kick and in other ways show their extreme disapproval.[16] To say no to a child's request often creates a small bundle of fury (see it happen in any supermarket). Some rationalize this behaviour by saying that the child is simply in the process of discovering its own will and is testing the limits within which it is allowed to operate, or that it doesn't understand why it is being denied what it wants. One has to ask, however, why a severe clash of wills or ignorance, which

---

[16] Of course, when emphasizing these characteristics, in the context of the problem of evil, I am not denying that children do show tenderness and generosity. My point is that it is the aggression that needs explaining not the affection and kindness.

leads to anger, frustration and misery, has to be a normal part of childhood, unless there is some deeply abnormal condition within the child's psyche in the first place. Why should children see their parents or siblings as rivals? Why is it necessary for them to draw attention to themselves? Why should they, on occasion, be cruel or vindictive towards their playmates? I suspect we have become so accustomed to the way young children behave that we do not even consider that it could have been different.

Another piece of evidence comes with adolescence. As anyone with teenage children knows, a young person tends to be almost completely absorbed in his or her own world. The life of the family is often manipulated, in order to satisfy teenage desires. It seems as if, given the opportunity, a young person will spend as much money as possible on clothes, music, electronic goods and entertainment for themselves. The battle of wills with the parents, seen first at about the age of two, continues with renewed vigour. In early teenage years the young person often seems little interested in the world beyond a circle of friends, though there are significant examples of youngsters caring for others and gradually most, as they approach adulthood, become genuinely aware of the need to do something about injustices and suffering. Again, our culture tends to accept the adolescent years as a normal phase through which children eventually turn into adults. We excuse behaviour which is erratic, self-centred, often bombastic and arrogant, sometimes violent, on the grounds that teenagers cannot cope with the physical changes that are happening to their bodies; or that they are simply apeing the consumerist priorities of their parents and the adult world in general;[17] or that they are venting their frustration on a world which does not allow them to satisfy their needs and fulfil their potential. However, the closer we come to affirming that behaviour destructive of human relations is an inevitable part of a growing process the closer we are to confirming the Christian thesis that human beings, from the earliest years, have an egoistic bias.

---

[17] It is interesting that one of the arguments for the deregulation of 'soft' drugs, taken, according to surveys, by as many as one in three teenagers, is that the consumption of alcohol (preferred by adults) is both legitimate, abused and dangerous to health and safety.

Our final piece of evidence (space forbids a wider survey) is the economic system which dominates the world. Apologists for capitalism candidly admit that economic life prospers best when each individual is pursuing to the maximum his or her own self-interest. It is based on the principle that, everything else being equal, all people will always tend to act in the market to enhance their own benefit as they see it. Conversely, an economic system which deliberately sets out, under strict democratic control, to take away the surplus owned by the relatively rich and redistribute it to the relatively poor is said to have no chance of working efficiently. This is tantamount to admitting that creating wealth, distributing resources, manufacturing goods and supplying services can be achieved effectively only in response to the motivation of self-concern and self-gratification.

It is, apparently, inconceivable that people could agree to work and create wealth in part, at least, so that the fruits of their labour might go to meet the needs of people struggling to overcome adverse circumstances. What a comment on human nature! Of course, a defender of capitalism will respond that redistribution of wealth is a matter of individual philanthropy not of state coercion, for a giving to others which is forced upon the individual has no moral value. However, most people do not engage in regular, generous, sacrificial giving to others. It is true that many respond nobly to disaster appeals, and out of the best of motives. However, what is at stake is something much more fundamental, something akin to the ideal of the religious tithe, where individuals or families put aside a percentage of their income for the benefit of others *before* they spend a single penny on themselves. The real test of generosity is what we do with our entire income rather than with the residue left after satisfying our many needs, real or supposed.

These examples are but a small fraction of the evidence that a Christian would adduce to demonstrate the inescapable bias towards self-preoccupation which exists at the very centre of the human psyche. This is a message that most people would rather not hear. Surrounded by life's daily disasters, most of us want to derive some comfort from the fact that we are not as bad as others. We are inclined to find causes external to ourselves to explain the tragedies that occur in our lives or those of others. In stressing the reality and seriousness of moral failure, Christians are accused of a misanthropic outlook on life and of gaining pleasure from provoking guilt complexes. But the best Christian belief and practice is nothing like this; for Christians believe that the most adequate way of coping with the predicaments and alienations of life is to face their reality with transparency and robustness. Our modern world sets great store by empirical evidence in other fields; why should we be unwilling to accept the substantial signs that a profound disorder has pervaded the remotest recesses of our own personalities?

Assuming that the Christian explanation of evil is the only one that does full justice to the complex dilemmas of human experience, what difference does this make to our practice of freedom? There are at least three corollaries that follow. First, nobody is internally free to choose a life completely dedicated to the selfless service of others. A person can imagine the good and wish that they were spontaneously generous towards others simply out of compassionate concern for their highest well-being. There will, however, always be a fatal gap between desire and fulfillment. The will to self-preservation and self-indulgence will take over sooner or later to block the realization of our good resolutions.

Secondly, the Christian description of the way evil works in people's lives delivers us from the fatalism of imagining that error, wrong, misfortune and suffering are usually caused by factors external to ourselves. We noted that it was a central characteristic of existentialism that it held people responsible for their own decisions and actions. Therefore, contrary to contemporary wisdom, to find people personally responsible and therefore truly guilty of inflicting wounds upon themselves and others is not psychologically cruel and damaging but ultimately humane in the proper sense of the word: it tells them that they are real people, whose actions make a difference to life, not automatons driven by forces beyond their control. In other words, guilt is one of the consequences of being a fully human person accountable for one's own actions. Whereas a verdict of 'diminished responsibility' implies a lack of freedom and is passed upon a person judged not to be in control of his or her own actions. Thus, paradoxically, the doctrine of 'original sin' holds out a greater prospect of personal freedom than do doctrines that suggest that our human attitudes and actions are largely conditioned by factors external to our own inner impulses.

Thirdly, acknowledging the bias towards selfishness alerts us to the dangers of allowing human beings to concentrate too much power in their own hands. Thus we are encouraged to defend freedoms, especially those of vulnerable and powerless peoples, against the tendencies to self-aggrandizement which lead others to limit those freedoms in their own interests. Belief in the corroding presence of sin in the heart of all has always been one of the major reasons why Christians have called for checks and balances in the exercise of government. It is not fortuitous that those nations which were most deeply influenced by the Protestant Reformation with its teaching on the pervasive operation of sin were also those which took the most elaborate steps, and succeeded best, to counteract the corruptions of political power. It is unfortunate that many of the heirs of the Reformation, fanatic proponents of free-market economics, do not seem to see the same corrupting influences at work in the exercise of economic power.

The Christian understanding of sin is thus at the centre of a Christian understanding of freedom. But this is true only in so far as it supplies the necessary context in which freedom may, or may not, be exercised. For the Christian, freedom ultimately means being wholly available for the purposes for which God created human beings: creativity, scientific endeavour, right human relationships, self-giving for others, enjoyment of God's presence and of the natural world. As sin destroys in some measure all these ventures, we cannot claim to be truly free until we have been freed from the corrosive power of sin. If our analysis of the human condition at its most fundamental and influential level is correct – and the case rests not only on the message given by the Hebrew prophets and the Christian apostles, but on the observable, intractable nature of human conduct – then freedom becomes a reality more as a gift received than as something that can be created and sustained by human imagination and power.

That is why Christians speak about salvation in terms of *liberation into freedom*. In the last analysis, such liberation can be given only by someone who is entirely free from all trace of evil and corruption and who has overcome its cunning temptation and relentless power. In the whole history of humanity, the Christian story alone speaks of such a person. It maintains that he continues to be active in the world, setting those people on the path to real freedom who are willing to accept his transforming presence in their lives and in the life of human communities and social structures. Freedom is achieved ultimately by freely serving the liberating purposes of the One who is both the source, the goal and *the meaning of freedom.*

# Appendix

# Methods and Approaches in the Exploration of the Theme

One of the most basic concerns motivating this study has been the desire to allow the message of Christian faith to engage sympathetically and dialogically, but also critically, with the pervading assumptions of modern, secularized societies. A serious gulf has arisen between the implicit or explicit intellectual beliefs that drive those societies that have accepted a modern outlook on life and the beliefs that Christians deem to be true, and therefore fitting for all aspects of human existence. Whereas inter-religious dialogue is considered to be essential at different levels among the followers of the major religious traditions of the world, one cannot say as much of the upholders and purveyors of secular convictions.

There are various likely reasons why this kind of dialogue is not happening. One has to do with the offence that some powerful Christian churches have given in the past through their attempts to stifle open debate about the natural world, the meaning of life and moral values. Any kind of open conversation may in consequence be seen by some as another devious way by which the churches can claw back some of their lost influence. Another reason is the tacit presumption that somehow Christian faith belongs to an age that is past, being a relic that continues to survive, but in the long term doomed to extinction because it cannot properly adapt to an alien world. A third may derive from the well-nigh universal conviction that, although in some circumstances (e.g. major human tragedies) religion may have an instrumental, public role to play in society by providing symbols that can comfort and heal, it is in general marginal to society's 'daily round and common task'.

Those who believe, both for practical and intellectual reasons, that the message of Jesus Christ is ultimately the only source that reveals the full meaning and purpose of human living find such coyness, if not indifference, exceedingly frustrating. Like many other Christians, I am chastened but not perturbed by the frontal onslaught on belief in the supreme reality of another mode of existence that has marked the beginning of the modern period of human history. Critical engagement with faith convictions suggests that, at the least, they are being taken seriously but indifference or, even worse, nonchalant dismissal, is hard to take.

This book explores ways whereby people who live on the basis of secular assumptions may come to understand the importance of establishing an open, transparent and unrestricted dialogue with Christian perspectives concerning some of the most important human issues that affect us all, whatever our motivations for living. The theme that has been chosen is freedom; with dialogue in mind, it might well have been some other reality that shapes the belief and behaviour of the citizens of the modern world – ethnic consciousness, economic policies, marriage and family matters, technological change, artistic endeavour, fashion, sport or a host of others. There are two major reasons for focusing on freedom: first, the meaning, achievement and practical realization of freedom are largely taken for granted, but not analysed; secondly, a good case can be made out for the thesis that the pursuit of freedom has been the dominant global movement within human cultures during the last quarter of a millennium, and this preoccupation shows little sign of abating. On the one hand, freedom is conceived to be an enormously influential and significant concept which inspires and drives human communities to new enterprises and ventures. On the other hand, the intricacies of its meaning and the ambiguities of its practice have not been examined with the rigour and care that such an important perception deserves.

The shape and content of this book are conditioned by the desire to engage, as discussed above, in a significant piece of dialogue – though such a purpose is not overtly proclaimed in the course of the presentation. Indeed, some Christians, who have kindly read drafts of the whole text, have asked why I have not declared my own Christian position much earlier in the book. In my estimation, given possible sensitivities over the subject under discussion, such a procedure would be more likely to foreclose than open up a real conversation.

The approach has also been criticized for not announcing towards the beginning the ambiguities and negative aspects of the way freedom is conceived and lived in contemporary societies. The text, as it stands, has been judged to take a naive view of the near-universal benefits of freedom as understood within the culture of nations that have experienced liberal democracies. However, I believe that the adoption *ab initio* of a largely negative apologetic towards the phenomenon of secularization has hindered the possibility of the kind of dialogue I am advocating and made an adequately comprehensive account of the history and processes of freedom difficult to achieve. Thus, in a number of Christian discussions about the effects of Westernization, freedom is too easily assumed to be the main cause of economic injustices and too simplistically identified with individualism.

Ultimately a sober assessment of freedom is indeed necessary. However, my intention has been to try first to understand why this notion, perhaps beyond all others, has made such a colossal impact on modern human consciousness. There is both a pre-history and a history to freedom as experienced in the Western world. Far from having evolved by an effortless progression into its present forms, it has emerged as the result of both real, physical conflicts and intense intellectual confrontations. Of course, few imagine that there is one unequivocal understanding of what freedom means. I acknowledge both the disputed interpretations and the wide variety of contexts in which freedom has found expression. I try to do this by allowing the different advocates to speak for themselves in their own language, whilst at the same time pointing out some of the assumptions on which theory and practice are based.

Further into the discussion, I allow my own Christian convictions to help guide both the choice of the material which I believe is most worthy of consideration (given that the topic is almost inexhaustible) and the criteria by which it may be assessed. But it is part of my convictions that in many instances the freedom I am describing is, precisely from a Christian perspective, a positive gain that should be cherished and defended against encroaching structures and ideas that slowly or dramatically dissolve its beneficial nature.

My dialogical approach culminates in what I consider to be the mutual challenge which secular faith and Christian faith ought to offer one another. As a matter of fact, I do not see these as two independent extremes on some imaginary line. Historically, and contemporaneously, there has been a subtle interaction between the two, which is still going on. Secularism, as a more or less self-conscious stance, may have arisen as a polemical counterbalance to an absolutist Christianity reluctant either to cede political and social power or admit its errors, but so have a number of groups within the Christian tradition itself. There is a strong case to be made out for Max Weber's celebrated thesis that 'Christianity has dug its own grave', i.e. that its own message is the well-spring and necessary condition for the kind of social space which enables people to decline to believe and practise faith without incurring political or cultural sanctions.

Moreover, the modern tradition of freedom has helped to expose the many alienating and oppressive features of religious belief and practice. Again, it has created the space in which people may stand back, look at what they see and declare it to be ugly and dehumanizing. Human beings have rights over against the imposition of religion. Purged of false imperialistic tendencies, inherited from corrupted views of power, Christian faith ought to be able to accept such rights without creating internal contradictions and then urge other religions to make a similar acknowledgement. Finally, a secular view of freedom should stimulate Christians constantly to review critically their tendency to split reality into two domains, the secular and the sacred, and then to favour the latter over the former. Too often notions of the sacred have been manipulated to achieve dominance within the Church for a clerical caste that has been able to decide what is, and is not, permissible within the boundary of the community. Laicization is not only a phenomenon of a modern society but a positive step for the Church to take if it seriously wishes to follow the message of freedom entrusted to it from the beginning.

On the other side, Christian faith has a vital and irreplaceable role in ensuring that the meaning of freedom is grounded in and sustained by a proper understanding of the reality of human existence. This means that freedom must be linked to the actuality of truth. There is more than enough evidence from the last two centuries to confirm the premise that freedom is neither self-authenticating as a notion nor self-sustaining as a practical reality. It cannot be preserved by an appeal to its own internal logic alone. Inevitably freedoms conflict in such a way that one freedom can be used in countless ways to deny others. Indeed, the very rhetoric of freedom has been skilfully and cynically exploited to introduce the totalitarian regimes of communism, fascism and religious fundamentalism. The danger for modern, secular societies is that they forget the foundations of their own existence and pretend that the momentum of the past will magically maintain itself without further input. I argue that one of the most important, if painful, contributions that Christian faith can make to the dialogue is to uncover for the secular world the nature of its own illusions. In other words, even though it might sound pretentious or condescending to put the matter this way, modern culture is in peril of succumbing to a terminal disease engendered by its own success, unless it is willing in a new spirit to engage in a forthright dialogue with the Christian message. My desire is that this book should be part of this process.

# Bibliography

The following selection of books relates to the various topics that have been tackled in the different chapters. It does not profess to be a comprehensive list. It includes those that I have quoted in the notes and some more which I have consulted and found helpful, but not directly referred to.

M.J. Adler, *The Idea of Freedom*. New York. Doubleday. 1958–61.
A. Ahmad, *Modern Islam in India and Pakistan 1857-1964*. London. OUP. 1967.
A. Ahmed, *Discovering Islam: Making Sense of Muslim History and Society*. London. Routledge and Kegan Paul. 1988.
   *Post-Modernism and Islam: Predicament and Promise*. London. Routledge and Kegan Paul. 1992.
S. Akhtar, *Faith for All Seasons*. London. Bellew Publishing. 1990.
N. Anderson, *Freedom under the Law: The Role of Law in Man's Quest for Freedom*. Eastbourne. Kingsway. 1988.
I.G. Barbour, *Religion in an Age of Science*. London. SCM Press. 1990.
R. Bellamy (ed.), *Theories and Concepts in Politics: An Introduction*. Manchester. Manchester University Press. 1993.
A. Bennett, *Readers and Reading*. Harlow. Longman Group. 1995.
I. Berlin, *Four Essays on Liberty*. Oxford. Oxford University Press. 1969.
H. Bertens, *The Idea of the Postmodern: A History*. London. Routledge. 1995.

R. Bhaskar, *Philosophy and the Idea of Freedom*. Oxford. Blackwell. 1991.

A. Bloom, *The Closing of the American Mind*. Harmondsworth. Penguin. 1987.

P. Bocock and K. Thompson, *Religion and Ideology*. Manchester, Manchester University Press. 1987.

A. Bowie, *Aesthetics and Subjectivity: From Kant to Nietzsche*. Manchester. Manchester University Press. 1990.

J. Bowker, *Is God a Virus? Genes, Culture and Religion*. London. SPCK. 1995.

S. Brittan, *A Restatement of Economic Liberalism*. Atlantic Highlands. Humanities Press International. 1988.

D. Carson and J. Woodbridge, *God and Culture*. Grand Rapids. Eerdmans. 1994.

A. Carter, *The Political Theory of Anarchism*. London. Routledge and Kegan Paul. 1971.

R. Carter, *Language and Literature: An Introductory Reader in Stylistics*. London. George Allen and Unwin. 1982.

R. Carter and B. Simpson, *Language, Discourse and Literature: An Introductory Reader in Discourse Stylistics*. London. Unwin Hyman. 1989.

O. Chadwick, *The Secularization of the European Mind in the 19th Century*. Cambridge. CUP. 1975.

V. Chappel (ed.), *The Cambridge Companion to Locke*. Cambridge. CUP. 1994.

K. Cragg and Speight, *The House of Islam*. London. Wadsworth Publishing Co. 1987.

M. Cranston, *The Romantic Movement*. Oxford. Blackwell. 1994.

R. Dahrendorf, *The New Liberty: Survival and Justice in a Changing World*. London. Routledge and Kegan Paul. 1975.

R. Dawkins, *The Selfish Gene*. Oxford. OUP. 1989.

H. Djait, *Europe and Islam*. Berkeley. University of California Press. 1985.

E. Dussel, *A History of the Church in Latin America; Colonialism to Liberation*. Grand Rapids. Eerdmans. 1981.

T. Eagleton, *Ideology*. Harlow. Longman Group. 1994.

R. Eatwell and A. Wrig, *Contemporary Political Ideologies*. London. Pinter Publishers. 1993.

M. Fakhry, *Ethical Theories in Islam*. Leiden. Brill. 1991.

V. Fiddes, *Science and the Gospel*. Edinburgh. Scottish Academic Press. 1987.

M. Fischer and M. Abedi, *Debating Muslims: Cultural Dialogues in Postmodernity and Tradition*. Wisconsin. University of Wisconsin Press. 1990.

D.B. Forrester, *Theology and Politics*. Oxford. Blackwell. 1988.

P. Freire, *Cultural Action for Freedom*. Harmondsworth. Penguin Books. 1972.

M. Friedman, *Capitalism and Freedom*. Chicago. University of Chicago Press. 1962.

E. Fromm, *The Fear of Freedom*. London. Routledge and Kegan Paul. 1960.

F. Fukuyama, *The End of History and the Last Man*. London. Hamish Hamilton. 1992.

J.K. Galbraith, *The Anatomy of Power*. London. Hamish Hamilton. 1984.

A. Gilbert, *The Making of Post-Christian Britain: A History of the Secularization of Modern Society*. London. Longman. 1980.

M. Ginsberg, *On Justice in Society*. Harmondsworth. Penguin Books. 1965.

J. Glover, *Responsibility*. London. Routledge and Kegan Paul. 1970.

G. Grant, *Technology and Justice*. Concord. Aransi. 1986.

J. Gray, *Liberalism*. Milton Keynes. Open University Press. 1986.

B. Griffiths, *The Creation of Wealth*. London. Hodder and Stoughton. 1984.

R. Gross, *Themes, Issues and Debates in Psychology*. London. Hodder and Stoughton. 1995.

J.J. Gumperz, *Discourse Strategies*. Cambridge. CUP. 1989.

S.M. Haider, *Islamic Concept of Human Rights*. Lahore. The Book House. 1978.

S. Hall and B. Gieben, *Formations of Modernity*. Cambridge. Polity Press. 1992.

D. Harti, *Basic Genetics*. Boston. Jones and Bartlett. 1991.

D. Harvey, *The Condition of Postmodernity: An Enquiry into the Origins of Cultural Change*. Oxford. Blackwell. 1990.

S. Hauerwas, *After Christendom?* Nashville, Abingdon Press. 1991.

F.A. Hayek, *The Constitution of Liberty*. London. Routledge and Kegan Paul. 1976.

   *Law, Legislation and Liberty: A New Statement of Liberal Principles of Justice and Political Economy*. London. Routledge and Kegan Paul. 1979.

A. Heywood, *Political Ideologies: An Introduction.* Basingstoke. Macmillan Press. 1992.

J.R. Hinnels (ed.), *A Handbook of Living Religions.* Harmondsworth. Penguin Books. 1991.

R. Hodge and G. Kress, *Language as Ideology.* London. Routledge and Kegan Paul. 1993.

M.F. Hoffmann, 'Assumptions in Sex Education Books', *Educational Review,* 27,3, June 1975.

I. Hore-Lacy, *Creating Common Wealth: Aspects of Public Theology in Economics.* Sutherland (Australia). Albatross Books. 1985.

J. Horton and S. Mendus, *Aspects of Toleration: Philosophical Studies.* London. Methuen. 1985.

G.F. Hourani, *Reason and Tradition in Islamic Ethics.* Cambridge. CUP. 1985.

R. Hughes, *The Shock of the New: Art and the Century of Change.* London. Thames and Hudson. 1991.

*Independent, The* (and others), *Leonardo: The Age of Discoveries.* London. *The Independent.* 1992.

J.C. Keene, *The Western Heritage of Faith and Reason.* New York. Harper and Row. 1963.

J.A. Kirk, *Loosing the Chains: Religion as Opium and Liberation.* London. Hodder and Stoughton. 1992.

A. Kleinman, *Patients and Healers in the Context of Culture.* Berkeley. University of California Press. 1980.

N. Koshy, *Religious Freedom in a Changing World.* Geneva. WCC. 1992.

C. Lasch, *The Culture of Narcissism: American Life in an Age of Diminishing Expectations.* New York. Norton and Co. 1979.
  *The Minimal Self: Psychic Survival in Troubled Times.* London. Picador Books. 1985.
  *The True and Only Heaven: Progress and its Critics.* New York. Norton and Co. 1991.

V.B. Leitch, *Deconstructive Criticism: An Advanced Introduction.* London. Hutchinson. 1983.

R. Levitas (ed.), *The Ideology of the New Right.* Cambridge. Polity Press. 1986.

R.C. Lewantin, *Biology as Ideology: the Doctrine of DNA.* Concord. Artansi. 1986.

J. Lively and A. Reeve, *Modern Political Theory from Hobbes to Marx: Key Debates.* London. Routledge. 1993.

R. Lockyer, *Habsburg and Bourbon Europe 1470-1720*. Harlow. Longman. 1993.

J.R. Lucas, *The Freedom of the Will*. Oxford. Clarendon Press. 1971.

*Freedom and Grace*. London. SPCK. 1976.

*Responsibility*. Clarendon Press. Oxford. 1993.

D. Lyon, *The Steeple's Shadow: On the Myths and Realities of Secularization*. London. SPCK. 1985.

A. MacIntyre, *After Virtue: a Study in Moral Theory*. London. Duckworth. 1987.

*Whose Justice? Which Rationality?* London. Duckworth. 1988.

J. Maquet, *The Aesthetic Experience: An Anthropologist looks at the Visual Arts*. New Haven. Yale University Press. 1986.

D. Martin, *A General Theory of Secularization*. Oxford. Blackwell. 1978.

M. Marty and R.S. Appleby, *Fundamentalisms Observed* (Vol. I). 1991; *Fundamentalisms and Society: Reclaiming the Sciences, the Family and Education* (Vol. II). 1993; *Fundamentalisms and the State: Remaking Politics, Economics and Militance* (Vol. III). 1993. Chicago. University of Chicago Press.

*Accounting for Fundamentalisms; The Dynamic Character of Movements*. Chicago. University of Chicago Press. 1994.

A. Mazrui, *Cultural Forces in World Politics*. London. James Currey. 1990.

McKeon, *Freedom and History*. Chicago. University of Chicago Press. 1990.

D. McLellan, *Ideology*. Milton Keynes. Open University Press. 1995.

S. McMurrin (ed.), *The Tanner Lectures on Human Values (Vols. I and II)*. Cambridge. CUP. 1980–1.

J.C. Merrill, *The Imperative of Freedom: A Philosophy of Journalistic Autonomy*. New York. Freedom House. 1990.

M. Midgley, *Heart and Mind: The Varieties of Moral Experience*. Brighton. Harvester Press. 1981.

*Evolution as Religion: Strange Hopes and Strange Fears*. London. Methuen. 1985.

J. Milbank, *Theology and Social Theory: Beyond Secular Reason*. Oxford. Blackwell. 1990.

B. Mitchell, *Morality: Religious and Secular*. Oxford. Clarendon Press. 1980.

J. Moltmann, *The Way of Jesus Christ: Christology in Messianic Dimensions*. London. SCM Press. 1990.

H. Montefiore (ed.), *The Gospel and Contemporary Culture*. London. Mowbray/Cassell. 1992.

M. Morgan, M. Calnan, N. Manning, *Sociological Approaches to Health and Medicine*. London. Routledge. 1985.

M. Moriarty, *Roland Barthes*. Cambridge. Polity Press. 1991.

H.J. Muller, *Issues of Freedom: Paradoxes and Promises*. New York. Harper Row. 1960.

T. Munck, *Seventeenth Century Europe: State, Conflict and the Social Order in Europe 1598-1700*. Basingstoke. Macmillan. 1990.

L. Newbigin, *Truth to Tell: The Gospel as Public Truth*. Geneva. World Council of Churches. 1991.

B. Nicholls (ed.), *The Unique Christ in our Pluralist World*. Exeter. Paternoster Press. 1994.

C. Norris, *The Truth about Postmodernism*. Oxford. Blackwell. 1993.

R. Norris, *Deconstruction and the Interests of Theory*. London. Pinter Publishers. 1988.

R. Nozick, *Anarchy, State and Utopia*. Oxford. Blackwell. 1974.
   *The Examined Life: Philosophical Meditations*. New York. Simon and Schuster. 1989.

O. O'Donovan, *Resurrection and Moral Order*. Leicester. IVP. 1986.

F.E. Oppenheim, *Dimensions of Freedom: An Analysis*. London. Macmillan. 1961.

H. Osborne, *Abstraction and Artifice in Twentieth Century Art*. Oxford. OUP. 1979.

D.H. Pennington, *Seventeenth Century Europe*. London. Longman. 1970.

B. Pimlott (ed.), *Fabian Essays in Socialist Thought*. London. Heinemann. 1984.

M. Polanyi, *Personal Knowledge: Towards a Post-Critical Philosophy*. London. Routledge and Kegan Paul. 1958.
   *The Tacit Dimension*. London. Routledge and Kegan Paul. 1967.

J. Polkinghorne, *Reason and Reality: The Relationship between Science and Theology*. London. SPCK. 1991.

Pollis and Schwab, *Human Rights: Cultural and Ideological Perspectives*. New York. Praeger. 1979.

G. Ponton and P. Gill, *Introduction to Politics*. Oxford. Blackwell. 1984.

K. Popper, *Conjectures and Refutations: The Growth of Scientific Knowledge*. London. Routledge and Kegan Paul. 1963.

R.H. Preston, *Religion and the Persistence of Capitalism*. London. SCM Press. 1979.

J. Robert, *The Triumph of the West*. London. British Broadcasting Corporation. 1985.

F. Rosenthal, *The Muslim Concept of Freedom prior to the 19th. Century*. Leiden. Brill. 1960.

P. Sampson, V. Samuel, C. Sugden, *Faith and Modernity*. Oxford. Regnum Books. 1994.

L. Sanneh, *Encountering the West. Christianity and the Global Cultural Process: The African Dimension*. London. Marshall Pickering. 1993.

Z. Sardar and M.W. Davis, *Distorted Imagination: Lessons from the Rushdie Affair*. London. Grey Seal. 1990.

E.P. Sanders, *Paul*. Oxford. Oxford University Press. 1991.

G. Scambler (ed.), *Sociology as Applied to Medicine*. London. Tindall. 1991.

H. Schlossberg et al., *Freedom, Justice and Hope: Towards a Strategy for the Poor and Oppressed*. Westchester (Illinois). Crossway Books. 1988.

M. Schluter and D. Lee, *The 'R' Factor*. London. Hodder and Stoughton. 1993.

B. Schwartz and S.J. Robbins, *Psychology of Learning and Behaviour*. New York. W.W. Norton. 1995.

A.J. Simmons, *The Lockean Theory of Rights*. Princeton. Princeton University Press. 1992.

Skinner, *Beyond Freedom and Dignity*. Harmondsworth. Penguin. 1971.

A. Storkey, *A Christian Social Perspective*. Leicester. Intervarsity Press. 1979.

B.F. Stowasser (ed.), *The Islamic Impulse*. London. Croom Helm. 1987.

C.R. Strain (ed.), *Prophetic Visions and Economic Realities: Protestants, Jews and Catholics Confront the Bishops' Letter on the Economy*. Grand Rapids. Eerdmans. 1989.

G. Strawson, *Freedom and Belief*. Oxford. 1986.

R.F. Strawson, *Freedom and Resentment and Other Essays*. London. Methuen and Co. 1974.

C.B. Strozier, *Apocalypse: On the Psychology of Fundamentalism in America*. Boston. Beacon Press. 1994.

L. Swidler (ed.), *Religious Liberty and Human Rights in Nations and Religions*. Philadelphia. Ecumenical Press. 1986.

Syed Muhammed Naquib al-Attas, *Islam, Secularism and the Philosophy of the Future*. London. Mansell Publishing. 1986.

B. Tibi, *The Crisis of Modern Islam: A Preindustrial Culture in the Scientific-Technological Age*. Salt Lake City. University of Utah Press. 1988.

G. Tinder, *The Political Meaning of Christianity*. New York. Harper Collins. 1989.

Various, *Sex Education in the School: The Religious Perspective*. Cambridge. The Islamic Academy. 1991.

A. Walters, *All You Love is Need*. London. SPCK. 1984.

Wan Mohd Nor Wan Daud, *The Concept of Knowledge in Islam and its Implications for Education in a Developing Country*. London. Mansell Press. 1989.

C. Ward, *Anarchy in Action*. London. 1973.

M. Waters, *Modern Sociological Theory*. London. Sage Publications. 1994.

W.M. Watt, *Islamic Political Thought*. Edinburgh. Scottish Academic Press. 1980.

*Islam and Christianity Today: A Contribution to Dialogue*. London. Routledge and Kegan Paul. 1983.

*Islamic Philosophy and Theology: An Extended Survey*. Edinburgh. Edinburgh University Press. 1987.

*Islamic Fundamentalism and Modernity*. London. Routledge and Kegan Paul. 1988.

A.J. Wensinck, *The Muslim Creed: Its Genesis and Historical Development*. London. F. Cass. 1965.

P. White (ed.), *Personal and Social Education: Philosophical Perspectives*. London. Kegan Page. 1989.

N.T. Wright, *The New Testament and the People of God*. London. SPCK. 1992.

C.T. Yu, *Being and Relation: A Theological Critique of Western Dualism and Individualism*. Edinburgh. Scottish Academic Press. 1987.

R. Zakaria, *The Struggle within Islam: the Conflict between Religion and Politics*. Harmondsworth. Penguin Books. 1988.

# Index